INTERNET AUCTIONS FOR DUMMIES®

by Greg Holden

IDG Books Worldwide, Inc.
An International Data Group Company

Foster City, CA ◆ Chicago, IL ◆ Indianapolis, IN ◆ New York, NY

Internet Auctions For Dummies®

Published by
IDG Books Worldwide, Inc.
An International Data Group Company
919 E. Hillsdale Blvd.
Suite 400
Foster City, CA 94404
www.idgbooks.com (IDG Books Worldwide Web site)
www.dummies.com (Dummies Press Web site)

Library of Congress Catalog Card No.: 99-63197

ISBN: 0-7645-0578-5

Printed in the United States of America

10 9 8 7 6 5 4 3 2 1

1B/QZ/QX/ZZ/IN

Distributed in the United States by IDG Books Worldwide, Inc.

Distributed by CDG Books Canada Inc. for Canada; by Transworld Publishers Limited in the United Kingdom; by IDG Norge Books for Norway; by IDG Sweden Books for Sweden; by IDG Books Australia Publishing Corporation Pty. Ltd. for Australia and New Zealand; by TransQuest Publishers Pte Ltd. for Singapore, Malaysia, Thailand, Indonesia, and Hong Kong; by Gotop Information Inc. for Taiwan; by ICG Muse, Inc. for Japan; by Norma Comunicaciones S.A. for Colombia; by Intersoft for South Africa; by Eyrolles for France; by International Thomson Publishing for Germany, Austria and Switzerland; by Distribuidora Cuspide for Argentina; by Livraria Cultura for Brazil; by Ediciones ZETA S.C.R. Ltda. for Peru; by WS Computer Publishing Corporation, Inc., for the Philippines; by Contemporanea de Ediciones for Venezuela; by Express Computer Distributors for the Caribbean and West Indies; by Micronesia Media Distributor, Inc. for Micronesia; by Grupo Editorial Norma S.A. for Guatemala; by Chips Computadoras S.A. de C.V. for Mexico; by Editorial Norma de Panama S.A. for Panama; by American Bookshops for Finland. Authorized Sales Agent: Anthony Rudkin Associates for the Middle East and North Africa.

For general information on IDG Books Worldwide's books in the U.S., please call our Consumer Customer Service department at 800-762-2974. For reseller information, including discounts and premium sales, please call our Reseller Customer Service department at 800-434-3422.

For information on where to purchase IDG Books Worldwide's books outside the U.S., please contact our International Sales department at 317-596-5530 or fax 317-596-5692.

For consumer information on foreign language translations, please contact our Customer Service department at 1-800-434-3422, fax 317-596-5692, or e-mail rights@idgbooks.com.

For information on licensing foreign or domestic rights, please phone +1-650-655-3109.

For sales inquiries and special prices for bulk quantities, please contact our Sales department at 650-655-3200 or write to the address above.

For information on using IDG Books Worldwide's books in the classroom or for ordering examination copies, please contact our Educational Sales department at 800-434-2086 or fax 317-596-5499.

For press review copies, author interviews, or other publicity information, please contact our Public Relations department at 650-655-3000 or fax 650-655-3299.

For authorization to photocopy items for corporate, personal, or educational use, please contact Copyright Clearance Center, 222 Rosewood Drive, Danvers, MA 01923, or fax 978-750-4470.

About the Author

Greg Holden is founder and president of a small business called Stylus Media, which is a group of editorial, design, and computer professionals who produce both print and electronic publications. The company gets its name from a recording stylus, which reads the traces left on a disk by voices or instruments and translates those signals into electronic data that can be amplified and enjoyed by many.

One of the ways Greg enjoys communicating is through explaining technical subjects in non-technical language by writing computer books, which help other people use the Web to share their own personal and professional interests. *Internet Auctions For Dummies* is his tenth book.

In the past year, Greg has also coordinated a chat event on the Internet, prepared content for a CD-ROM tutorial that shows small-business owners how to create their own Web sites, and helped produce technical manuals on Java and Lotus Notes.

Greg balances his technical expertise and his entrepreneurial experience with his love of literature. He received an M.A. in English from the University of Illinois at Chicago, but that only gave him an official credential for what he had been doing since he was a tiny tot. As a preschooler, barely big enough to hold the book, he was displayed by his proud but rather puzzled parents as the kid who read from the encyclopedia to impress his relatives at family gatherings.

After graduating from college, Greg became a reporter for his hometown newspaper, first covering sewers and school boards and then working his way up to having his own column (called "So It Goes") in which he voiced his perspective on the world. Working at the publications office at the University of Chicago was his next job, and it was there that he started to use computers. He discovered, as the technology became available, that he loved desktop publishing (with the Macintosh and LaserWriter) and, later on, the World Wide Web.

Collecting and tinkering have been time-honored traditions in his family, and Greg was delighted to discover the many ways that he could use the Web in general and online auctions in particular to further his interests. Greg loves to travel and has researched vacation sites and bought tickets on the Web. He spends a lot of time browsing sites that give him tips for the rehabbing that he has been doing for many years on the old house in Chicago where he lives with his family. He still can't drive by a sign for a garage sale or flea market without stopping to take a gander at the merchandise, but online auctions have helped him add hard-to-find items to his collections of pens, cameras, radios, and hats. He also is delighted to meet new friends in virtual communities who share his interests. For example, he is an active member of Jewel Heart, a Tibetan Buddhist meditation and study group based in Ann Arbor, Michigan.

ABOUT IDG BOOKS WORLDWIDE

Welcome to the world of IDG Books Worldwide.

IDG Books Worldwide, Inc., is a subsidiary of International Data Group, the world's largest publisher of computer-related information and the leading global provider of information services on information technology. IDG was founded more than 30 years ago by Patrick J. McGovern and now employs more than 9,000 people worldwide. IDG publishes more than 290 computer publications in over 75 countries. More than 90 million people read one or more IDG publications each month.

Launched in 1990, IDG Books Worldwide is today the #1 publisher of best-selling computer books in the United States. We are proud to have received eight awards from the Computer Press Association in recognition of editorial excellence and three from Computer Currents' First Annual Readers' Choice Awards. Our best-selling ...For Dummies® series has more than 50 million copies in print with translations in 31 languages. IDG Books Worldwide, through a joint venture with IDG's Hi-Tech Beijing, became the first U.S. publisher to publish a computer book in the People's Republic of China. In record time, IDG Books Worldwide has become the first choice for millions of readers around the world who want to learn how to better manage their businesses.

Our mission is simple: Every one of our books is designed to bring extra value and skill-building instructions to the reader. Our books are written by experts who understand and care about our readers. The knowledge base of our editorial staff comes from years of experience in publishing, education, and journalism — experience we use to produce books to carry us into the new millennium. In short, we care about books, so we attract the best people. We devote special attention to details such as audience, interior design, use of icons, and illustrations. And because we use an efficient process of authoring, editing, and desktop publishing our books electronically, we can spend more time ensuring superior content and less time on the technicalities of making books.

You can count on our commitment to deliver high-quality books at competitive prices on topics you want to read about. At IDG Books Worldwide, we continue in the IDG tradition of delivering quality for more than 30 years. You'll find no better book on a subject than one from IDG Books Worldwide.

John Kilcullen
Chairman and CEO
IDG Books Worldwide, Inc.

Steven Berkowitz
President and Publisher
IDG Books Worldwide, Inc.

Eighth Annual Computer Press Awards ≥1992

Ninth Annual Computer Press Awards ≥1993

Tenth Annual Computer Press Awards ≥1994

Eleventh Annual Computer Press Awards ≥1995

Author's Acknowledgments

I'm a freelancer who spends a lot of my time alone in my computer room. But the irony is that, as a member of many thriving virtual communities, I'm never really alone. One of the things I like best about this book is the chance it gave me to connect with many interesting new friends.

Trust is the cornerstone upon which online auctions are built. The popularity of this way of doing business is due not only to the probability that with a little skill and a little luck you can find a bargain, but also because you can form gratifying relationships with others without ever meeting face to face. This is also a community that is defined by the way it shares stories and knowledge. I was struck by the fact that the most successful online auction entrepreneurs also tended to be the ones who were the most generous with their time and experience. They taught me that the more helpful you are, the more successful you'll be in return.

I want to thank all those who were profiled or contributed comments to the book, particularly William Crockett, Alex Fan, Bill Fulkerson, Matt Goebel, Tessa Hebert, Shawn Morningstar, Jim Robinson, Marty Scriven, Edith Shaefer, Robbin K. Tungett, and Connie Varco.

I would also like to acknowledge some of my own colleagues who helped prepare and review the text and graphics of this book, and who are important members of my personal and professional communities. Thanks to Lucinda Scharbach, Nathan Wesling, and Aya Iwai who made many important contributions, especially to the Internet Directory section.

For editing and technical assignments, I was lucky to be in the capable hands of the folks at IDG Books Worldwide: my always-supportive and helpful project editor Wendy Hatch, copy editor Kathleen Dobie, technical editor Jim McCarter, CD guru Joell Smith, and Carmen Krikorian, the Queen of Permissions.

Thanks also to Neil Salkind and David and Sherry Rogelberg of Studio B, and to Joyce Pepple and Sherri Morningstar of IDG Books for helping me add this book to the list of those I've authored and, in the process, broadened my expertise as a writer.

Last but certainly not least, I want to thank my two daughters, Zosia and Lucy, for putting fun in my life by allowing me to share their ever-widening circle of loving friends, as well as my mother and father, and my main supporter and partner Ann Lindner, who helps me every step of the way.

Publisher's Acknowledgments

We're proud of this book; please register your comments through our IDG Books Worldwide Online Registration Form located at http://my2cents.dummies.com.

Some of the people who helped bring this book to market include the following:

Acquisitions, Editorial, and Media Development

Associate Project Editor: Wendy Hatch

Acquisitions Editors: Sherri Morningstar; Joyce Pepple

Copy Editor: Kathleen Dobie

Technical Editor: Jim McCarter

Media Development Editor: Joell Smith

Associate Permissions Editor: Carmen Krikorian

Editorial Manager: Jennifer Ehrlich

Media Development Manager: Heather Heath Dismore

Editorial Assistant: Alison Walthall

Production

Project Coordinator: Maridee Ennis

Layout and Graphics: Thomas R. Emrick, Barry Offringa, Angela F. Hunckler, Brent Savage, Janet Seib, Dave McKelvey, Brian Torwelle, Dan Whetstine

Proofreaders: Nancy Price, Marianne Santy, Toni Settle

Indexer: Liz Cunningham

Special Help
Publication Services, Inc.

General and Administrative

IDG Books Worldwide, Inc.: John Kilcullen, CEO; Steven Berkowitz, President and Publisher

IDG Books Technology Publishing Group: Richard Swadley, Senior Vice President and Publisher; Walter Bruce III, Vice President and Associate Publisher; Steven Sayre, Associate Publisher; Joseph Wikert, Associate Publisher; Mary Bednarek, Branded Product Development Director; Mary Corder, Editorial Director

IDG Books Consumer Publishing Group: Roland Elgey, Senior Vice President and Publisher; Kathleen A. Welton, Vice President and Publisher; Kevin Thornton, Acquisitions Manager; Kristin A. Cocks, Editorial Director

IDG Books Internet Publishing Group: Brenda McLaughlin, Senior Vice President and Publisher; Diane Graves Steele, Vice President and Associate Publisher; Sofia Marchant, Online Marketing Manager

IDG Books Production for Dummies Press: Michael R. Britton, Vice President of Production; Debbie Stailey, Associate Director of Production; Cindy L. Phipps, Manager of Project Coordination, Production Proofreading, and Indexing; Shelley Lea, Supervisor of Graphics and Design; Debbie J. Gates, Production Systems Specialist; Robert Springer, Supervisor of Proofreading; Laura Carpenter, Production Control Manager; Tony Augsburger, Supervisor of Reprints and Bluelines

◆

The publisher would like to give special thanks to Patrick J. McGovern, without whom this book would not have been possible.

◆

Contents at a Glance

Cartoons at a Glance

By Rich Tennant

"He and Fendleman in Marketing are in a bidding war over a rare Xena lunch box."

page 9

REVEREND DAVIS PAUSES DURING HIS SERMON TO BID ON A DUKES OF HAZARD SMOKIN' GENERAL LEE SNOWBOARD.

page 83

"Mr. James! Mr. James! I know you're in there—I can hear you breathing over the partition. If you don't stop outbidding me on those Tae-Bo workout videos..."

page 235

"Cool! My last-second snipe bid for that Swiss chalet you and Mom were admiring earlier made it through."

page D-1

"I learned the hard way that you should always use an escrow service when you're the high bidder on the Venus de Milo."

page 115

Fax: 978-546-7747 • E-mail: the5wave@tiac.net

Table of Contents

Introduction

· ·

*F*rom the get-go, surfing the Internet has been exciting for me. I love the feeling of power when I find information online that answers a question that's been bugging me. I get an even more powerful positive surge when a knowledgeable person takes the time to help me out individually with one of my many specific concerns.

But when I made my first bid at an Internet auction in late 1997, I found out what an adrenaline rush is really all about. I collect fountain pens (as well as other archaic treasures too numerous to mention). After driving (sometimes for hours) to an antique store or flea market, I may be lucky enough to uncover one or two pieces of interest. When I discovered online auctions, a whole new world opened up. Suddenly I had my choice of pens that previously, I could only drool over in catalogs. My heart pounded as my bid appeared online, and I found it hard to concentrate on anything else as I waited for the auction to end. Would I experience the thrill of success or the agony of defeat? (Oh, no! How dare you outbid me at the last minute!)

Not only was I delighted with the additions to my beloved collection, but I was meeting new friends. I loved interacting with sellers, who were often in exotic locations around the world. I was suddenly a member of a thriving community of people who share my passions. I was hooked.

Today thousands (perhaps even millions) of individuals are discovering Internet auctions for themselves. Auctions are one of the hottest areas in the exploding field of electronic commerce.

The Internet research group Jupiter Communications estimates that the online auction market will soar to 6.5 million buyers purchasing $3.2 billion of merchandise by 2002. According to Jupiter, online shoppers bought more than $461 million in merchandise from auction sites in 1998, and PC hardware and software combined amounted to 12.9 percent of that figure.

One of the challenges of writing this book is that it was like hitting a moving target. As I wrote, several new big auction sites came online, including The Sharper Image and Amazon.com Auctions, and eBay purchased the prestigious auction house Butterfield & Butterfield. Online auctions are an area of Internet commerce that is still settling out. Of course, that makes it exciting as well.

Another challenge is that so many different types of auctions are available on the Internet. Person-to-person auctions of the sort provided by eBay are only the most obvious example. Many people frequent the totally different kinds of auctions offered by the computer and electronics services like Auction Universe (www.auctionuniverse.com) or Onsale (www.onsale.com).

Most of the examples in this book focus on eBay because it is by far the most popular auction site on the Internet, and clearly the one that people think about first when they consider getting into Internet auctions. Other auction services are giving eBay a run for its money, but it is so well-established and has such a wide range of users, services, and features that it's likely to hold off the competition and continue to thrive.

Internet auctions are becoming so popular that celebrity items like baseball star Mark McGwire's home run baseballs, Michael Jordan's basketball jerseys, and even O. J. Simpson's Heisman trophy are being offered online to the highest bidder. Long-established auction services like Sotheby's are feeling the competition and starting their own online auction sites. Everyone wants a piece of the action. It's not too late for you to join in the fun, too.

Where this Book Is Coming From

Internet Auctions For Dummies provides you with a practical, user-friendly guide to buying and selling at auction sites on the Net. Even though auctions have been conducted in cyberspace for only a few years, many of the people who frequent them regularly are veterans who can provide you with some stiff competition, whether you're a buyer or seller.

Cyberspace is the perfect place for individuals who like to use computers to find bargains as buyers and make a few extra dollars as sellers. It doesn't take much money to get started. If you already have a computer and an Internet connection, you can participate in auctions for only a small investment of time and money. You may be able to pay your bills or round out your collection of Pez dispensers. You don't have to buy a lot of special equipment, and you aren't faced with sizable fees beyond what you already pay to go online. You're quite likely to make some friends, too.

With each month that goes by, the number of Internet users increases exponentially. Whether you believe the surveys that count 40 million users or the ones that provide a "conservative" estimate of 20 million users, a lot of people are out there in cyberspace. We are now beginning to reach that critical mass where _most_ people begin to use the Internet regularly for everyday shopping and other financial activities. Very soon, the Internet will be a powerhouse for shopping online.

This book explains how to start bidding and selling. It does not simply concentrate on eBay, but also describes the many other kinds of auction sites that are springing up in cyberspace.

To get you up to the auction block quickly and help you avoid pitfalls that can arise along the way, this book guides you through the following steps:

- ✔ Picking the auction that best fits your buying/selling needs.
- ✔ Registering with auction sites and maintaining your privacy online.
- ✔ Avoiding losing time, money, or merchandise to deadbeat bidders or fraudulent sellers.
- ✔ Scanning images, writing descriptions, and formatting auction listings to maximize sales.
- ✔ Knowing how to use "sniping," proxy bids, and reserve bids to win auctions.

How to Use this Book

One of the great things about using the Net to find what you want, whether you're shopping for auction treasures or looking up the history of ancient Egypt, is that you don't have to move in a straight line from beginning to end. The Net doesn't work that way, and neither does this book.

Feel free to skip around this book's contents based on your level of experience with the Internet and what you want to get from online auctions. Need an overview of how Internet auctions work? Begin with Chapter 1. Just taking your first baby steps in cyberspace and don't know what kind of equipment you need? Jump over to Chapter 2. Primarily interested in selling at auction? Take a look at Chapter 6. Need some tips on getting the best bargains? Check out Chapters 4 and 11. You don't have to read each chapter from start to finish, either. I've tried to make this book an easy-to-use reference tool that you can be comfortable with, no matter what your experience with buying and selling, with auctions, or with the Internet.

Foolish Assumptions

In this book, I assume that you aren't starting from Ground Zero, but perhaps from Ground One, as far as computers and the Internet are concerned. In other words, I assume you have access to a computer, whether you own the machine yourself or use one at a public library, your office, or an Internet café. I also assume that you're familiar with the Internet and have been surfing for a while. You may even have put out some information of your own in the form of a home page.

I also make the following bold assumptions:

- ✔ **You're looking for a new and exciting way to buy and sell.** Whether you want to find a bargain, uncover a rare collectible, or reach a potential audience of millions of customers, Internet auctions can help you meet your goals.

- ✔ **You have just enough technical know-how.** You don't have to know your DHCP from DHTML to join the Internet auction bandwagon. This book can help you understand the basics of how to place bids and sell your items to the highest bidders.

What's Where in this Book

In each chapter of this book, you find step-by-step instructions and icons that present short bits of useful information. Here are the parts of the book and what they contain:

Part I: Stepping Up to the Auction Block

Part I gives you an overview of the exploding field of online auctions. In Chapter 1, I tell you how auctions on the Web differ from traditional auctions and how to decide which auctions are best for your needs.

Subsequent chapters detail the hardware and software you need to get in on the auction, so to speak; and how to win friends and influence your buyers and sellers by joining online communities.

Part II: Buying at Internet Auctions

This part of the book describes how to find what you want at online auctions without getting carried away in the thrill of the chase. I share strategies for finding what you want and explain how you can avoid being defrauded by sellers who don't follow through on your purchase by shipping you the goods. I also explain how escrow services can facilitate successful transactions by acting as intermediaries between buyers and sellers.

Part III: Selling at Internet Auctions

Selling on the Internet is a booming business. Some eBay sellers are virtual professionals. In order to compete, you have to know how the system works and how you can make it work for you. In this part of the book, you find out how to place your merchandise on the virtual auction block, how to control the terms of your auction sale, how to create Web pages to promote yourself and dress up your auction listings, and how to provide good customer service that enhances your reputation and ensures repeat customers. I also explain how to deal with overseas bidders and how to keep track of your earnings and expenses with accounting software.

Part IV: The Part of Tens

Filled with tips, cautions, suggestions, and examples, the Part of Tens chapters present some insider secrets and show you how to avoid trouble when using online auctions.

Appendix

The CD-ROM that accompanies *Internet Auctions For Dummies* includes plenty of software for auction sellers, shoppers, and all Web surfers, for that matter. It also includes a set of links to all sites listed in this book's Internet Directory. The Appendix explains how to install the programs on the CD.

The Internet Auctions For Dummies Internet Directory

How do you choose the auction service that's right for you? How do you find computer equipment, rare coins, antique rugs, and other specialized merchandise? Not to fear: Everything you need is in this directory. The *Internet Auctions For Dummies* Internet Directory contains reviews and descriptions of many different auction-related sites, reporting on fees charged to sellers, restrictions on what you can sell, and more. Auction services are organized according to what they sell. (You'll find a set of links to all the sites listed on the CD that accompanies this book.)

Conventions Used in this Book

I wrote most of this book with Windows 95/98 and Macintosh users in mind, but most of the software included on this book's CD or referred to in the text can be used by Windows 3.1 or NT users, too.

Important bits of information are formatted in special ways to make sure you notice them right away.

When I talk about choosing a menu option, I represent the choice with an arrow between the options. For example, File⇨Open translates to "Choose the Open option from the File menu." When I tell you to insert a bit of text — for example, "Type the keyword **Collectibles**" — the text you should type is bold.

When I describe activities or sites of interest on the World Wide Web, I include the address or Uniform Resource Locator (URL) in a special typeface like this: `http://www.idgbooks.com`.

Keep in mind that the newer versions of popular Web browsers, such as Netscape Navigator and Microsoft Internet Explorer, don't require you to enter the entire URL. For example, if you want to connect to the IDG Books Worldwide site mentioned in the preceding example, you can get there by simply entering the following in your browser's Go To box:

`www.idgbooks.com.`

Remember that not all URLs begin with "www." Here's an example:

`primecom.net`

Don't be surprised if your browser can't find an Internet address you type, or if a Web page depicted in the book is no longer where I say it is. Although the sites were current when the book was written, Web addresses (and sites themselves) can be pretty fickle. Try looking for a "missing" site by using an Internet search engine. Or try shortening the address by deleting everything after the `.com` (or `.org` or `.edu`).

Icons Used in this Book

Internet Auctions For Dummies uses special graphical elements called icons to get your attention. Here's what they look like and what they mean:

Points out some technical details that you may find of interest. A thorough understanding, however, is not a prerequisite to grasping the underlying concept. Non-techies are welcome to skip these details altogether.

Calls your attention to general time-saving or money-saving suggestions of interest to both auction buyers and sellers.

Points out potential pitfalls that can develop into major problems if you're not careful.

Alerts you to facts and figures that are important to keep in mind.

Provides you with tips and strategies for bidding online.

Provides Internet auction sellers with suggestions for how to maximize their sales success.

Alerts you to slang and jargon used by auction insiders so you can start speaking like a pro.

Calls your attention to tips and success stories from online entrepreneurs who buy and sell at Internet auctions.

Points out software and other goodies on the CD-ROM that accompanies this book.

We're in It Together

Person-to-person contact is key when it comes to online auction sales. By the same token, you should feel free to contact this book's publisher and author, too. With this book, I hope to help you make connections and find new commercial opportunities in the exciting new medium of the Internet and to remind you that you're not alone. We're all consumers, after all.

Let IDG Books know what you think about this book by sending an e-mail to feedback/dummies@idgbooks.com. And remember to check out the ...*For Dummies* Web site at www.dummies.com.

You're welcome to contact me directly if you have questions or comments. Send e-mail to Greg Holden at gholden@interaccess.com.

Part I

Stepping Up to the Auction Block

The 5th Wave   By Rich Tennant

"He and Fendleman in Marketing are in a bidding war over a rare Xena lunch box."

In this part . . .

You've heard the hype and you've heard the horror stories. Now it's time to separate the myths about Internet auctions from the realities.

This part starts by establishing a firm foundation of knowledge about the difference between online auctions and those conducted by traditional auction houses. Then I help you draw up a shopping list of hardware and software you need to step up to the virtual auction block.

But there's more to online auctioning than digital bids and bytes. You also join an active community of real folks, many of whom share your interests. You find out how to get the most out of your auction experience, as well as how to play by the rules.

Chapter 1

Getting in on the Auction

. . . .

In This Chapter

▶ Uncovering the differences between traditional and Internet auctions

▶ Delving into the ins and outs of Internet auctions

▶ Choosing the type of Internet auction that's right for you

▶ Enjoying the auction experience

. . . .

*O*ne of the most exciting and potentially lucrative ways to join the business revolution that's sweeping the Internet is to participate in online auctions.

Internet auctions are taking the world by storm. Celebrities in the worlds of sports and show business regularly conduct online auctions of choice memorabilia for profit or charity. But regular folks like you and I can buy or sell practically anything through Internet auctions, too.

Most people know how traditional auctions worked in the B.I. era (Before the Internet). A person with something to sell let interested buyers gather to inspect the item and bid on it. The bidders traded offers, and the person willing to pay the highest price won the item, handed over the money, and took the treasure home.

Traditional auctions still occur, but increasingly, Internet auctions provide a practical alternative. In an Internet auction, merchandise is offered for sale on the World Wide Web. Prospective buyers use their Web browsers to connect to the auction site and submit bids to the site by filling out a Web page form. Millions of sales have been conducted smoothly in recent years, and thousands of satisfied buyers and sellers can attest that the system is usually a good one.

Of course, fraud happens. Sometimes. To some people. You can minimize your chances of being one of the unlucky ones by understanding how Internet auctions work, picking the type of auction that's right for you, and getting auction advice from the experienced buyers and sellers who contributed to this book. This chapter gives you an overview of how the whole Internet auction process works.

What Makes Traditional Auctions Tick?

Before you get your mouse clicking in the hopes of buying the object of your dreams at an Internet auction, you need a little background on traditional live auctions of the sort held for decades by venerable institutions like Christie's, Butterfield & Butterfield, and Sotheby's.

What is a traditional auction?

An auction, as defined by C. Hugh Hildesley, auctioneer for Sotheby's, in *The Complete Guide to Buying and Selling at Auction,* is "the method of selling by which property passes from the seller to the buyer at the highest price offered in a public forum."

People have been trading at auction for thousands of years. It's a way for a seller to get maximum value for a piece of merchandise and for a buyer to get rare and desirable items, occasionally at bargain prices.

How do traditional auctions work?

At traditional auction houses, you can touch, examine, and otherwise interact with the items on display. These houses also employ experts who evaluate the sales items and can advise both buyers and sellers of an item's worth. In a traditional auction house, the item is photographed, and a description and photo are published in a sales catalog. This type of catalog is being adapted for the Internet as big auction houses start realizing the potential of the Internet as a marketing tool (and not merely a source of competition). Figure 1-1 shows an online auction page from the Butterfield & Butterfield Web site at `www.butterfields.com`.

Traditional auction experts look for certain qualities when setting prices and preparing auction descriptions. Considering the following criteria is just as important to online auction participants:

- **Historical importance.** An item's value often depends on its connection to an historical figure or event, and how well that connection is documented.

- **Rarity.** The scarcity of an item, combined with its beauty, condition, and other qualities, directly affects its value.

- **Authenticity.** In the world of antiques, this is one of the most important criteria, one that is best determined by experts. (In an online auction, this is one of the most difficult qualities to evaluate.)

Figure 1-1:
Auction
houses'
Web sites
blend
traditional
sales
catalogs
with the
Internet's
marketing
and
publicity
potential.

✔ **Provenance.** Who owned the item previously sometimes comes into
play in both traditional or online auctions. The pen shown in Figure 1-2
is described as having never been offered at auction before, which
makes it more desirable to die-hard collectors like me.

How Are Online Auctions Different?

Traditional auctions are held periodically in locations around the world. The
purchaser must either attend the auction or find someone to represent him
on-site in order to make a bid. Bidders are given *paddles* to hold up when
they want to bid. The auctioneer must be skilled in pacing bids and handling
last-minute bidding, and he has the right to extend the auction when bids
come in "as the hammer is coming down."

Online auctions certainly have merchandise and bidders, and sometimes flur-
ries of last-minute bids, but the timing and location of auctions are less
relevant on the Internet. Items can be offered for sale at any time, and it mat-
ters not at all where buyer and seller are located as far as offering the item
and bidding on it are concerned. When an auction takes place online, you can
participate without leaving the comforts of home. In the following sections, I
explain the ins and outs of Internet auctions.

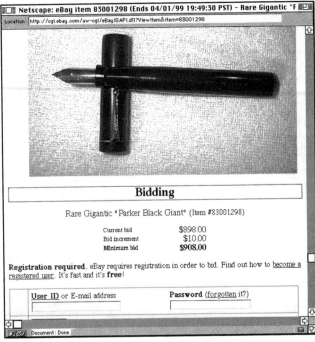

Figure 1-2:
You can find
rarities and
household
bargains
alike at
eBay, one of
the most
popular
Internet
auction
sites.

Understanding How Online Auctions Work

The procedure for participating in online auctions differs depending on the type of auction you use (see "Understanding the Different Types of Internet Auctions," later in this chapter). Each auction service has its own set of rules for bidding and selling. Read these guidelines carefully. They don't make for exciting reading, but they are important. Check out the bidding rules. Some auctions keep track of the time you first bid on an item, and subsequent bids can "bump" someone at the same price who's first bid was later than yours. Also, note the shipping charges, which can be excessive and can raise the actual value of your bid. See Parts II and III of this book for a more detailed look at bidding and selling at online auctions.

Bidding is a breeze

I cover bidding in greater detail in Chapter 4, but the following numbered list explains the bidding process in a nutshell:

1. **Register.** Typically, you provide the auction service with a username and password that you then use to login or place bids, as well as an e-mail address. You also provide the site with your real name and address in case it needs to contact you. Auction houses that function as the seller (many of which specialize in computer and other electronics equipment) usually require a credit card number when you register.

2. **Shop.** You search the selection of sale items in one of two ways: You can click links that denote categories of merchandise until you find the specific merchandise you're looking for, or you can search for particular brands or models by entering keywords in a search box.

3. **Place a bid.** You fill out a form on a Web page and submit your bid along with your registered username and password to the site. If you're the high bidder (or in the case of a Dutch auction, one of the low bidders) your bid is recorded on the Web page on which the auction item is displayed.

4. **Track your bid.** While the auction is going on, you can find out whether anyone has outbid you. Some sites automatically send you an e-mail message if this happens. Software programs are available to help you track your auctions (see AuctionTicker on this book's CD, for example).

5. **If you're the winning bidder, make payment and shipping arrangements with the seller.** The seller tells you how much to pay (your winning bid plus shipping) and where to send payment.

Selling is simple

I cover selling in Chapter 6, but the following steps explain the general process:

1. **Register.** This is the same as registering as a bidder. However, depending on the site you may have to submit credit card information to set up an account as a seller.

2. **Post an item.** "Posting" means that you place your description on the auction site's Web server by filling out a form in which you specify the length of the auction and describe what you're selling. You also make a link to an image of the item, if you have one.

3. **Watch the bids pour in.** Depending on your level of interest and available time, you can check in as often as you like by connecting to the auction Web page on which your merchandise is displayed. If you reconnect often, choose View⇨Reload or View⇨Refresh from your browser's menu bar to see the changes since your last visit.

4. **End the auction.** Some sites let you end the auction before your ending time, but this can get you negative feedback from disgruntled buyers.

Let the auction end at the time you originally chose. See if the high bid meets or exceeds your reserve price, if you specified one. Contact the high bidder with purchasing information.

5. **Get paid.** The most common forms of payment are cashier's checks or postal money orders. If you have a merchant account with a bank and can accept credit cards, so much the better. If you use an escrow service, the buyer can pay the escrow service with a credit card, and the service pays you after the shipment has been received and accepted.

6. **Deliver the goods.** It's important to pack your merchandise well and ship it in a way that lets you track its progress. You may also want to insure the item.

Understanding the Different Types of Internet Auctions

The following sections describe some of the auction types you may encounter.

Reserve price auctions are playing fair

If you're selling an item at auction, one of your primary questions (after the inevitable "Will I actually get my money?") is, "Am I going to get what I think this is worth?" In other words, what happens if the high bid is less than the amount you wanted to sell the item for? Do you *have* to sell it?" Not if you offer your merchandise in a reserve price auction.

A *reserve price auction* is a way for a seller to protect his investment. The *reserve price* is the lowest price at which a seller is willing to sell an item. The reserve price usually isn't disclosed to bidders, although some sellers actually tell bidders what the reserve price is in an item's description.

To win a reserve price auction, you must not only have the highest bid but must also meet or exceed the reserve price that the seller set. If the reserve price isn't met, neither the seller nor the high bidder is under any obligation to complete the deal. This isn't a hard and fast rule, however. Nothing prevents the high bidder and the seller from negotiating a compromise price.

Open reserve auctions protect the price

An open reserve auction is a common variation on the reserve auction concept. In an *open reserve auction,* the starting bid is set at the reserve price. The seller sets the minimum bid to guarantee that he'll get at least that amount and doesn't have to sell the item for less than the indicated starting price.

In some auctions (for example, Yahoo! Auctions at `auctions.yahoo.com`) the seller may choose to lower the starting price to meet your bid before the auction closes.

Yankee auctions are dandy

Onsale (`www.onsale.com/atauction`), one of the first Internet auction sites, uses a Yankee auction type. Many of its sales are for high-tech equipment such as digital cameras, computers, or CD players. Typically, the initial bids are far below the retail price of the merchandise offered and bidding often doesn't heat up until the very end of the auction.

In a *Yankee auction,* bids are ranked by price first. The number of successful bidders is equal to the number of items offered. Usually, more than one sample of the same item is auctioned at a time. For example, if the site offers 20 notebook computers, the 20 highest bidders win if each of them bids on a single item. The bids may range in price (say, from $899 to $1,099), so some winners pay less than others.

If two or more bids are for the same price, the bid for a larger quantity of items takes precedence over a bid for a smaller quantity. For example, if three computers are being auctioned and the first bidder bids $800 for one computer and the second bidder bids $800 each for all three computers, the second bidder wins all three computers for $800 each. If bids are for the same price and quantity, then earlier initial bids take precedence over later initial bids. For example, if two bidders offer $10 per pair for five pair of orange and green striped socks being offered, the bidder who submitted his bid first gets to buy the socks (and wear them with his purple and yellow suits, perhaps?).

Time-based auctions make deadlines your friends

Time-based auctions are the most common types of auctions on person-to-person auction services such as eBay. A *time-based auction* lasts for a definite period of time, such as a week.

Onsale (www.Onsale.com), for example, has a QuickBid feature. You can find printer cartridges, videocassettes, and tennis balls posted for sale at fixed prices. These products are offered in limited quantities and are available until the posted sale closing time or as long as supplies last. (Note that Onsale doesn't wait until the posted closing date to process your order — it's processed the same day.)

Dutch auctions don't tilt at windmills

Suppose you have a dozen copies of a rare and desirable Beanie Baby bear named Greg the Grump (hey, it could happen!). You want to sell to the dozen highest bidders. The way to sell multiple identical items is to offer them in a *Dutch auction.*

Dutch auctions seem similar to Yankee auctions, and they are, with one difference: The seller in a Dutch auction specifies the minimum successful price for an individual item as well as the number of items available. Potential buyers can bid at or above that minimum for the quantity they're interested in. At the close of the auction, the highest bidders purchase the items at the lowest successful price (that is, the lowest bid that is still above the minimum price).

In the aforementioned example, if the minimum bid for Greg the Grump is $20, and twenty people bid $20, the first twelve successful bidders win. If six people bid $30, three bid $27, three bid $25, and four bid $21, only the twelve people who bid $25 and over win. Things get more complicated if someone bids, say $25 for six items. That person would not get all six items, because nine individuals already placed higher bids. Rather, the six at $25 bidder would get only three Greg the Grumps.

Private auctions in a plain brown wrapper

In a *private auction,* bidders' e-mail addresses aren't disclosed on the item screen or bidding history screen. When the auction is over, only the seller and the high-bidder are notified via e-mail.

You can get practically anything online, and X-rated material is without a doubt one of the most prevalent online offerings. eBay, accordingly, provides users who want to buy or sell in the Erotica, Adults Only category with a special *restricted access auction.* You need a credit card on file with eBay to both view and bid on these items. In addition, sellers can't list adult auctions without credit card verification.

If it sounds like Adults Only auction restrictions are going to prevent your kids from seeing inappropriate content, guess again. There are so many places to find "adult" stuff online, it's downright scary for parents like me with young children. Products like Net Nanny (www.netnanny.com) can help by blocking sites and words that you label as off-limits. These products are not a perfect solution because e-mail, newsgroups, chat rooms, and the whole Internet universe provide so much content. Wouldn't it be nice if auction sites or browser manufacturers provided users with an option that would let you set up preferences to block naughty stuff?

Live Auctions! Auctions! Auctions!

Want to have the excitement of sitting in a "real" auction house and bidding on items in real time rather than participating in the week-long or three-day auctions commonly found on Internet sites? Online *live auctions* recreate this excitement.

If you want to increase your heart rate in a hurry, check out the live auctions at LiveBid.com (www.livebid.com). You equip your computer with special software and hardware so you can actually hear — or even watch — the auction take place. Listen as the auctioneer calls the bids and says, "Going, Going, Gone!"

Premium or featured auctions when only the best will do

Many auction houses have a special category for more desirable items. Sellers pay a special rate to advertise their items in the highlighted area, and they tend to pass along higher prices to buyers in the form of reserve prices or minimum bids. For example, Yahoo! Auctions teamed with Butterfield & Butterfield to launch a Premium Auctions category. Through this partnership, Yahoo! Auctions now offers appraised jewelry, antiques, memorabilia, and rare and unique collectibles. Buyers have to pay a 10-to-15 percent fee in addition to the final high bid, and they must pay for their purchases in a specified amount of time.

Butterfield & Butterfield (www.butterfields.com) has a free photo appraisal service; send the auction house a photo of your item, and it will tell you what the item is worth.

Finding your niche in the eBay auction categories

Auctions on eBay come in many different flavors. The garden-variety "regular" auctions are the ones that most everyday collectors and shoppers frequent. There are more than 350 categories of these by my rough estimate, and you can find a lengthy list of them at listings.ebay.com/aw/listings/overview.html.

Sellers can make their items appear exceptional by placing their listings in special categories. Featuring an item in these specialized categories costs extra, and items offered for sale in these categories tend to cost more, too. But the merchandise in these featured categories generally is unique and hard to find.

Featured Auctions

Featured Auctions listings appear at the top of the main Listings page, which is accessible from the menu bar at the top of every page on eBay. Additionally, some Featured Auctions listings are randomly selected to appear on the eBay home page. However, there's no guarantee when or whether a certain item will appear in this well-traveled, highly popular location. Featured Auctions items aren't necessarily more unique or notable than other auction items. They are "featured" only because the seller paid the $99.95 listing fee to have them placed in the special location.

Featured Auctions have restrictions: The seller must have ten or more positive feedback comments, and the merchandise listed can't include adult items or things that eBay judges to be "illegal, illicit, or immoral." Find out about Featured Auctions and Category Featured Auctions (more information on these is coming up next) at cgi.ebay.com/aw-cgi/eBayISAPI.dll?Featured.

Category Featured Auctions

Sellers must have a feedback rating of at least ten to list items in Category Featured Auctions, but they aren't subject to the other restrictions that apply to Featured Auctions.

Category Featured Auctions appear at the top of the first Web page for the eBay category in which they fall. Paying the extra $14.95 listing fee is a good way to get attention for an exceptional item, particularly if the listings in its category run to 30, 40, or even more Web pages. As with Featured Auctions, the seller decides whether an item is special enough to fall into this category.

The Gallery

The eBay Gallery is a photo album showing JPEG images that users submit with their auction listings. Including an image in the gallery doesn't cost anything, and it's an easy way to get a little attention for what you have to sell. To add your image to the gallery, simply save your image in JPEG format and check a box when you list your item. (See Chapter 7 for more information about graphics formats.)

Big-Ticket Items

These are especially high-priced items, such as rare automobiles or jerseys signed by sports stars, that go for several thousand dollars and up. As this book was written, all the items on this page (pages.ebay.com/aw/big-ticket.html) were selling for $5,100 or more.

If you're a seller, you don't have to do anything special to get your object of great value listed on this page other than offer it for an initial bid of more than $5,000. If the bids go over that amount on their own, the item gets listed here.

Gift Section

Sellers pay an extra dollar to have a gift icon included with their listing title and to have the items included in the gift category (pages.ebay.com/aw/gift-section.html). These items are supposed to be suitable for gifts for Mother's Day, birthdays, or other occasions. However, remember that the sellers themselves determine whether these are really "gift" items or not, so you don't have an impartial jury doing the judging here.

Club99 Auctions

A group of eBay users came up with their own auction within the eBay auction universe. The home-grown auction, called Club99, takes place the second Saturday of every month. Merchandise is offered at an opening price of 99 cents with no reserve price. The auctions last a week.

You won't find exotic Italian sports cars or Babe Ruth autographed baseballs here. The typical Club99 auction listing is for a single item, such as a book, CD, alarm clock, shirt, or other household or personal item. Find out more about this special Saturday event at `members.ebay.com/aboutme/club99`.

Premium Auctions

As I was writing this chapter, eBay announced its purchase of the prestigious Butterfield &

Butterfield auction house, which specializes in the appraisal and sale of fine art, antiques, and objects in many collecting categories, including paintings, furniture, and jewelry.

eBay's announcement indicated that the purchase would enable users to access higher-end items as well as Butterfield's appraisal services. Look for the new alignment to result in a separate category of premium items on eBay. The items will be from Butterfield & Butterfield and other auction companies. Keep checking eBay's Web site if you're looking for a place to unload that original Renoir painting tucked away in your attic.

Adults Only Listings

Yes, Virginia, there is "adult" material for sale on eBay, in the Miscellaneous: Adults Only category. Shoppers must have credit card information on file with eBay to both view and bid on the items in this category. Sellers also must have credit card information on file so that eBay can verify their identities.

Finding the Auction Site that's Right for You

The variety and number of online auction sites are growing constantly. The growth feeds on itself: As sites get more popular and indicators of success like eBay's stock skyrocket, new sites go online hoping to get in on the auction themselves. The following sections help you determine which site is right for you.

Do your homework

By now, you may be — no, *should* be — excited about either finding bargains or making money through online auctions. So what's your next step?

Read some general overviews of Internet auction sites. As I write this book, there aren't too many of these online because the industry is so new. Try one of the following resources:

- **The Mining Company's Online Auction page** (www.miningco.com). Go to the Mining Company page and search for "auction." You get a fairly good selection of auction sites — although at the time I visited, the biggest auction service of all, eBay, wasn't included for some strange reason.

- **Auction Guide** (www.auction-guide.com). This site concentrates on computer equipment auctions, but it contains good general tips for buyers at any online auction.

- **Jesse Berst's Anchor Desk** (www.zdnet.com/anchordesk/story/story_3108.html). This article about online auctions provoked a lively series of comments in the Talkback section.

- *PC Magazine* **Web Auction Sites article** (www.zdnet.com/pcmag/features/auction/index.html). This article provides a good introduction to using online auctions.

- **PlanetClick's Auctions & Bargains section** (www.planetclick.com). This site gets really specific about specialty and "home-grown" person-to-person auctions. It also provides customer reviews of sites. Go to the PlanetClick home page and search for "auctions." You'll be amazed at the auction listings you find on specialty items such as wine, stamps, Oriental rugs, and much more.

Check out any discussion group or bulletin board features provided by an auction house to get the real lowdown on the pros and cons of the organization. eBay's bulletin boards are the best around. You can probably go there and ask about a site you like. Also check out *PC Magazine*'s suggestions of "The Best Auction Sites for..." at www.zdnet.com/pcmag/features/auction/bestfor.html. Some of the services that let you search multiple auction sites at one time contain brief descriptions of each service; these descriptions often (though not always) contain tips and critical evaluations. BidFind has one at www.bidfind.com/af/af-list.html.

Auction sites come in many flavors

Characterizing auction site types succinctly is difficult because the lines between them blur. The following sections provide some brief descriptions of the kinds of sites you can find online.

The fact that so many auction services exist can work to your advantage. Don't search just a single location for a particular item you want. Instead, use a service that lets you search multiple services at the same time. Try BidFind (www.bindfind.com) and Auction Connect (auctionconnect.lycos.com).

Company auctions

Auctions are becoming so popular that many existing retailers are getting in on the fun by offering select items of their own stock for sale to the highest bidder in *company auctions*. (*PC Magazine* calls these "House" auctions.) Companies may also sell their wares online in the conventional way.

This is a relatively new field; as I started working on this book, Sharper Image had just opened an auction service (`auction.sharperimage.com/ osauction.shtml`). The company's online auction offerings were just a selection of items from their catalog — they weren't even as varied as the items on the company's regular retail site.

When you visit these sites (several are listed in this book's Internet Directory) read the fine print carefully. Find out if you're bidding on merchandise that has been returned or refurbished. There's nothing wrong with such items, necessarily; it's just good to know what you're getting.

Computer auction services: It all computes

Everyone on the Internet needs and uses computer equipment, so it's hardly surprising that one of the most popular treasures you can bid on is computer equipment and software, as well as other electronics. One of the oldest of these is Onsale's atAuction site (`www.onsale.com`), shown in Figure 1-3.

Figure 1-3: Onsale goes well beyond computers, offering everything from appliances to vacations.

A fair number of auction sites act as resellers: They buy equipment from OEMs (Original Equipment Manufacturers) or VARs (Value Added Resellers). An *OEM* purchases product components from one or more companies and builds a product that it then sells under its own company name. Sometimes, the component manufacturers themselves (such as IBM) function as OEMs, so this can get confusing. A *VAR* also uses original components but adds "value" in the form of a computer application or other feature before it resells the product.

It's common to see ads on the front pages of computer auction sites that advertise a piece of hardware for $1. This is only the opening bid. The price is likely to go up dramatically as the end of the auction nears. Don't expect to get a brand-new laptop or digital camera for $1. Bidders can get caught up in such bargains and drive the price up to or even beyond the retail price — which means you no longer have a bargain.

Also keep in mind that you're probably dealing with merchandise that's currently out of date or refurbished. This isn't necessarily bad. For one thing, it means you can get an item for far less than the suggested manufacturer's retail price. It also means the device probably has been checked and repaired by the manufacturer.

Person-to-person auctions

Person-to-person auctions let buyers and sellers deal with one another directly. The auctions run on eBay, Yahoo! Auctions, and Amazon.com Auctions have the backing of the auction service's feedback, insurance, and other services. Person-to-person auctions can get really wild and crazy — and that can result in tremendous bargains for buyers or huge moneymaking moments for sellers.

The big difference between person-to-person auctions and company auctions is that the seller is not a company but an individual who may sell items either as a hobby or as a business. A few sellers have their own companies, and some even make a living doing auctions. A few of these more serious sellers accept credit cards, but the majority don't.

The overwhelming majority of sellers and buyers on person-to-person auctions are collectors or amateur dealers who are trying to make a deal or uncover a bargain. It's completely up to the seller to decide whether an auction item must sell for a predetermined minimum amount (called a *reserve;* see "Reserve price auctions are playing fair," earlier in this chapter) or whether it will go to the highest bidder. The seller can also choose whether the auction format is a traditional time-based auction or a Dutch auction (see "Understanding the Different Types of Internet Auctions," earlier in this chapter).

Most of the time, person-to-person auctions proceed smoothly. But occasionally, sealing the deal can be a problem. Sellers and buyers alike can perpetrate fraud either by refusing to ship the auctioned item and pocketing the money, or by refusing to pay or sending a "rubber" check. Keep this risk in mind when you sell or bid, especially when high-ticket items are involved.

The uncertainty with resolving person-to-person auctions is relieved considerably through feedback. Buyers and sellers record comments about whether the individual at the other end of the transaction performed his part well and seems reputable, or whether the person did something dishonest. See Chapters 3, 4, and 5 for more information about the types of problems you may encounter and how to avoid them.

Personal, "home-grown" auctions

The riskiest type of auction is a *personal auction,* which is arranged by an individual who wants to get rid of a lot of items, or maybe just a few scattered things. The seller could be a big business, and it could be a single individual who just started a commercial Web site. It's impossible to tell the difference on the Internet anyway.

Home-grown auctions may be perfectly reliable, but they aren't subject to any kind of regulation other than the commonsense business practices observed by any company that wants to stay in business. I strongly recommend using either a credit card or an escrow service to purchase from one of these sites, and that you buy only merchandise within your field of interest and expertise.

A good place to find individual sellers' auction pages is on the PlanetClick Web site (`www.planetclick.com`). Search for the type of item you want to buy, and chances are that the list of matches will include some individual sellers as well as big auction services like eBay.

Feeling the Lure of the Online Gavel

Who should take part in auctions on the Internet? Why should you venture into this brave new entrepreneurial world? The following sections provide some good reasons to participate in online auctions.

Experience the thrill of bargain hunting

You don't have a lot of money to spend. You need to get the best deal you can get on an item of value to you. Many auction enthusiasts are savvy shoppers who need to save money on things they purchase either for personal or business use.

My mother (hi, Mom) is an example of someone who searches months and even years, traveling to stores and flea markets around the United States hoping to find both everyday necessities and that one hidden masterpiece she wants to complete one of her collections. I sometimes do some shopping for her on the auction sites; I haven't quite gotten around to buying a computer for her and getting her online. You, however, can now search for your heart's desire online and, because so many people are gathered in one place and so many auctions are held all the time, your chances of finding what you want are excellent.

Take Jim Robinson, for instance. Jim is the CEO of Robinson & Muenster Associates, Inc., a research and telecommunications company headquartered in Sioux Falls, South Dakota. He's been buying online at auctions since early 1998. He estimates that in that first year, he purchased more than $100,000 worth of merchandise for his company — primarily computer hardware/software, peripherals, and electronics. He estimates that he's saved at least $50,000 over previous purchasing methods. He reports especially good experiences with Fair Auction (www.fairauction.com), a popular auction Web site that offers computer equipment online. (See Figure 1-4.)

But Jim doesn't stop there. He also frequents Internet auctions to buy household items (he recently purchased a carpet cleaner, for example), books and movies, camping and sporting goods, and games. He sometimes sells items, too. (See the sidebar "Auctions for personal and business benefit" for more details about Jim's online auction success.)

Figure 1-4:
Auction Web sites are great places to obtain computer and technical equipment at bargain prices.

Find rare treasures

You're actively seeking rare items to add to your collection. You don't have time to schlep around the country for months or years visiting antique stores, flea markets, and sales to find them. I collect rare pens and used to have to wait for the annual special collectors' auction to come to town. Now I shop for pens online. They don't exactly give things away online, especially since Internet auctions are growing in popularity and more and more collectors are flocking to them. The nice thing is finding those rare items *at all.* The pen in Figure 1-2 is an example of an offering that isn't cheap, but is so rare that even finding it is difficult.

Maximize your investment

You know you have treasures, and you want to make as much money as you can selling your merchandise. One of the best and most exciting benefits of online auctions is that buyers and sellers now have a huge database of information on which to draw to help determine how much an item is worth or what constitutes desirable merchandise. For example, you can search the eBay site (www.ebay.com) for an item that's sold and see what people have paid for it over the past weeks and months. Online auctions take appraisals out of the hands of professionals and put information at your fingertips so you can be an informed purchaser.

Find potential customers

If you're a seller, you need to expose your items to collectors or enthusiasts who may be looking for exactly what you have and will pay a premium for them.

Some people who frequent Internet-based auctions are individuals who love to shop for the things they love. I tend to shop for old watches and fountain pens, for example. My nephew looks for Beanie Babies to add to his collection. No matter what floats your boat, shopping for what you want is a thrill, whether it's a rare antique or a computer modem at half the retail price. If you're a seller, your adrenaline starts to rush when you anticipate having bidders who will offer you far more than you ever expected for what you have to sell.

Meet people with similar interests

The online world brings together many different communities made up of users with similar interests. Auction services can be a wonderful place to meet people who love to collect or sell the same things you do, who love bargain-hunting just as much as you do, and who are willing and happy to compare notes and talk about their experiences. You meet your fellow auction denizens at places like the eBay Cafe, where buyers and sellers alike can post messages to one another on online bulletin boards.

eBay calls its message boards "chat rooms," but this is misleading. As any teenager who has participated in Internet Relay Chat (or "chat" for short) can tell you, real chat on the Internet involves a number of users who connect to the same site on the Internet and communicate by typing messages that appear in a matter of seconds to everyone else connected to the site at that time. Typically, when the conversation is over, the messages are no longer visible. eBay's message exchanges don't occur in real time. They remain visible for a matter of hours and more closely resemble bulletin boards, where people "converse" in a more leisurely fashion.

A random look at eBay's "chat room" for book enthusiasts (see Figure 1-5) turned up lots of useful information, including a notice for an upcoming book fair, United Parcel Service shipping tips, warnings about poor packaging of books shipped from various sellers, and lots of book reviews.

Chapter 3 describes how getting into the world of online auctions can help you make new connections, even new friends, in the auction world.

Auctions for personal and business benefit

Jim Robinson, the CEO of a high-tech company, has this to say about his experience with Internet auctions:

"I buy all kinds of computer hardware, software, and networking parts for my business. Personally, I buy household items (I just purchased a carpet cleaner last month), books and movies (lots and lots of books and movies), camping and sporting goods and games. I will sell about anything (except books and movies — I have quite a library!). This weekend I'm listing a new digital camera.

"Internet auction transactions are always exciting for me, especially if I can finally buy something at a price far below what I have been seeing on the Net.

"I would tell auction newcomers to avoid getting auction fever and buying stuff just to win the auction. Even hard-to-find items will repeat online, so it's silly to pay too much for something just to beat the other guy.

"Second, be patient. Auctions sometimes take a week, so don't put out too high a bid right away — you can always go back to the auction site on the last day and see how things are.

"Third, know your merchandise. Go to a store or someplace to check something out before bidding on a high-ticket item. I see people buy computer systems that sound really neat but have an inferior computer processor (one that doesn't do computations as fast as the latest versions) in them. This isn't the seller's fault — it's the buyer's.

"Four, have some fun with this stuff! Get to know people. You'll be surprised how nice most are. I even hired a staff person who was referred to me by someone I had bought computers from. It's worked out great."

Ensuring a Positive Auction Experience

Buyers and sellers can reach their goals — whether those goals are to find a rare antique, save a few bucks, make some extra money, or uncover new customers for an existing business — by following some general rules. By following these guidelines, you dramatically reduce your chances of getting swindled. The risks aren't eliminated entirely, but lots of people use auctions all the time without ever running into trouble. It's far more common to have a good experience than a bad one. Just use common sense and be careful, and you should be okay.

To increase your chances for a good outcome and dramatically reduce your chances of getting swindled (although not eliminate them entirely) follow the guidelines in this section.

Understand how Internet auctions work

Lots and lots of specialized auctions are online, and they operate very differently, each with its own tricks and quirks. Some sites let you purchase only with credit cards; on other sites you have to send buyers or sellers a check or money order. Some sites provide lots of customer support options. Others give you a single e-mail address for all inquiries and complaints.

Figure 1-5: Online discussion forums like this don't look glamorous, but they're among the friendliest and most useful sources of information you can find.

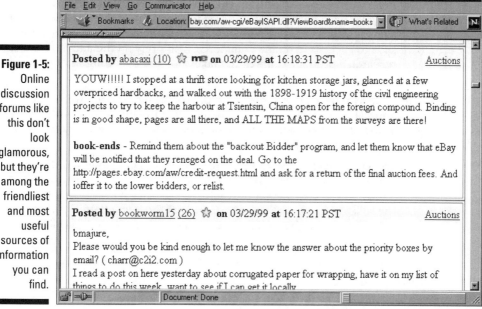

The moral of the story: Don't start placing bids without knowing what's involved first. Be sure you read a site's User Agreement or its rules for buyers or sellers to know what you can and can't do.

Keep a level head

It's hard not to get emotional when you're bidding at auction. The item catches your eye; you get excited. If you get involved in a bidding war, you can easily get carried away. Make sure that you get a good deal at a price with which you are satisfied. If you're a seller, this means selling the item for the price you want — not less. If you're a buyer, it means paying the price you want — and no more.

Auctions can also be addictive: Bargain-hunting can be like horse-racing, stock trading, or other thrilling activities. When you bid, ask what it is that attracts you. Are you really in love with the item at hand? Make a cold-blooded appraisal. Keep a clear head.

Know the risks

Thrills and bargains don't come for free. Internet auctions are fun and exciting, but they're also risky in several respects. Some aspects that may work against you are:

- **Poor customer service from the auction service.** Many Internet auction services have gone online only recently and know nothing about how to provide good customer service and personal interaction, which are the keys to success in online commerce. Don't rely on the auction house; research a product yourself to make sure you're getting what you want at a good price.

- **Your own lack of experience.** In the traditional auction world, experts appraise and vouch for the authenticity of the items they put up for sale. These checks are not available online. You have to be your own expert and do your own research so that you don't get ripped off.

- **You can't touch what you buy.** You can see an item online and ask questions about it, but you can't actually interact with it as you can at a garage sale or flea market or traditional auction. It's up to you to research the seller to be as sure as you can be that the item offered is what the seller claims it to be, and that the advertised quality and condition is accurate.

> ✔ **Closing a transaction can be difficult.** This applies whether you are selling or buying. For sellers, the deadbeat bidder — who places the high bid on an item but never follows through with payment, or who sends a bad check — is the most common problem. For buyers, potential trouble abounds in the form of fraudulent sellers. See Chapter 3 for suggestions on how both buyers and sellers can protect themselves against being cheated. See Chapters 5 and 8 for more information on how to close a transaction successfully.

Practice safe auctioning

Problems with Internet auctions were the most frequent source of complaints received in 1998 by Internet Fraud Watch, a service of the National Consumers League. Most of these complaints concerned sellers who received payment in the form of a check or money order and then failed to deliver the goods purchased. Chapters 3, 11, and 12 are chock-full of suggestions for how to avoid these sorts of problems.

 Read more about auction complaints received by Internet Fraud Watch, as well as suggestions for how to avoid trouble online, in the article at www.fraud.org/internet/9923stat.htm.

Take advantage of electronic gimmicks

Because Internet auctions are online, they make use of high-tech tricks that may seem a little intimidating but can maximize your chances of a successful transaction.

For one thing, auction services can communicate with you automatically by e-mail. Some services, like eBay or Auction Universe (www.auctionuniverse.com) automatically notify you if someone outbids you on an item. You can then place another bid before the auction ends.

Other services, like Bid-4-It (www.bid4it.com), use computer programs called *agents* to automatically notify you about items that you want to find. Whenever such an item appears, you can receive a notification about it.

Make sure that what you see is what you get

The online equivalent of traveling to the site of the auction and viewing the sales merchandise beforehand is to open a digital version of the image in your Web browser window.

The clarity of the image you see depends on the clarity of your computer monitor and the quality of your computer's video card. (I discuss these and other hardware requirements for participating in Internet auctions in Chapter 2.)

Because the image is broken down into tiny segments of digital information called *pixels,* and the visual details have been compressed into special graphics formats used on the Web in order to get them online (see Chapter 7), you don't get a perfect representation of the item when you see it online. If a seller provides more than one image, so much the better. Often, though, you see only one photo of an item. If you're lucky, the seller at a person-to-person auction provides you with one or more clear images of the item, such as the sharp close-up shown in Figure 1-6.

No matter how clear the images are, there's no substitute for your own knowledge, much of which is provided by or augmented by research. Often, no photo of the item is available on the auction page or the Internet ad. If the item is offered by an individual, ask him or her questions. Then, you can look up prices at sites like Pricewatch (www.pricewatch.com). Also read the Winning Strategy Guide at the Auction-Guide Web site (www.auction-guide.com).

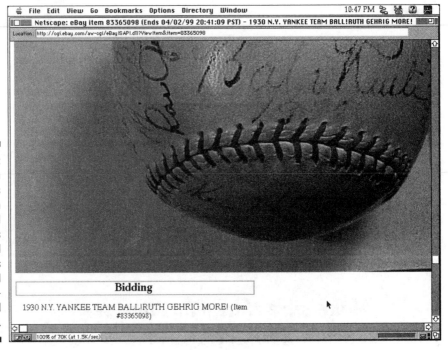

Figure 1-6: Auction sales depend on good descriptions and digital images displayed online, supplemented by research.

1930 N.Y. YANKEE TEAM BALL!RUTH GEHRIG MORE! (Item #83365098)

Bidding

Chapter 2

Getting Online and Up to Speed

● ●

In This Chapter

▶ Getting your computer hardware up to speed

▶ Choosing an Internet service provider

▶ Protecting your security and privacy

▶ Choosing Web browsers and auction software

● ●

*B*efore you can step up to the auction block, you need to connect to the Internet, and in order to do that, you need some basic computer hardware and software.

The transformation from regular folk to online auction maven is akin to going from game show couch contestant to actual player. You have to forsake the familiar and learn new skills: Instead of walking from the kitchen to the couch, you have to hop in your car, or board a plane, or somehow travel to the show. When you reach the studio, you have to do more than operate your remote: You get to push buttons, speak into a microphone, maybe spin that wheel of fortune.

In short, you learn to be a participant instead of a spectator. Rather than watching from afar on the small screen, you're an active player in the game, and people are watching *you*.

When it comes to online auctions, your computer hardware, your Internet connection, and your Web browser are the technological tools that transport you to the auction site. After arriving at your destination, you use your Web browser to play the game, and your monitor to keep track of how you're doing.

If you're happy with your Internet connection and equipment, you can skip this chapter. This chapter is for those of you who are eager to start wheeling and dealing but aren't sure what equipment you need.

What sort of computer hardware do you need to participate in online auctions? What if you don't even own a computer — is it worth shopping for and purchasing a new one? Do you need special hardware to do business online?

Find the answers to these questions in the following sections.

Getting the Right Hardware

Buying and selling through online auctions, like other types of electronic commerce, don't require a machine with the latest super-fast processor and multimedia bells and whistles.

Nevertheless, the speed and quality of your computer, monitor, and other hardware can affect your auction experience. If your machine is slow and your modem a crawler, you could come up the loser in a last-minute bidding battle. If you can't inspect a detailed screen image of that work of art you want, you may end up with a Whiner instead of a Whistler. Make sure you have, at the very least:

- A reasonably fast computer — that is, one with a 166 MHz processor at the very least. If you're on a Macintosh, try to get one with a PowerPC processor.
- A good monitor and video card (see the section "Monitor-ing the Action" for more details).
- A reliable Internet connection.

I give you merely an overview of your equipment needs in this section. For more detailed explanations of hardware terms and suggestions for what to buy, look no further than *PCs For Dummies,* 5th Edition, by Dan Gookin, or *Upgrading & Fixing PCs For Dummies,* 4th Edition, by Andy Rathbone, both published by IDG Books Worldwide.

Lots of people access the Internet from their offices. On the plus side, such users are likely to have a fast connection, a computer with a speedy processor, and a big monitor.

But, as any supervisor will tell you, there's a big downside to using your office equipment for auction or other personal Web surfing: You slow down network access for the rest of your colleagues, and you waste time that could be spent on, well . . . work.

To stay out of the doghouse, set up an inexpensive, basic system in your home.

More is better with memory

Computer memory comes in many varieties, but the most important for your purposes are hard disk storage and RAM.

Computers on the auction block

When you're looking for good deals on computer equipment, consider online auctions. Many auction outlets include computers in their bidding categories, and some even specialize in hardware and software.

Often, you can shop online for integrated computer-monitor packages that have lots of memory and fast processors. The figure in this sidebar shows an example from ONSALE.com (`www.onsale.com`).

The Internet is teeming with good deals on hardware. A great place to start is the CNET Shopper.com Web site (`www.shopper.com`). Also visit the Inter-Mart Computer Store (`www.buysoftware.com/intermart`). And if you're looking for bargains on used hardware, don't forget the newsgroups devoted to

equipment for sale, such as `alt.ads.forsale.computers` and any of the groups whose names begin with `misc.forsale.computers`.

You can find plenty of other auction sites for computer equipment in this book's Internet Directory.

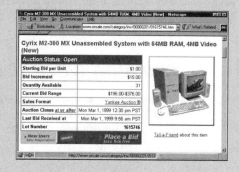

Hard disk storage space isn't an issue for most new computers, which come with hard disk drives that store one or more *gigabytes* (GB) of data. (A gigabyte is a thousand megabytes.) Any hard disk capable of storing a gigabyte or more should be fine for your needs. (Many new computers come with hard disks of 3, 6, or more gigabytes.) If you're buying a used computer, beware. Don't come home with less than a gigabyte of storage space, or you'll run out of room before you know it.

Random Access Memory (RAM) is the memory your computer uses to temporarily store the information needed to operate programs. The more RAM you have, the more programs you can run at the same time. If you don't have enough RAM to operate all the programs you have open at any one time, your computer slows to a crawl.

Going online, using a Web browser, and shopping for auction treasures doesn't require huge amounts of memory. But if you plan to put goodies up for sale, you need some additional software, and each program requires RAM. For example, you may want to do one of the following (all of which require RAM):

  ✔ **Create a Web page.** A Web page or Web site can help advertise you or your business, if you have one (see Chapter 7).

  ✔ **Run an auction ticker.** Some programs let you track bids on goods you have for sale (see Chapter 7).

✔ **Capture digital images.** You're likely to get more bids if you provide a clear computerized image of your items by scanning them or using a digital camera (see Chapter 7).

Bottom line: If you plan only to buy through auctions, you can get by with 32MB of RAM. However, to be an auction seller, install a minimum of 48MB. In either case, make sure that your auction "vehicle" has as much RAM "fuel" as you can afford to give it.

When you shop for memory or other computer hardware, save your receipts. If you make money selling through auctions and have to report the income to the IRS, you may be able to itemize computer equipment purchases as business expenses on your tax return. Check with your tax advisor.

Speeding when it counts

Computer processors are getting faster all the time. Every month, it seems, some manufacturer comes out with a faster chip that's supposed to make games leap off the screen, perform all your functions in half the time, and wax the kitchen floor, besides.

The speed at which a processor operates is measured by the number of electronic pulses its clock emits per second. This speed is expressed in terms of a million cycles per second, or megahertz (MHz). Don't be overly impressed by a computer's clock speed, however. Sure, you're wise to purchase the fastest computer you can afford, but don't obsess about getting the latest and fastest processor on the block. By the time you get your computer home, another, faster chip will have been released.

A super-fast Pentium chip helps primarily when you have to perform scads of calculations, fill out spreadsheets, and deal with other number-crunching tasks. For basic business needs, Web surfing, and viewing graphics, concentrate on getting lots of memory — not speed — for your computer.

The Pentium chip is a popular processor introduced in the early 1990s by the Intel Corporation to replace its 486 processor. Faster versions of the original Pentium — the Pentium Pro, Pentium II, and Pentium III — have since come out. Pentium processors are great, no doubt about it. But in my experience you can still surf the Web, exchange e-mail messages, and update Web pages with a 486 processor in your computer. When should you upgrade to a Pentium? If your computer already has 32 to 48MB of RAM, you have a 56 Kbps modem, and you're still crawling slowly from one Web page to another, consider taking your machine to a computer service center and having your 486 upgraded to a Pentium chip, which is becoming more practical and reasonable in cost as time goes on.

Protecting your investment

You can spend all the money you want on top-notch computer equipment, but if you plug your expensive machines into a substandard electrical system, your investment can (almost literally) go up in smoke.

Protect your equipment against electrical problems that can result in a loss of data or substantial repair bills. A *power surge* or *spike* (a sudden increase in voltage) can damage your equipment. Electrical storms can damage ungrounded equipment, and blackouts can put you offline and prevent you from getting work done, which can hit you in your pocketbook.

At the very least, make sure that your home office has grounded three-prong outlets. (Even if the rest of your house has the old-fashioned outlets, pay an electrician to upgrade the line to your office.)

Upgrading means more than just changing the outlets; it means using grounded cable to get the electricity to the outlet. Your whole electrical system should be grounded, which is most often accomplished by having your main electrical box connected to a copper spike buried in the ground. In case your house is struck by lightning, or an electrical appliance shorts out, the electricity runs harmlessly into the ground, and not into your computer, TV, or toaster.

Another must-have is a *surge suppressor,* a device that guards your equipment against power surges and other electrical problems. A common variety is a five- or six-outlet strip with a built-in protection device. You can find surge suppressers at hardware and computer stores.

Don't worry about multimedia add-ons

Multimedia is more important to your children's computer games than it is to participating in online auctions. Just make sure that you have the basics: a sound card and a built-in speaker or a set of external speakers.

You probably don't need to worry about purchasing special sound cards, external speakers, or adding audio-video goodies when you're first starting out. At a later stage, when and if your online business transactions become more sophisticated, you may want to try Web browser add-ons that require you to be able to listen to audio and conduct voice communications online, such as the conferencing and whiteboard technologies built into Netscape Communicator and Microsoft Internet Explorer. A whiteboard is a computerized version of an overhead projector used to make presentations at a meeting. It lets one person make presentations and show them to others on a network. Conferencing lets you communicate by voice with other Internet users in real time, almost as though you're using your computer to make an online phone call.

Monitor-ing the action

When it comes to buying online, a good monitor and a video card are two of the most important investments you can make. In order to know whether an item is exactly what you want, you have to be able to see it clearly. Sometimes, too, the only reference you have for an item's quality is an onscreen image.

It's tempting to scrimp on computer monitors, especially if you're a bargain hunter like me. You can find cheap monitors for $100, or even less if you buy a used one. But, because monitors are so important to your auction experience, don't scrimp on this important component. If you can afford it, purchase a 15- or 17-inch monitor instead of the smaller 14-inch variety. Even an extra inch makes a huge difference whether you're looking at word-processing documents or Web pages.

A monitor's quality depends on several factors:

- ✔ **Resolution.** A computer monitor's resolution refers to the number of pixels it can display horizontally and vertically. A resolution of 640 x 480 means that the monitor displays 640 pixels horizontally and 480 pixels vertically. Anything less than 640 x 480 is unusable these days. (Check out the "Pixel perfect" sidebar for more on pixels.)

- ✔ **Size.** As with a television, monitor size is measured diagonally. Monitor sizes up to 32 inches are available. A 15-inch or 17-inch monitor can display most Web pages fully.

- ✔ **Refresh rate.** This is the number of times per second that a video card redraws an image on screen. Look for a monitor with a refresh rate of at least 60 Hz (Hz is a common abbreviation for hertz, a way of measuring electrical pulses in cycles per second).

Pixel perfect

Computer monitors display graphic information that consists of little units called *pixels.* Each pixel appears in a computer image as a small dot. The pixels are so small that they're hard to see with the naked eye unless you magnify an image to look at details close up. Together, the patterns of pixels create different intensities of light and different ranges of color in an image. The more pixels per inch (ppi), the higher a monitor's potential resolution. The higher the resolution, the closer the image appears to a continuous-tone image such as a photograph.

A monitor *resolution* of 1280 x 1024, for example, refers to the number of pixels per inch that the monitor displays. *Dot pitch* refers to the distance between any two of the three pixels (one red, one green, and one blue) that a monitor uses to display color. The lower the dot pitch, the better image resolution you obtain. A dot pitch of .28 millimeters is a good standard for a 17-inch monitor.

Your perfectly good monitor may display a distorted view due to an inadequate video card. I recently upgraded my video card from one that uses 2MB of video RAM to one that uses 4MB and improved my Web page viewing immensely.

Connections count with modems

A modem is a hardware device that translates your computer's digital data to signals carried over other types of electronic cables. A conventional analog modem translates the digital computer information into analog data that can be sent over ordinary phone lines. Other kinds of modems translate digital data differently. An ISDN terminal adapter connects a computer to a digital data line, and a cable modem carries signals over fiber optic cables. If you already have a modem that you use to connect your computer to the Internet, you don't necessarily have to purchase a new and faster one just because you're delving into online auctions. For most auction adventures, a simple dialup modem connection is adequate. But the faster the connection, the faster you can place a bid, update a sale description, or receive e-mail inquiries. The following sections discuss analog and other types of modems to help you decide which modem type is right for you.

When shopping for a modem, you may encounter the term bandwidth. *Bandwidth* refers to the amount of data an Internet connection can transmit. Bandwidth is usually measured in bits per second (bps). Different kinds of modems provide varying amounts of bandwidth.

To get up to speed on modem speeds and related topics, consult *Modems For Dummies* by Tina Rathbone and Andy Rathbone, published by IDG Books Worldwide.

Conventional (analog) modems

The simplest and most straightforward way to connect to the Internet is to use an analog modem — either external or built in to your computer. Unfortunately, using a dial-up modem is also the slowest way to Web surf. If you have an analog modem, I recommend that you keep your existing device and try it for a while before shopping for a faster modem. Place a bid on an item and refresh your Web browser's screen display immediately to see whether your bid was recorded. (If you use Netscape Navigator, choose View➪Refresh. For Microsoft Internet Explorer, the command is the same but the hotkey is different: View➪Refresh.)

Checking the refresh speed isn't a strictly scientific test because the speed of the data transfer also depends on the speed of the computer that provides the auction listings. But if you find that placing a bid takes too long, consider getting a faster modem. A 28.8 Kbps (kilobits per second) or 36.6 Kbps modem should be adequate, but a 56 Kbps device is much better.

Alternatives to conventional modems

Most people on a budget use a regular dial-up modem connection (see the previous section). A far better way to connect to the Internet is through a *direct line,* which keeps you connected at all times, rather than just for the length of your modem's phone call. Besides freeing up a phone line, a direct connection with a cable modem line is typically a lot faster than a dial-up modem connection.

The following sections discuss some faster alternatives to conventional modems.

The cable company does modems

Cable modems receive data from the Internet through a cable TV company's existing underground fiber optic cable. This is an extremely fast, attractive option — if it's available in your area. Cable modem connections are relatively new, but they're already demonstrating many advantages: A cable modem provides a direct connection, frees up a phone line, and is super fast. Cable modems have the capacity to deliver 4 or 5MB of data per second. In reality, the speed is less than that because you share access with other users. But a cable modem is still almost certainly faster than your dial-up connection.

In my neighborhood in Chicago, a company called 21st Century (www.21stcentury.com) offers basic cable TV service for $29.45 a month and/or Internet access for an additional $44.95 per month, plus a $125 installation fee that includes the cable modem device itself. You need an Ethernet network card installed in one of your computer's internal card slots in order to use the cable modem, however, so make sure you have a slot available if you need to buy the card as well.

ADSL: Not just alphabet soup

Asymmetrical Digital Subscriber Line (ADSL) technology, sometimes simply called DSL, is a cost-effective "starter" type of direct connection to the Net that uses conventional telephone lines to transfer data at very high speeds. An ADSL transmits data using the part of your phone line that your voice transmissions don't use — the part that transmits signals of 3000 Hz (hertz) or higher. ADSLs can *upload* (send) data to another location on the Net at 1.088 Mbps (megabits per second), and *download* (receive) data at more than twice that rate: 2.560 Mbps.

Of course, you can't just use your existing telephone to connect via ADSL. You need to buy and install special hardware at your end, and the telephone company needs to have the same piece of ADSL hardware at its end. Where you live also makes a difference: You must live relatively close to a telephone switch that supports ADSL technology.

Check with your telephone provider to see whether ADSLs are available in your area.

What's on TV? The Web

Web TV is a network service that enables you to connect to the Web and view Web pages through your TV monitor. With Web TV, you purchase a set-top box, a hand-held controller, and a keyboard. You sign up with the Web TV network and pay a monthly access fee. You may also want to install another phone line or get call waiting — Web TV uses a regular telephone jack, so callers get a busy signal if they call while you're online and you don't have a second line or call waiting.

The advantage of Web TV is that is gives you a way to surf the Web and use Internet software without having to purchase a computer. You see the same content that other surfers see with Web browsers and computers. In fact, if you already have a computer, Web TV frees up your regular computer so someone else in the family can do homework — or you can work on your business site — while someone else surfs the Web. You can also create Web pages through Web TV.

ISDN: It's a simply divine network

ISDN (short for Integrated Services Digital Network) service is a practical alternative for many individuals or small businesses who need a faster connection to the Internet than conventional dial-up modems provide that's still affordable. ISDN enables your computer to connect to the Net at 64 or 128 Kbps by means of a special phone line and line-switching equipment installed by your phone company. Check with your phone company to find out whether it provides ISDN service.

In my opinion, the best thing about ISDN setup is that the device that connects your computer to the ISDN line, which is called a terminal adapter rather than a modem, comes with two POTS (Plain Old Telephone Service lines), which I use for my fax machine and extra phone connection. I rarely use the 128 Kbps option because my Internet service provider charges a higher rate and I find 56Kbps to be fast enough for my basic needs. My ISP charges an extra monthly fee for ISDN service, and so does my telephone company. If I had to do it over again, I'd probably purchase a 56 Kbps modem and an extra phone line rather than installing an ISDN.

Go wireless with DirecPC

DirecPC is a satellite-based Internet access service that beats ISDN when it comes to speed, offering download rates of as much as 400 Kbps. You need to purchase a satellite dish, which comes with the service. However, DirecPC does not provide unlimited access to the Net with any of its three service plans: One gives you 25 hours free per month, and the other two include 100 and 200 hours, respectively. Additional hours cost $1.99 each. Find out more at www.direcpc.com/about/index.html.

Additional hardware for sellers

Hardware requirements for auction sellers are a bit more extensive than those for buyers. You need a way to take images of the merchandise you want to sell and capture those images as digitized computer files. After you have an image in the form of a computer document, you can transfer it to a Web site to let potential buyers take a look (see Chapter 7).

Sure, plenty of auctioneers list items online without photos, just descriptions. But most marketing gurus agree that a picture is worth a thousand mega-bytes of information, in online terms. Including a clear, sharp image on your Web site greatly increases your chances of selling your product or service. You have two choices for digitizing:

- ✔ Taking photos with a digital camera and saving the image files on your computer.
- ✔ Taking photos with a conventional camera and then scanning them into your computer.

Your choice depends on your budget and your needs; the following sections discuss the advantages and disadvantages of each method.

Saying cheese, digitally

If the objects you want to auction are three-dimensional or won't fit on a scanner (ever try to scan an automobile, house, or box of candy? In the case of the candy, it's possible, but be careful not to squish your delicacies! Don't try this at home!), you need either a digital camera or a scanner that can scan an ordinary photo of the object. The advantage of using a digital camera is that it's portable and convenient. A digital camera connects directly to your computer, so you can save images right to disk. You can get photos online in a matter of minutes without spending money or time having them processed and printed conventionally.

Not so long ago, digital cameras cost thousands of dollars. These days, you can find good digital cameras made by reputable manufacturers like Nikon, Fuji, Canon, Olympus, and Kodak in the $300 to $700 range. You have to make an investment up front, but this particular tool can pay off for you in the long run. Not only can you use the camera for your auction offerings, but with the addition of a color printer, you can even print your own photos, which can save you a pile in photo lab costs.

Don't hesitate to fork over the extra dough to get a camera that gives you good resolution. It doesn't pay to cut corners and end up with images that look fuzzy. Most low-cost devices have a resolution of 640 x 480 pixels, at best. Look for a camera like the Epson PhotoPC 600, which costs about $500 and has a top resolution of 1,024 x 768 pixels. Others, such as the Fuji MX-700 or Agfa ePhoto 1280, can take photos at a resolution of 1,280 x 1,024 pixels, and the Kodak Digital Science DC260 can reach 1,536 x 1,024. But keep in mind that the higher the resolution, the fewer photos your camera can store at any one time, because larger image files require more memory.

As with other computer hardware, online auctions are good places to do some comparison shopping for digital cameras (see Figure 2-1).

Scanning for the perfect scanner

If you plan to auction photos or other flat objects, you can *scan* them. Scanning is the process of turning the colors and shapes contained in an image such as a photographic print or slide into digital information (that is, bytes of data) that a computer can understand. You place the image in a position where the scanner's camera can pass over it, and the scanner turns the image into a computer document that consists of tiny bits of information called *pixels.*

Scanners have been around for a while, which, in the world of computing, means that prices are going down at the same time that quality is on the rise. The bargain models are well under $100, and I've even seen a couple (including the Microtek ScanMaker E3) priced under $135. This book's tech editor reports purchasing one for only $49.95 after a $30 manufacturer's rebate. Now that's a deal!

Scanners come in many different types. Some devices scan slides, but most accept photographic prints. The one that I find easiest to use is a flatbed scanner. The photo or other image is placed on a flat glass "bed," just like the one on a photocopier. An optical device moves under the bed and scans the photo. The flatbed scanner shown in Figure 2-2 showed up on eBay.

If you already have a video camera for home use and need a way to get your photos on the Web, consider a neat little device called Snappy Video Snapshot, which lets you select still images from your videotapes and save them in digital format so that you can display them on your Web pages. Snappy, by Play Incorporated (www.play.com), is a software and hardware package that works only with PCs, not Macs.

Figure 2-1:
You can find digital cameras at bargain prices at Internet auction houses.

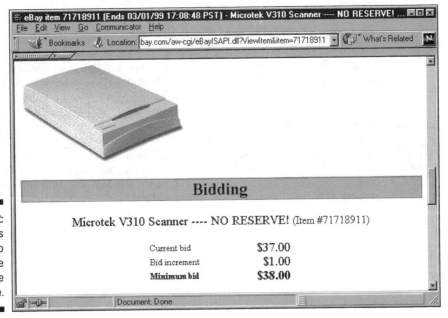

Figure 2-2:
Scanners continue to drop in price and are easy to use.

Making the Right Internet Connections

After you purchase the computer hardware you need, you need to connect it to the Internet. Your Internet connection's reliability is important. Make sure you sign up with an Internet Service Provider (ISP) that:

- Gives you many different dialup numbers (in case one line is busy or not responding, you can dial in on another line).

- Provides round-the-clock technical support.

- Gives you space on a computer called a Web server where you can publish your own Web pages. If you plan to create your own auction Web pages or provide Web-based content that supplements your auction sales listings, look for an ISP that gives you Web page space.

- Has a reputation for consistent, reliable connections. You don't want an ISP with a history of technical glitches that keep customers offline for hours at a time.

I'm not going to go into detail here about finding an Internet Service Provider. You can check out my books — *Starting an Online Business For Dummies* or *Creating Web Pages For Kids & Parents* — or *Creating Web Pages For Dummies* by Bud Smith and Arthur Bebak for suggestions. All are published by IDG Books Worldwide.

Probably the most important telephone- or connection-related decision you can make is to install a second phone line for your online buying and selling. Unless you have an ADSL or cable modem connection, having a second line is pretty much a necessity if you plan to do business online regularly — or if your children or significant other uses your existing phone line even on a semi-regular basis. (The digital modem that you need when you install an ISDN line comes with two extra analog phone lines — that is, the kind you use for normal voice and dial-up modem connections. The extra lines come with the ISDN terminal adapter and don't require any special installation; however, you have to pay the phone company to use them, the same as any other phone lines. See "ISDN: It's a simply divine network," earlier in this chapter.)

Because you use your modem to dial the same one or two access numbers provided by your Internet Service Provider, confirm with your telephone company that your Internet access number is truly local — not a number for which you pay a toll fee.

If you don't already pay a flat fee for unlimited local calls, be sure to ask your telephone company whether a call pack is available. A *call pack* allows you to make a large number of local calls to the same number for the same rate: 100 calls per month for a flat $10 fee, for example.

Maintaining Online Security and Privacy

Connecting to the Internet is a snap after you have the right equipment in place. Unfortunately, it's also a snap for an unscrupulous individual to make unauthorized use of any personal information sent over the Internet. When buying and selling is one of your primary reasons for connecting to the Internet, you need to protect yourself. This section describes some simple ways in which you can make your Internet activities safe and secure.

Choosing a good password

Passwords are an essential part of online auctions, just as they are for connecting to the Net, retrieving e-mail, and many other Web surfing functions. Picking a password that thieves won't be able to crack is essential.

One good method for choosing a password is to take a phrase that's easy for you to remember and then use the first letters of each word to form the basis of a password. For example, the phrase Early to Bed and Early to Rise would be ETBAETR. Then, you can mix upper- and lowercase letters and add punctuation, and you wind up with eTb[a]ETr. If you *really* want to make a password that's hard to crack, add some numerals as well, such as the last two digits of the year you were born: eTb[a]Etr59.

Getting some privacy

Working at home is safer in many ways than driving to a remote office. You don't have to brave the highways and byways commuting from one place to another.

But when your workplace is the same as your living space, you run into new challenges, not the least of which is privacy. For example, to your kids and your spouse, the computer may be a place to do homework, play games, or surf the Net. But to you, it may be a place to make money or to go treasure-hunting. The ultimate solution is to have separate machines — one for personal use and one for business use. Then set up your system so you have to log on to your business computer with a username and password.

If you don't have multiple computers available and different individuals want to use the same machine but with different e-mail addresses or other settings, you can set up different user profiles for your copy of Netscape Communicator. That way, your kids won't receive your business e-mail while they're surfing the Net, because you'll have different e-mail inboxes. If you're on Windows, choose Start➪Programs➪Netscape Communicator➪Setup New User Profile.

Are you insured?

You insure your house and car, so it only makes sense to protect your business investment by obtaining insurance that specifically covers you against hardware damage or theft and loss of data. You can also go a step further and obtain a policy that covers the cost of data entry or equipment renewal necessary to recover your business information. Write a list of all your hardware and software and how much each item cost, and store the list in a safe place. Take photos of your computer setup in case you need to make an insurance claim. Investigate the computer hardware and software coverage provided by Data Security Insurance (www .data-security.com) and Safeware, The Insurance Agency Inc., 1-800-848-3469.

Whatever you do, don't use passwords that appear in a dictionary. A clever hacker can run a program that uses every word in an online dictionary as your password and eventually discover it. Plus, be sure not to use something as obvious as your own name, username, or e-mail address. Also avoid using the same password at more than one site. If you use the same password all the time, and your password to one site on the Internet is compromised, all your password-protected accounts are in jeopardy. Finally, use at least six characters. The more letters in your password, the more work code-crackers have to go through.

Encryption: Use it to keep from losing it

Like the secret agents who populated TV in the '60s, computers can be set up to use a process of encoding and decoding to protect information they exchange on the Internet.

The term _encryption_ refers to the process of encoding sensitive data, such as credit card numbers. Information is encrypted by means of complex mathematical formulas called _algorithms_. Such a formula can transform a simple-looking bit of information into a huge block of seemingly incomprehensible numbers, letters, and characters. The gobbledygook can only be decoded by someone who has the right formula, called a _key_, which is itself a complex mass of encoded data.

Here's a very simple example: Suppose that my credit card number is 12345, and I encode it using an encryption formula so it looks like the following:

1aFgHx203gX4gLu5cy

The formula essentially says: "Take the first number, add x letters to it, multiply it by x numerals, take the second number, divide it by x, add x characters to it," and so on. (In reality, the formulas are far more complex than this, which is why you usually have to pay a license fee to use them. But this is the general idea.) Someone who has the same formula can run it in reverse, so to speak, in order to decrypt the encoded number and obtain the original number, 12345.

In practice, this kind of encryption is used by businesses, but individuals selling or buying online can use encryption by:

✔ Obtaining a personal certificate (see "Using certificates," later in this chapter).

✔ Encrypting e-mail messages (see "Encrypting your e-mail messages," later in this chapter).

Feeling insecure? Read on to find out some easy ways to verify that your data is encrypted.

Figuring out whether your data is encrypted

For consumers, the most important signal that a site such as an auction service uses encryption to protect your credit card numbers and other personal information is the security indicator found in the status bars of the two most popular Web browsers, Microsoft Internet Explorer and Netscape Navigator.

Both browsers alert you when you enter a "secure" area of a site. Typically, an alert message pops up in your browser window to tell you that you are either entering or leaving the part of the Web site that uses encryption. For consumers, this is a good thing: You should see this alert message or another security indicator before you submit any personal information to the site. The security indicator displayed by both Navigator and Internet Explorer, an icon that looks like a lock, appears "locked" when you are in the secure part of a site.

Using certificates

In the real world, you carry a passport or a state ID, and retailers use these documents to check your identity. The solution in the online world is to obtain a personal certificate, also called a *Digital ID*, that you can send to Web site visitors or append to your e-mail messages.

Understanding what a certificate is

A *certificate,* which is also sometimes called a Digital ID, is an electronic document issued by a certification authority (CA). The certificate contains the owner's personal information as well as a public key that can be exchanged with others online. The public key is generated by the owner's private key, which the owner obtains during the process of applying for the certificate.

A certificate assures the people with whom you trade that you are the person you say you are, and protects your e-mail communications by enabling you to encrypt them.

You don't often see certificates offered by people you meet on online auctions, but as certificates become more mainstream and fraud becomes more of a concern, they are likely to become more of a household word.

Certificates might make sense in one of the following auction scenarios:

- ✔ You operate a business Web site and, in connection with your business, you offer some items on auction. You include a link to your Web site on your auction listings. Visitors to your site can elect to receive your certificate to verify that your business is real and you are who you say you are.

- ✔ You exchange e-mail with a buyer or seller and exchange Digital ID numbers or encrypted e-mail.

The following section explains how to obtain a certificate.

Getting a certificate from VeriSign

Obtaining a certificate is remarkably easy. If you use Microsoft Internet Explorer 5, you don't have to do anything; one of the most widely used Certificate Authorities (CAs), VeriSign, Inc., now includes a certificate with this version of Microsoft's browser. Otherwise, you obtain a certificate by applying and paying a licensing fee to a CA. VeriSign lets you apply for a certificate called a Class 1 Digital ID on its Web site (www.verisign.com).

A VeriSign personal certificate, which you can use to authenticate yourself in e-mail, news, and other interactions on the Net, costs $9.95 per year, and you can try out a free certificate for 60 days. To get a VeriSign certificate, follow these steps:

1. **Connect to the Internet, launch your Web browser, and go to the VeriSign, Inc. Products page at** www.verisign.com/products/index.html.

2. **Click the Digital IDs link under the Individual Certificates section of the page.**

   The VeriSign Digital ID Center page appears.

3. **Click the Enroll Now button.**

   A security alert message appears, and your browser's security icon changes to show that you are entering a secure site (see the section, "Figuring out whether your data is encrypted," earlier in this chapter, for more information).

   The Digital ID Enrollment page for your browser appears (see Figure 2-3).

4. **Follow the steps described on the Web site.**

Another way to obtain a certificate is to purchase a personal encryption program. PGP Personal Privacy, which is owned by McAfee Associates, uses the popular Pretty Good Privacy (PGP) encryption system (available at the McAfee Web site at www.mcafee.com). The program lets you protect the privacy of your e-mail messages and file attachments by encrypting them so that only people with the proper authority can decipher the information. You can also digitally sign the messages and files you exchange, which ensures that they have come from the person who allegedly sent them and that the information has not been tampered with on its way to you.

The program costs $39.95 by itself, but it is also available with a group of programs called Nuts & Bolts Deluxe — a package that includes a useful program that checks your system for Year 2000 compliance and fixes the problem, if necessary. Nuts & Bolts Deluxe costs $59.95 and runs on Windows 3.1 or higher. The program requires 8MB of RAM and 20MB of disk space. You can download and try an evaluation version from the McAfee Web site before buying the program — but be aware that this is a 6MB file!

PGP Personal Privacy is a *plug-in,* an application that works with another program to provide added functionality. You can integrate the program with popular e-mail programs such as Eudora and Microsoft Outlook (although Netscape Messenger is notably absent from the list of supported applications).

Figure 2-3:
VeriSign's
Digital ID
Center
detects
whether you
are using
Netscape's
or
Microsoft's
Web
browser and
presents the
appropriate
page.

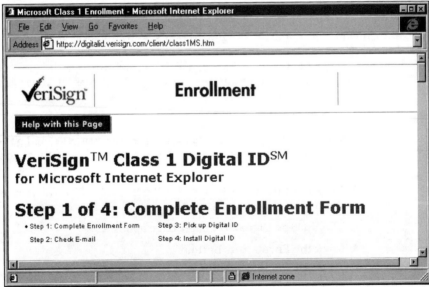

After you have your Digital ID, what you do with it? One practical use of a certificate is to ensure your identity by submitting the certificate to sites that accept such submissions. Some sites that require members to log in use secure servers that give you the option of submitting your certificate instead of entering the usual username and password to identify yourself. You can also attach your Digital ID to your e-mail messages. See your e-mail program's Help files for more specific instructions.

Encrypting your e-mail messages

If you use an e-mail program that supports the S/MIME (Secure Multipurpose Internet Mail Extensions) protocol such as the Big Two browser packages, Netscape Communicator and Microsoft Internet Explorer, you can encrypt your own e-mail messages.

Sending secure messages with Netscape Messenger

If you use Netscape Messenger, the e-mail application that comes with Netscape Communicator, you can do the following:

- ✔ **Send a digital signature.** You can digitally shrink-wrap your e-mail message using your certificate in order to assure the recipient that the message is really from you.

- ✔ **Encrypt your message.** You can digitally encode a message to ensure that only the intended party can read it.

To better understand how to keep your e-mail communications secure, read the online Secure E-mail Reference Guide at www.verisign.com/ securemail/guide.

If you use Netscape Messenger, follow these steps to encrypt your e-mail messages or include your certificate with them:

1. **With Messenger running, click the Security button in the toolbar of any of the Messenger windows.**

   A Security dialog box appears.

2. **Click Messenger in the list of topics on the left side of the Security dialog box.**

   The following security options appear in the right half of the dialog box:

   - Encrypt Your E-mail Messages
   - Sign Your E-mail Messages with Your Digital ID
   - Sign Your Discussion Group Messages with Your Digital ID

3. **In order to activate Messenger's security features, check one or more of the boxes; then click OK.**

   The security dialog box closes. You return to the Messenger window that you were in previously.

As long as you have a certificate, you can follow a similar set of steps to encrypt your outgoing e-mail using Microsoft Internet Explorer's e-mail program, as explained below.

Sending secure messages with Outlook Express

Microsoft Outlook Express also enables you to send encrypted and digitally signed messages. After you obtain your own Digital ID, open Outlook Express and then follow these steps:

1. **Choose Tools⇨Options.**

   The Options dialog box opens.

2. **Click the Security tab.**

   The Security options jump to the front (see Figure 2-4).

3. **In the Secure Mail section of the Security dialog box, check one or both of the boxes next to Digitally Sign All Outgoing Messages or Encrypt Contents and Attachments for All Outgoing Messages.**

4. **Click OK.**

   The Options dialog box closes, and you return to the Outlook Express window, where you can now compose an encrypted message.

For more detailed information about Outlook Express's security options, choose Help⇨Contents and Index and search the program's Help file for the topic "Automatically encrypting and/or digitally signing messages."

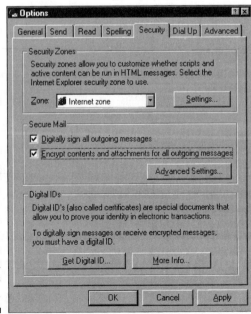

Figure 2-4:
If you have a Digital ID, you can encrypt outgoing mail messages by selecting options in this Outlook Express dialog box.

By checking one or more of the options in the Security dialog box presented by either Messenger or Outlook Express, you activate the e-mail program's built-in security features for *all* of your outgoing messages. In order to actually verify or undo those features (that is, if you want a message to be unencrypted or to be sent without a digital signature) in Messenger, deselect the Encrypted box after clicking the Message Sending Options button: In Outlook Express, deselect Encrypt and/or Digitally Sign, which appear as options under the Tools menu.

Getting the Right Software

The software you need to participate in online auctions is pretty much the same as the software you use to surf the Web, exchange e-mail, or engage in any number of online activities. The programs you use online are inexpensive (sometimes free) and easy to use and install, and are continually updated.

In addition, a small but growing selection of applications specially targeted at auction buyers and sellers is also available. The following sections describe some of the software you may need to participate in Internet auctions.

Software for both buyers and sellers

The following programs come in handy whether you visit online auction sites primarily as a shopper or want to sell some items to the highest bidders.

Browsing with your browser

A *Web browser* is software that serves as a visual interface to the images, colors, links, and other content contained on auction sites and the rest of the World Wide Web. The two most popular programs are Microsoft Internet Explorer and Netscape Navigator. Your Web browser is your primary tool for communicating and locating information online. When it comes to using Internet auction services, though, you have to run your software through a few more paces than usual. You need your browser to:

- Display sale items you want to buy or sell.
- Preview any personal Web pages you create.
- Support some level of Internet security, such as encryption or secure transactions (see Chapter 2).

In addition to having an up-to-date browser with the latest features, having more than one kind of browser installed on your computer is often a good idea. For example, if you use Microsoft Internet Explorer because that's what came with your operating system, be sure to download the latest copy of

Netscape Communicator as well. That way, if you have problems with one program, you can try the other. Having two programs also enables you to test any Web pages you create so you can make sure that they look good no matter which browser your visitors use.

Sealing the deal with e-mail

Although a Web browser provides you with a port of entry for getting involved with auctions, e-mail often seals the deal. E-mail communication is essential for exchanging both pre-sale and post-sale information between buyers and sellers. You can, and should, ask sellers for background information about items in which you're interested.

After the sale, you need to provide shipping information and (in the case of a reserve auction where the reserve price is not met) possibly renegotiate the final sale price. You do this through e-mail. It pays to be proficient with some of the finer points of e-mail communication, such as the following:

- **Quoting.** Almost all e-mail programs let you quote from a message to which you're replying so you can respond easily to a series of questions.

- **Attaching.** Attaching a file to an e-mail message is a quick and convenient way to transmit information from one person to another. For instance, it's common to e-mail a photo of an item that isn't displayed on the Web. If you do this, be sure to send the image in a common graphics format your recipient can view, like GIF, JPEG, TIF, PCX, or BMP.

- **Signature files.** Make sure that your e-mail software enables you to automatically include a simple electronic signature at the end of your messages. Businesspeople use this space to list their company name, their title, and Web site URL. Auction buyers and hobby sellers like you can include your name, e-mail address, a few words about what you collect or sell ("Dealer in Rare Coins," for instance), and a link to your Web page if you have one.

Both Outlook Express, the e-mail component of Microsoft Internet Explorer, and Netscape Messenger, part of Netscape Communicator's suite of programs, include most or all these features. Because these functions are all essential aspects of providing good relations with buyers or sellers, I discuss them in more detail in Chapter 3.

Comparing notes with discussion group software

A discussion group, often called a newsgroup, is a collection of messages about a particular subject. Newsgroups are part of Usenet, an extensive and popular part of the Internet. In order to read and post messages to Usenet discussion groups, you need newsgroup software, which is built into Netscape Communicator and Microsoft Internet Explorer.

Newsgroups are a lively and often exciting place where participants can compare notes and share their passion for things they collect or trade in online auctions. Newsgroups can also be a place to do more trading. See Chapter 3 for more information about the online auction community.

Avoiding viruses that make your computer sick

Lots of good things can come to you from Internet auctionland, but unfortunately, some bad things can invade your computer, too. These include harmful programs called *viruses, macros,* or *Trojan Horses,* each of which can rob you of data or disable your computer in some way.

Every computer that's regularly connected to the Internet needs to be equipped with some sort of virus protection software. Such programs detect a virus if it's downloaded to your machine from the Net. Usually, the software notifies you when it detects a virus and disables the virus.

Because new viruses keep cropping up, it's important to buy a program that provides you with free upgrades to catch the latest harmful things. Here are some good bets:

- **VirusScan** by Network Associates, Inc. (Go to `www.mcafee.com/products/` and click the VirusScan link).

- **Dr. Solomon's Anti-Virus** (`www.drsolomon.com/vircen/index.cfm`).

- **Norton Anti-Virus** by Symantec (`www.symantec.com/nu/index.html`).

One way to deal with computer trouble, in case you do encounter it, is to record serial numbers and make/model information for all your equipment. This is not only important for insurance purposes in case something is lost or stolen, but it helps when you need to tell service people exactly how much memory your computer has and what kind of peripheral hardware is attached to the machine.

Making it all add up with accounting software

If you regularly sell via Internet auctions, you essentially create and operate an online business through your computer. If that's the case, it only makes sense to keep track of your finances on your computer, as well.

You don't necessarily have to purchase special accounting software to do this. You can set up a table in Word or Word Perfect, or use Microsoft Works or Excel. But with luck, you'll need to keep track of lots of orders and will want a more powerful financial software package. For something more elaborate, try programs like QuickBooks (a trial version of which is included on this book's CD-ROM), Quicken, Peachtree Accounting, or one of the other popular software packages described in Chapter 10.

Additional software for sellers

In order to get the highest price possible for the items you put up for auction, you need to make the items as attractive as possible. Providing customers with background information about you and your business, if you have one, also helps customers feel as though they can trust you to deliver the items you promise. The following programs can help you build credibility and attract bidders.

Web page editors

Some auction services — eBay, for example — help sellers create Web pages that provide additional information for potential customers. One way to create such pages is to use a program called a *Web page editor.* These programs help you format text, add images, create hyperlinks, and do all the fun assembly steps necessary to make your Web site a winner.

Most good Web page editors let you create Web content without having to learn *HyperText Markup Language* (HTML), a set of markup instructions used to format text, images, and other Web page elements so Web browsers can correctly display them.

You'll find Microsoft FrontPage Express, HotDog Express, HotDog Professional, and Macromedia Dreamweaver on this book's CD-ROM. Also see Chapter 7 for further suggestions of good Web page tools you can use.

Image editors

You need a graphics editing program either to create original artwork for your Web pages or to crop and adjust your scanned or digitally photographed images. The software you need to adjust or crop photographic image files almost always comes bundled with a scanner or digital camera, so you don't need to buy separate software.

In the case of graphic images, the first question to ask yourself is: Am I really qualified to create my own graphics? If the answer is yes, think shareware first. Two programs I like are LView Pro by Leonardo Haddad Loureiro (www.lview.com) and Paint Shop Pro by Jasc, Inc. (www.jasc.com). (Paint Shop Pro is included on this book's CD-ROM, in fact.) You can download both of these programs from the Web to use on a trial basis. After the trial period is over, you're asked to pay a small fee to the developer in order to register and keep the program. LViewPro costs $40; Paint Shop Pro costs $69 for version 3.12 or $99 for version 5.01.

The ability to download and use free (and almost free) software from shareware archives and many other sites is one of the nicest things about the Internet. Keep the system working by remembering to pay the shareware fees to the nice folks who make their software available to individuals like you and me.

Auction programs

If you plan to present lots of auction items for sale on the Web and envision a full-fledged online business that includes customer service options and online purchases, you may want to look into software specially designed to help you present items for sale, track bids, or even set up your own auction service.

Auction programs take most of the work out of designing Web pages and putting them online. These programs often provide you with pre-designed Web page formats, called *templates,* that you can customize with your own content.

Chapters 6 and 7 examine some of the programs available for participants of eBay and other auction services.

Chapter 3

Joining the Online Auction Community

*O*ne of the nicest things about participating in Internet auctions is the fact that you're never alone. You may *feel* like you're alone, sitting at your computer in your home, hotel room, or office, but that's just an illusion. Help, advice, and support are only a mouse click or two away.

When you register for one or more auction services and start buying or selling online, you actually join a community — a rapidly growing, increasingly computer-savvy community of individuals who are doing pretty much the same thing (exploring the Web, shopping for bargains, trying to make some auction sales) that you are.

This chapter discusses how to participate as a fully functioning member of the Internet auction community, and how your participation can benefit your transactions. The more buyers and sellers communicate, the better their chances of successfully completing transactions — and making new business contacts and widening their circles of friends.

Mastering the Art of Auction Feedback

Anyone who thinks the world of Internet auctions is a cold, technological place run by computers probably doesn't know about the feedback system employed by many auction services.

What is auction feedback?

A feedback system provides the users (both buyers and sellers) of an auction service with a way to register comments about their transactions with specific individuals. Customers type evaluations (positive or negative) into an online form. The auction service then posts this feedback on its site along with accumulated reports from other users. The feedback stays online for a period of time and may influence others deciding whether to do business with a particular person. Figure 3-1 shows feedback posted on eBay for yours truly. (See "Leaving feedback," later in this chapter, for more information about how to leave feedback.)

When it comes to online auctions, feedback can make or break a reputation. In the "real world," your next door neighbor may recommend the antique store around the corner, and you can visit the store and talk with its proprietor to decide whether you trust him and want to do business with him. However, when it comes to conducting business over the Internet, you usually can't get a referral from Mrs. Jones next door, or determine a person's integrity from his screen name, so you must depend on what others say about the way he behaves online and their experiences with him — the way he communicates via e-mail, the speed with which he delivers payment or goods purchased, the quality of the goods sold, and so on.

Figure 3-1:
eBay, like
many
auction
services,
lets users
register
feedback
about one
another.

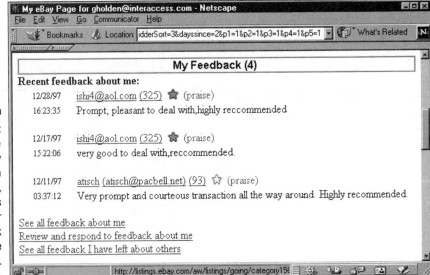

Viewing feedback

I've been buying and selling through online auctions for a couple of years, and I depend a lot on feedback. eBay probably has the best-known and most extensive structure for rating auction users via feedback comments. You can view feedback about individuals in a couple of ways. The easiest is to simply click either a link next to a seller's name or the name itself. Figure 3-2 shows a computer disk drive offered on eBay by Edith Shaefer, who goes by the username Egyptian and is profiled in the "A great way to make friends" sidebar in this chapter.

The term "Feedback Profile" is usually seen on eBay, though sites like Yahoo! Auctions and Amazon.com's auction service also use feedback. Feedback Profile refers to the total number of comments — positive, negative, and neutral — left for an auction user by people who have done business with him. See the "Understanding feedback rating systems" section later in this chapter for more.

Figure 3-2: eBay users get a star next to their name if they accumulate enough positive feedback.

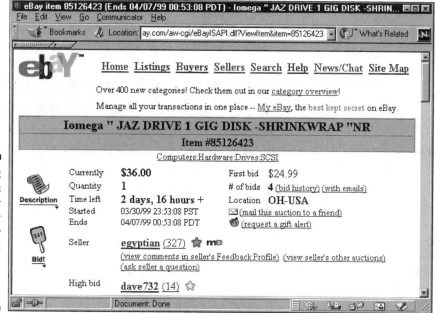

The simple-looking Web page shown in Figure 3-2 offers a veritable bushel basket full of options for interacting with others and researching the reputation of both buyers and sellers. In most cases, eBay requires you to enter your eBay-registered username and password to receive the e-mail addresses of other users. Here are just a few examples of the ways you can find out more about other auction participants:

- ✔ Click the With Emails link (on the `# of bids` line) to get a record of the bidders on the displayed item, along with their e-mail addresses.

- ✔ Click the username (such as `egyptian`) to find out about this individual's previous transactions on eBay.

- ✔ Click the *feedback rating number,* the number in parentheses next to the username (in this case, `327`), to see that user's *feedback profile* — a history of the comments left by users who have conducted transactions with the individual. (See the next section, "Understanding feedback rating systems," for more about this rating number.)

- ✔ Click the `me` graphic next to a user's name to link to that person's About Me eBay page. (See Chapter 7 for more on the About Me feature and creating Web pages to support your auction activities.)

- ✔ Click the star next to the user's name to view a chart that interprets what the star's color means — like the one shown in Figure 3-3.

Figure 3-3: A star tells you that a user has received a substantial number of positive comments — but look at the complete feedback profile to make sure.

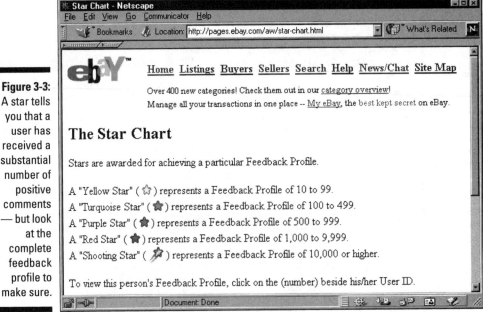

It is important for buyers and sellers to accumulate positive feedback. eBay's "star chart" encourages users to keep getting positive comments over hundreds, or even thousands, of transactions, as explained in the next section.

Understanding feedback rating systems

On auction service discussion boards, you often see comments such as "that seller had a +10 rating" or "she had a -1 feedback rating." Comments like these refer to the number of positive and negative feedback comments the individual has received.

Not every auction service provides its users with a feedback system. Such a system is most relevant on person-to-person auction services, where one individual deals directly with another, rather than "house" auction services, where a buyer deals directly with the auction house. (See Chapter 1 for further explanations of the types of Internet auctions.) When it comes to feedback, though, eBay has the most elaborate system; it's one that serves as a model for others to follow.

In eBay's system, the number that appears in parentheses (##) next to a person's User ID (or User Name) on the site is called a *feedback rating*. It represents the sum of points received, taking into account the positive, neutral, and negative points. A user receives feedback rating points as follows:

- ✔ One point (+1) is added for each positive comment.
- ✔ No points (0) are added or subtracted for neutral comments.
- ✔ One point (-1) is subtracted for each negative comment.

In theory, I suppose you can leave feedback for any registered eBay user, as long as you are a registered user yourself. But it makes sense to comment only on the people you've done business with.

Yahoo! Auctions has a ratings system for its buyers and sellers that resembles eBay's. Click the feedback number in parentheses next to a user's Yahoo! ID on any auction page to read the comments left by previous high bidders. (See Figure 3-4.) Amazon.com, like eBay, lets users register two kinds of feedback: personal comments (which any user can leave about another user) and numerical ratings (which only buyers who have won an auction or sellers whose auction received a winning bid can register). You access the feedback comments for a user by clicking the feedback symbol (usually a series of stars, which denote positive comments) next to the seller's username.

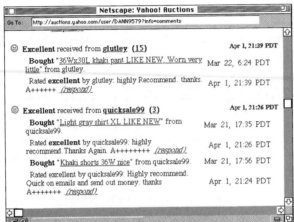

Figure 3-4:
Feedback
comments
are helpful
but often
repetitious.
If you want
more info,
e-mail the
commenta-
tor with
specific
questions.

I predict that more and more companies will use feedback because it's such an effective deterrent against fraud. The obvious goal is to reduce the number of deadbeat bidders (high bidders who don't follow through with a sale) and fraudulent sellers (sellers who take the high bidder's money and never deliver the goods).

Evaluating feedback ratings

There's no scientific way to evaluate the numbers of positive, neutral, or negative comments left for a user. The interpretation is up to you. Lots of positive comments are impressive, but after you get past a hundred or so, they are all equally reliable indicators of how much you can trust someone. On the other hand, if a person has several negative feedback comments, you should think twice before you sell to or accept a bid from him. (I usually disregard one or two negative comments because some people are never pleased, no matter what.)

Leaving feedback

Feedback is effective because it is so human and so personal. The response is as unique as each individual. You don't have to register a certain kind of comment or state it in a particular way; you don't, for that matter, have to leave any feedback at all. But if you are buying or selling through online auctions and have a moment or two to spare, please consider leaving some feedback because doing so is a very important step in the auction process.

When you want to leave feedback for someone on Amazon.com Auctions, you click that person's username (Amazon.com calls this his "nickname") to display his Customer Details page. Then click the Leave Feedback link on the left side of the page. The Leave Feedback page for that user appears. Fill out the form with up to 80 characters of comments.

The following sections offer tips for leaving helpful, effective feedback.

Be specific

The best auction feedback comments are brief and specific. Often, buyers and sellers tend to copy one another's stock phrases, such as "smooth transaction" or "fast response." There's nothing wrong with using these phrases. But consider describing, simply and briefly, your precise experience with the individual. Saying "Sent check on Monday; received item in only six days" or "Poor packaging; item arrived damaged" gives other users a better understanding of your transaction.

Be prompt

There's no rule for when you should leave feedback, but it's a good idea to do so shortly after the transaction is completed, so you don't forget about it. I usually wait a few days after I receive something, until I make sure everything is in good working order.

On the other hand, if it's taking a while to get your payment or shipment, be patient. It's embarrassing to leave negative feedback too quickly, and to have to correct yourself because what you were waiting for was just delayed.

Take a deep breath before complaining

If you have a bad experience with someone, you deserve to complain. You have every right to record, for example, that the person failed to follow through with a transaction, wasted your time, created problems, or made you suffer a financial loss.

Remember, though, that your comments reflect on you, too. Your username goes next to the feedback. So although waiting may be difficult, I advise you to "count to ten" before you record your comments. Be specific about what happened, but don't use profanity or other coarse comments that make you look bad. Simply explaining what happened should provide the negative feedback that can serve as a warning to other members of the auction community. Remember that your comments are meant to help other buyers or sellers. Unfortunately, leaving feedback won't get your money returned or your item shipped.

Be courteous

It's always a good idea to mind your manners, even when you're voicing a complaint. Remember that the feedback comments you leave reflect on you, and if you're profane or abusive, it can discourage traders from wanting to deal with you.

Besides that, you invite negative comments by being impolite. On eBay, other users can respond to individual feedback comments. Someone is likely to criticize you if you leave comments seen as silly or uncalled-for in some way.

Minding Your E-Mail Manners

E-mail is still one of the most popular types of communication on the Internet, and it's the primary way you contact prospective buyers or sellers as well as other members of the Internet auction community.

I don't intend to provide an in-depth discussion on sending and receiving e-mail messages here, but I do want to give you some tips that may come in handy. The following sections provide you with some suggestions for maintaining good relations with your auction friends.

Play it safe

Many e-mail programs, like Netscape Messenger, let you send and receive secure e-mail messages, which can help if you need to give out sensitive information such as credit card information, addresses, and phone numbers to the people with whom you do business. See Chapter 2 for more information.

Check your spelling

Outlook Express and Netscape Messenger include spell-checkers that automatically check for any boo-boos you make when composing and preparing to send an e-mail message. In Outlook Express, choose Tools⇨Options. In the Options dialog box, click the Spelling tab, and then choose the Always Check Spelling Before Sending option. In Netscape Messenger, click the Spelling toolbar button in the Message Composition window before sending your message.

Say hello and goodbye

These simple pleasantries may seem unimportant to online communication, but they aren't. Simply providing a greeting and a closing salutation can make a big difference in the tone of your e-mail message. Don't forget to say Hello, Cheers, Best, Sincerely, or whatever at the beginning and end of your communication.

People can't see you when you write an e-mail message. They don't get visual communication clues such as facial expressions and body language that they usually take for granted. For some people, this may be a good thing; nevertheless, go to a little extra effort to build goodwill in the absence of in-person contact. See the "Smileys, frownies, and other emoticons" sidebar in this chapter for tips on making your e-mail more expressive.

Add your electronic John Hancock

Snappy salutations and silly smileys are fun add-ons to e-mail messages, but if you're using auctions and e-mail for business purposes, a signature file is a must-have.

Smileys, frowneys, and other emoticons

When it comes to expressing emotion through e-mail, you can't beat those old-style computer tricks known as *emoticons*. These little typographical symbols, which also go by the name of smileys, provide your e-mail correspondence with little expressions you can insert into your messages by typing characters on your keyboard. (Confused? Tilt your head to the left, and the strange keyboard character combinations look like faces.) The list of emoticons is quite extensive, but only the real enthusiasts use the more obscure varieties. Here are just a few of the more popular ones that you're likely to use:

:-) This is the most popular smiley, used when you're making a joke or emphasizing that you're trying to be friendly.

:-(This is the frowney, which is used to convey: "I hate to tell you this . . ." or "This is getting me down."

:-0 This is used to convey surprise.

;-) The semicolon means that you're winking, as though to say: "I'm only kidding about this."

If you want a more extensive list of smileys and what they mean, check out members.aol.com/bearpage/smileys.htm.

A *signature file* is a standard bit of text or graphics that you can add to e-mail or discussion group messages. It quickly provides your readers with information about who you are, what you do, and where to find out more about you. A signature file is the electronic equivalent of sending a business card over the Internet. You can tell Outlook Express, Netscape Messenger/Collabra, or whatever e-mail software you use to automatically add a signature file to all your outgoing correspondence. For detailed instructions, see Chapter 8.

Gathering around the Virtual Watercooler

Being on the Internet is like any kind of activity where a lot of people gather and join in shared activities: You determine what you want to put into it. For the most part, I tend to watch the action from the sidelines and participate only occasionally. But you may be a party animal who's adept at making tons of cyber-friends.

Going beyond the usual buying-and-selling transactions and socializing with other auction lovers is a virtual piece of cake, especially because you tend to interact with individuals who share your own interests: You all collect baseball memorabilia or game cards, for instance. The makings of a club are right there in the people who place bids online. All you need is a way to communicate with the rest of the group. This section describes how to make use of the opportunities for group communication that already exist online.

When you discuss sales terms or exchange sales information via e-mail, you're establishing personal contacts that may be financially and personally beneficial. (See the "A great way to meet friends" sidebar in this chapter to hear one success story.)

Another way to meet people online is to engage in group communications. The Internet provides several ways of interacting with groups of individuals, and they are, for the most part, outgrowths of e-mail itself. The difference is that you type your message to many potential readers rather than just one. The following sections describe some of these opportunities to interact with your auction peers.

A great way to meet friends

Edith Schafer, a 74-year-old widow and grand-mother from Scottown, Ohio, is an antiques collector and dealer specializing in Fenton art glass. She also sells video and PC games on behalf of her son, who introduced her to selling on eBay. She describes Internet auctions as a "great activity for a senior citizen."

"Truly, auctions are not only places to buy and sell, but to meet people of similar interests and learn more about your hobby," says Mrs. Schafer. "For the most part, people are wonderful and honest. So far I have had a lot fewer bad experiences online than in real life.

"I speak with some people often via e-mail. One man in West Virginia has sold me some beautiful items. Another couple of ladies write me with inquiries about Fenton glass. I often enjoy sharing my knowledge with other collectors. One of my favorite people is a Fenton glass dealer in Kentucky, whom I met because of the auction. We do dinner, and love to sit and chat. Some older people could add a lot of meaning to their lives by taking part in an activity [internet auctions] that opens the doors of the world to them. It sure beats sitting around, reliving the old days. Seniors should not be afraid of technology!

"I have encountered some online fraud in the sense of not getting paid for items I sold. However, overall in the antique field, and for the most part all of eBay, you'll find honest people. Usually feedback is a good indication, though people can use that as a weapon to threaten you, if they get a product they're unhappy with. However again, if someone has 100+ positives, and one negative, it shows that you just cannot please everyone.

"The most exciting transaction was when I received a rare and special piece of art glass, and paid less than $20 for a piece worth 50 times that. My most shocking was when I paid $3.99 at a local (traditional, offline) auction for some JAZ drive disks, and got over $50 apiece for them on an Internet auction. That is still about 50 percent of retail, so both myself and the buyer won.

"The only major downfall is that this can get addictive. My living rooms are full of curios from eBay auctions. If you sell seriously, you can expect to spend a lot of time online. Overall, though, it is a fantastic concept!"

Auction "cafés"

Most auction sites aren't as social as eBay, but, then, they don't have as many users, either. As auctions grow in popularity, they're likely to include places for individuals to meet one another and compare notes, such as eBay's Café.

The Café is a lofty name for a simple feature that longtime Internet surfers know as *bulletin boards*. Bulletin board participants communicate by posting messages to the board and responding to messages already there. (*Posting* a message is the online equivalent of writing a note on a piece of paper and tacking it to a cork bulletin board.) A series of back-and-forth messages on a single topic results in a conversation called a *thread*.

You enter eBay's Café either through the front door (eBay's front door, that is, at `www.ebay.com`) and clicking the News/Chat link, or by going directly to `pages.ebay.com/aw/newschat.html`. Either way, your browser connects to the eBay News & Chat page. Scroll down the page and click the link for The eBay Café. The rather unappetizing eBay Café page appears (see Figure 3-5).

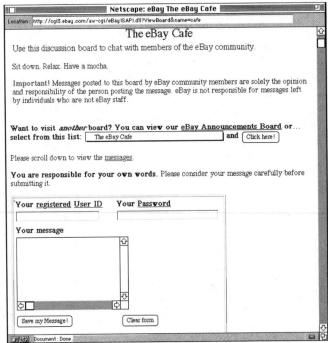

Figure 3-5:
It doesn't look like a watering hole, but the eBay Café lets you post or read messages from other auction users.

The nice thing about the Café is that you can read and post messages to the board using your Web browser, and don't need the special software required by Usenet newsgroups or old-fashioned bulletin board systems (BBSs). To post a message to the Café, fill out the form shown in Figure 3-5 with a comment or question and then submit your text to the eBay site by clicking the Save My Message! button. In a flash, your message is published on the Café page.

eBay has many different cafés. Most are targeted toward specific groups of users. Click the drop-down list on the main eBay Café page and select a group that interests you. If you aren't interested in having an online conversation and merely want to post an announcement about a new Web site or a special item for sale, click the eBay Announcements Board link near the top of the eBay Café page.

If you're the wallflower type and use eBay, you can still feel like part of a community by reading the *eBay Life* online newsletter (see Figure 3-6).

Figure 3-6:
The *eBay Life* online newsletter features profiles of individual users and tips for both buyers and sellers.

Acronyms are AOK

You may come across strange acronyms while reading e-mail messages, discussion groups, and newsgroups. Understanding what the acronyms stand for can help you understand what people are saying, when they're trying to be silly, and when they're making claims that you can safely ignore. Here are a few examples:

BBS: Be Back Soon

BTW: By The Way . . .

IMHO: In My Humble Opinion or In My Honest Opinion

LOL: Laughing Out Loud or Lots of Love

NR or <NoRes>: No Reserve price specified on this item

POOF!: I'm outta here!

ROTFL: Rolling On the Floor Laughing

TTFN: Ta Ta For Now

You can find explanations of these and other acronyms at `www.dworldonline.com/handbook.htm` (be aware that there's a sound file your browser will be asked to download, but you can cancel the download and still read the text).

Mailing lists

The discussion forums provided by auction services such as eBay are pretty freewheeling, but eBay staff members do participate occasionally to make sure that the discussions don't get out of hand. This can happen quite easily on unmoderated discussion groups or mailing lists so it's always a good idea to avoid "flaming" (that is, sending abusive and angry messages) that can hurt your reputation. You can choose to participate in a home-grown mailing list or discussion area instead, where you can say anything you want without interference.

A *mailing list* is a less immediate, and more involved way of communicating with a group of individuals on the Internet. First, you have to locate a list related to your area of interest. Then you have to subscribe to the list to receive the e-mail messages that members of the list send to one another. Usually, you subscribe by sending an e-mail message to the individual or the computer that routes the list's messages.

You can join two types of mailing lists on the Internet:

  ✔ **Moderated lists.** These lists are maintained by hard-working individuals who monitor discussions and manually add and subtract subscribers to and from the list.

  ✔ **Unmoderated lists.** An unmoderated list is owned by an individual but run by an automated mail server, sometimes called a LISTSERV.

Because mailing lists take some work to join, they tend to attract people who are really passionate or knowledgeable about the subject at hand, rather than casual users. If you feel strongly about your area of interest and want to find other experts, mailing lists are for you.

A high school biology teacher started the eBay Users Discussion List, an open, unmoderated discussion list open to all members of the eBay community — buyers, sellers, and browsers. Topics of discussion include successes, frustrations, the mechanics of using the eBay auction site, and anything else eBay-related that you want to discuss. Find out how to subscribe at `www.metronet.com/~cyn/ebay_users_list.htm`.

Some mailing lists can get really busy, thus resulting in a steady stream of e-mail messages. These messages can be distracting if you are at work and are looking for more urgent business correspondence. If you're feeling overwhelmed by your mailing list e-mail, see if the list provides subscribers with a *digest* version. A digest combines all the individual messages into a single message so that you receive one long message rather than many messages throughout the day.

AOL discussion groups

If you belong to AOL, you can talk about auctions either by typing real-time messages to others in a chat room or by posting messages in an online discussion group.

If you're into *chat,* which provides you with a way to type messages to other users in real time, and you are on AOL, go to Keyword: Collecting (select Go To⇨Keyword from the America Online menu bar) and double-click the Collector's Corner Chat Schedule link. (See Figure 3-7.)

This chat room meets often on specific topics but frequently holds chats on general collecting issues. The discussion, however, isn't terribly focused: It can range all the way from Pez dispensers to Jackie O. collectibles, as Figure 3-7 demonstrates. For more focused discussions on antiques and collectibles, go to Keyword: Antiques and click the Message Boards link. A long list of topics appears. Select one and double-click its name to view the current messages, and double-click a message to read it. Figure 3-8 shows a message board for collectors of antique buttons.

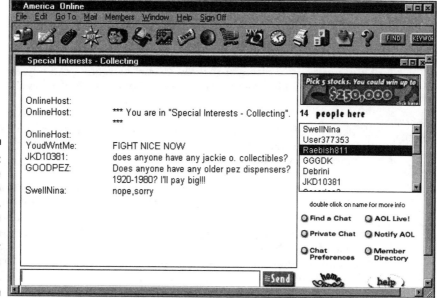

Figure 3-7:
If you're really into collecting, you can chat with other collectors on AOL.

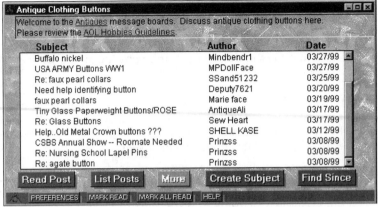

Figure 3-8:
AOL's
message
boards are
specific and
up-to-date,
and they
attract
knowledge-
able
collectors.

In my opinion, message boards are where the real action is for collectors. The AOL boards for collectors of fountain pens are really useful; the collectors even hold a chat on AOL once a week. You can talk about your experiences on Internet auction sites, find out about upcoming collector's shows in your area, and even buy or sell items to other enthusiasts.

Usenet newsgroups

I was surprised to discover that few Usenet newsgroups, if any, are devoted to the subject of Internet auctions. Before long, someone will get the nerve to start one.

Usenet (short for the User's Network) is a computer network that is part of the Internet, although it can also be accessed from outside the Internet using commercial online services such as AOL.

Usenet discussions resemble the bulletin board/message board systems described earlier in this chapter but with a couple of significant differences. Probably the biggest difference is that you need special software to locate and use Usenet newsgroups. You can't access them from within your Web browser, but both the big browser packages contain newsgroup software — Netscape Communicator's is called Collabra, and Internet Explorer uses Outlook Express.

An exception to the "special software" statement above applies to AOL users, who can often access newsgroups from within AOL. For example, if you connect to AOL and go to the Antiques page mentioned earlier (type **Keyword: Antiques**) you see a scroll-down list of newsgroups such as rec.antiques and rec.antiques.marketplace. Double-click a group's name, and AOL software connects you to the newsgroup and displays the current messages for you. You can also post your own new messages or reply to newsgroup messages using AOL's software.

To access Usenet, you must have access to a *news server,* a computer often called an NNTP server. Most Internet Service Providers give you access to a news server when you sign up for an account. You have to enter the name of the server in your Web browser's Preferences/Options area.

Another difference is in the naming of newsgroups. Most newsgroups have what is referred to as a hierarchical structure. Most individual groups belong to one of about eight main categories, as shown in Table 3-1.

Table 3-1	Newsgroup Categories
Abbreviation	*Description*
alt	Alternative or miscellaneous topics; it's easy to start your own group in the alt category, in contrast to starting a new group in other categories.
Comp	Computer issues.
misc	Miscellaneous issues. This differs from the alt category in that you can't simply start up your own newsgroup; you have to make a proposal and get feedback from people who run news servers, which is a time-consuming process.
news	Topics related to Usenet.
rec	Recreational activities, hobbies, and popular culture.
sci	Science.
soc	Sociology and anthropology.
talk	Groups in this category are devoted to debate, discussion, argument, and, well . . . talk.

I couldn't find a newsgroup devoted to auctions at this writing. If some enterprising reader wants to gain status points and start an alt.auctions or alt.ebay discussion group, connect to the alt.answers group and find the message titled So You Want to Create an Alt Newsgroup.

This is just a brief introduction to the extensive and often wild and crazy world of Usenet. Find out more in *The Internet For Dummies,* 6th Edition, written by John R. Levine, Carol Baroudi, and Margaret Levine Young (IDG Books Worldwide, Inc.).

Protecting Yourself Against Fraud

Edith Schafer, a senior citizen who enjoys Internet auctions (see her comments in the "Great way to meet friends" sidebar in this chapter), knows that most Internet auction participants are honest folks. But she also has first-hand knowledge about the dark side of the system.

"I have encountered some online fraud in the sense of not getting paid, and stuck owing the selling fees to eBay," she points out. "I was once given the runaround by one guy for more than four months until I got my order. It included a couple of items that had been misrepresented. They were junk." Her son, who introduced her to Internet auctions, later stopped participating because he was realizing only a 50 percent rate of successfully completed transactions.

A few of the longtime auction users I spoke to in the course of writing this book claimed that they never encountered fraud. But the majority had at least one hard-luck story to tell. Even my 12-year-old nephew told me with a combination of hurt and anger that he had once paid $10 for a Beanie Baby on eBay and never received it.

Is there any way to completely eliminate the chances of running into trouble? The realistic answer is no. However, you *can* minimize your chances of getting cheated by educating yourself about Internet security schemes that can protect your privacy and help you verify the identify of those you do business with online (see Chapter 2) and using the strategies I discuss in this section.

Using an escrow service is one of the best ways you can avoid becoming a victim of fraud. See Chapter 7 for details about setting up an escrow transaction.

Know who you're dealing with

In my experience, the best way to avoid getting ripped off by buyer or seller is to establish some sort of personal contact and get to know something about the person you're trading with.

On the Internet, you don't get to know people in person, and you can't always contact them where they live, but you can get to know people really well through e-mail. You can pose questions and carry on online conversations that get more in-depth and personal than they would on the phone or on the street corner.

Feel free to go beyond the simple facts of payment methods and delivery addresses, and engage the buyer or seller in conversation about things she collects or has purchased at auctions. You don't necessarily have to make friends with everyone you encounter; however, making personal contact probably discourages some people from backing out on you or failing to ship you what you've paid for.

If you're really concerned about dealing with people who live hundreds or even thousands of miles from you, only buy from or sell to people who are in your own geographical area. (If you're a seller, make sure that you specify any geographic limitations in your item descriptions.) It narrows your auction options, but it can be done. I'm continually surprised by the number of sellers on eBay who live in my home town, Chicago, or the surrounding area. Buying locally lets you arrange to pick up what you've purchased in person. Sometimes, sellers who are auctioning off heavy, bulky items (such as exercise equipment) prefer to deal with locals to save trouble and money shipping the goods.

Investigate feedback

One of the best ways to know something about your buyer or seller is to use the feedback system provided by eBay and many other auction services. Do a little digging to make sure that you deal with individuals who have accumulated a substantial number of positive comments from previous transactions. Bidding only on items being offered by sellers who have good feedback is a good strategy. Investigating a winning bidder's feedback can also prepare a seller for any potential snags. (I explain everything you need to know about auction feedback in "Mastering the Art of Auction Feedback," earlier in this chapter.)

If a person has one or two negative responses, that doesn't mean you should avoid him altogether. Sometimes negative feedback is left for quirky or insubstantial reasons. The proportion of positive to negative feedback is a more reliable indicator. If a person has 100 positive comments and only one or two negative ones, don't be afraid to work with him.

Check with consumer organizations

It's also a good idea, if you're really suspicious about an individual or a business, to see if any complaints have been registered about them by other consumers. Check the databases of the Better Business Bureau (www.bbb.org) or Internet Fraud Watch (www.fraud.org) for more information.

Keep the lines of communication open

Don't be afraid to communicate with a buyer or seller frequently during the auction. Too much communication is better than not enough. Ask questions. See what kinds of responses you get. If the responses are prompt and complete, you're very likely to have a good experience. If the responses are terse and unhelpful or you get no response at all, don't bid on that person's item or sell to that person. Chances are good that another similar item will come up later on.

Communication is just as important after the auction. Messages should be brief and businesslike. The seller should greet the high bidder and present preferred payment options and a mailing address. Or, if the reserve price was not met, the seller should discuss with the high bidder whether he must raise the high bid to the reserve level in order to receive the item.

The buyer can send an e-mail to the seller requesting payment and shipping information if he is particularly anxious to initiate the conversation, too. Remember that sellers can be very busy; many of them have multiple auctions ending at the same time and are dealing with others besides you. They'll appreciate it if you're brief and to the point.

When in doubt, verify

I know what you're saying: "Greg, I know it's good to look at feedback, but I've just got to have those Air Holden size 13½ racquetball shoes with the pump and the neon blinking lights, and they're being offered by this first-time seller. I can't pass them up. What do I do?"

In this case, take your cue from the arms control officials: When in doubt, verify. Make sure that the seller is who he claims to be. One of the scams that crops up on eBay and other services is that of the phantom seller: someone who simply registers with a fictitious name, scams some hapless customer, and when he receives negative feedback, simply re-registers to continue conducting scams under a different name.

There isn't necessarily anything wrong with someone having more than one registered username at an auction service such as eBay. eBay, in fact, allows sellers to have two registered names.

Let your mouse do the walking

When you're interested in items from less established sellers, make sure that you can independently verify the person's company, phone, and address. This will at least minimize, if not eliminate, the likelihood of fraud. At the very least, verify that someone is living at the stated address or in the advertised city using one of these handy lookup services:

✔ **Switchboard** (`www.switchboard.com`). This is the place I turn to first when I'm trying to find an individual's real-world address and phone number. I've found some long-lost friends through this service, as well as a shocking number of individuals bearing the name Greg Holden.

✔ **Yahoo! People Search** (`people.yahoo.com`). This service lets you search for individuals in the United States. Try one of the worldwide versions of Yahoo! to find people in other parts of our increasingly small world.

Verify that he's verified

Another way to make sure the person you are dealing with is legitimate is to deal only with verified users. eBay has a new Verified eBay User program (`pages.ebay.com/aw/help/help-faq-verify.html`). At this writing, the program had not yet begun, but plans were to introduce the verification service for $5 for a six-month period. That means you can register yourself as a verified user for six months. The verification is handled by a third-party service called Equifax Inc. (`www.equifax.com`) that also performs credit checks for individuals or business. Equifax even has its own automated verification service called Fraudscan that can check every transaction performed by individuals like you and me. The system alerts you when someone's phone number doesn't match his zip code, or when the address supplied is a mail-receiving service or a prison, for instance.

On Amazon.com Auctions, all participants' identities are verified by means of the credit card information they're required to submit when they register with the service. If the user doesn't have a valid credit card number and doesn't supply name, address, and other personal information, he can't participate.

It's especially good if the individual provides you with an electronic identification card called a personal certificate or Digital ID. These are mostly used by businesses that engage in electronic commerce, but they are available for individuals as well. (See Chapter 2 for details.)

Don't rush into a deal that's too good to be true

Auction sellers have different marketing styles. Some take the subtle approach. Others speak loudly and promote their products with lots of CAPITAL LETTERS and exclamation points!!!!! Still others make their merchandise sound like it's the best thing since sliced bread.

Keep in mind that if a deal sounds too good to be true, it probably is. As a buyer, time is on your side. You usually have several days before an auction ends. Take time to research what's being sold, either online or at the local library. Also look into the seller's feedback profile, as described in Chapter 5.

Patience is a virtue. A simple look at the records of past auctions on eBay tells you that if one item escapes your grasp — even if it's a rare and hard-to-find commodity — the same item is sure to turn up before too long. Don't rush into things and make impulse decisions that you may regret later.

Credit cards: Don't go online without them

Some auction users won't buy anything at an auction unless the seller accepts credit card payments. The credit card company sometimes serves as a buyer's final line of protection. If a seller doesn't deliver after billing your credit card, a company such as Visa International, MasterCard, or American Express can delete the charge. You might have to pay a service fee, but paying the fee is better than being out the entire purchase price.

Policies on refunds vary widely. Check with your own credit card company to see what level of protection is provided. The consumer credit cards offered by Visa International have services that vary by country and type of card; see `www.visa.com/pd/consumer/main.html` for detailed information. See features available to MasterCard card holders at `www.mastercard.com/consumer`. If you have an American Express card, go to the company's Web site (`www.americanexpress.com`) and choose Cardholder Benefits from the Personal drop-down menu.

The flip side of giving your credit card number over the Internet is the danger that it will be intercepted and misused by an unscrupulous someone along the way. Make sure you deal with someone with good feedback so you know you can trust them to handle your sensitive information responsibly. Also see Chapter 2, which discusses how to use encryption when sending sensitive information.

Giving to Charitable Causes

What better way to be part of a community than to give back to others? Happily, some auction sites give users the chance to do good by bidding on charity items (see Figure 3-9).

Yahoo! Auctions, for example, regularly features a charity auction on its home page (`auctions.yahoo.com`). eBay holds charity auctions to benefit TV talk show host Rosie O'Donnell's For All Kids Foundation. The Virtual Parrot Head Club (`VPHC.com`) for fans of singer Jimmy Buffet also conducts charity auctions on eBay.

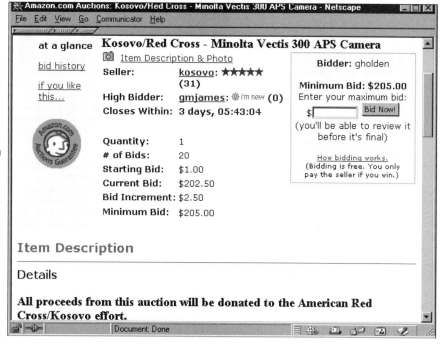

Figure 3-9:
Not all
Internet
auctions are
for-profit
occasions:
Charity
auctions are
available to
help others,
too.

Go to the eBay Classifieds Search page (`pages.ebay.com/aw/search.html`), enter **charity** or **for charity** in the Title Search section, and then click the Search button. You get a list of auctions for charity or charity-related subjects.

The *Internet Auctions For Dummies* Internet Directory (the yellow pages in this book) includes a section on Nonprofit/Charity auction services that hold auctions to benefit charitable causes. This service lets you bid on or offer items for auction to benefit nonprofit institutions and other good causes.

Part II
Buying at Internet Auctions

The 5th Wave   By Rich Tennant

REVEREND DAVIS PAUSES DURING HIS SERMON TO BID ON A DUKES OF HAZARD SMOKIN' GENERAL LEE SNOWBOARD.

In this part . . .

So you think you're ready to browse and click your way to the nearest Internet auction and start placing bids, right? Not quite. First, be sure to take a gander at some important do's and don'ts regarding the art of online auction shopping.

In this part I give you hints for choosing an auction and searching for the goods you want to nab. Then I describe the sorts of things you should and should not bid on and how to protect yourself against being defrauded or failing to receive what you've purchased at Internet auctions.

When you're ready to place an actual bid, the suggestions and tips I include in this part should fully prepare you for successful buying in the wild, wild world of Internet auctions.

Chapter 4

Making Your Bid a Winner

In This Chapter

▶ Researching merchandise so you can bid knowledgeably

▶ Coming up with a winning bid strategy

▶ Submitting your bid and waiting to win

*I*n my personal experience, bidding on auction treasures is one of the most exciting things I've done online, and I've been online a lot in the past several years. There was a period when I was on eBay every day, checking for items, seeing whether I'd been outbid. I got so obsessed with certain auctions that if I was outbid at the last minute I plunged into despair. I blush to confess that I once fired off an angry e-mail to the jerk/sneak who submitted a bid slightly higher than mine in the final minute of an auction. I realized the error of my ways and changed my approach (for the most part) when it dawned on me that by bidding rationally and knowledgeably, I was likely to get what I wanted.

Plenty of high bidders pay too much for what they purchase and end up feeling dissatisfied. The trick is to be a *savvy* shopper. This means not only finding what you want but also knowing how much the item is worth so you don't pay an unreasonable price for it.

One goal to keep in mind throughout the process is not to be overwhelmed by the excitement and addictive quality of bidding at auction. It's far better for your personal sanity as well as your pocketbook to take your time and avoid getting carried away. In this chapter, I tell you what you need to know before you enter the bidding arena and how to jump in on the auction once you get there.

Doing Your Homework

Before you start looking for treasures online and get caught up in a frenzy of clicking and bidding, do a little research. Find out which sites sell the items you're interested in, and familiarize yourself with the market value of those items so that you know whether you're getting a sweet deal or bidding on a lemon.

Know your item

One of the most important pieces of advice for auction buyers is this: Research what you want to buy. Read the specifications, compare prices, search through auction archives to see what previous items cost. Also take a page from the traditional auction sales described in Chapter 1 and make sure the merchandise you bid on is in good condition. Know exactly what constitutes a "good buy" and bid accordingly.

Condition, condition, condition

The real estate people say that "Location, location, location" is what rules. When it comes to bidding at auction, the maxim that often applies is "Condition, condition, condition."

I collect fountain pens (I already know that this is a strange hobby for someone who writes about computers and high-tech topics, so you don't have to remind me) and found one online that I really liked. I was impressed that the seller had provided several detailed, close-up photos of the pen and that he had gone out of his way to describe all the pluses and minuses of the pen's condition. It wasn't in perfect condition (which is why it was in my price range in the first place). I felt quite confident bidding on it. I didn't end up being the high bidder, but I felt I knew when to stop when the prices got too high for me.

If you're in any doubt as to the condition of the object on which you want to bid, ask the seller. If the merchandise is an antique, some blemishes are probably to be expected, and if the seller is an individual, be aware that he may not be an expert appraiser. Be as specific as possible about what you want to investigate, whether it's blemishes, discoloration, dents, tears, or other glitches.

If the seller is an auction house and the items are high-tech computer or electronics equipment, be aware that you're probably bidding on merchandise that is out of date or has been refurbished. Buying refurbished material is not necessarily a problem, because it means that a computer manufacturer has worked on it; the important thing is to realize that the equipment is probably not brand new.

Refurbished or outdated items can, and should, cost less than comparable new items. For example, if you're thinking of bidding on refurbished computer equipment, look for auction items offered at perhaps only half as much as their new counterparts.

When participating in computer auctions online, beware of bidding on outdated software. Always know what the latest release number is for software you wish to buy. Also be suspicious about new software being sold by individuals: Ask whether you are getting a copy of the program disk or CD, or the original. Also ask whether the software being sold is a bootleg copy or a valid, registered version. The original will have the genuine packaging and labels. It's safest to obtain software from reputable dealers rather than risk the possibility of an illegal transaction.

Don't be misled by "hot" items or featured products offered at special auctions. They may or may not be truly rare. These items are "featured" simply because the sellers pay an extra fee to have them listed up front in their particular category.

Price check on Aisle 3

Too many buyers win the battle but lose the war: They win the auction, but the price they pay is at or above what they would pay in a store for the same item. In other words, they lose the war. The solution? Do your homework before you start bidding.

You have several options for getting second/third/whatever opinions before you start bidding:

- ✔ **Call local stores and check on the best price for the item or a comparable item.** You may find that after shipping, insurance, and escrow charges are added to an auction item's price, you pay a lot more than you would at the mall.

- ✔ **Check Internet pricing resources.** Good bets are CNET's Shopper.com (www.shopper.com), Pricescan (www.pricescan.com) and PriceWatch (www.pricewatch.com).

- ✔ **Search through eBay's extensive archives of past auctions for an item that's similar to yours.** (Click the Search link at the top of nearly any eBay page to display the eBay Classifieds Search page. Scroll down to the Completed Search section at the bottom of the page, enter some search terms in the Words to Search for in Title box, and click the Search button. In a few seconds, a page appears with a list of completed auctions whose titles contain your search terms.) Make a note of what other high bidders have paid for similar items.

- ✔ **Consult consumer-oriented Web sites.** Try Consumer Guide (www.consumerguide.com) and Consumer Reports Online (www.consumerreports.com). The latter site has a good report titled Smart Cybershopping that can reduce your chances of falling victim to fraud (www.consumerreports.com/Special/Samples/Reports/9812shp0.htm). These organizations both excel in their product reviews.

- ✔ **Consult the International Society of Appraisers (ISA).** The ISA Web site's search page (www.isa-appraisers.org/search.htm) helps you find an appraiser in your area. You can also find out about courses in appraising and take a quiz to gauge your own appraisal expertise at www.isappraisers.org/value.htm.

> ✔ **Consult some of the traditional auction houses listed in this book's Internet Directory.** Christie's (www.christies.com) can set you up with one of its expert appraisers. Butterfield & Butterfield (www.butterfields.com) will appraise an item if you send them a photo. You can even send them a photo online, and they'll give you a price for free. It's a classic case of a small amount of effort possibly resulting in a big savings for you.

Find out where the best deals are

Get to know the kinds of auctions available and what each one of them sells. (Chapter 1 lists some good places to start your research.) Go through this book's Internet Directory and look through the various types of auction sites to get an idea of how the options match up with your shopping needs.

Table 4-1 shows the range of items you can bid on and a few places you can find them online.

eBay is a good place to start no matter what you're seeking.

Because new Internet auction sites are turning up continuously, it is virtually impossible to maintain an all-inclusive list: Table 4-1 provides just some examples of the kinds of specialized auctions out there in cyberspace. Many of these sites overlap; lots of them sell computers, for example, so check more than one category. Also, I'm not necessarily recommending these sites. I'm only suggesting starting points.

Don't be misled by the claims an auction house makes about itself. The words "Live Auction" are pretty much meaningless on the Internet — all online auctions are live. The difference is that some last an hour, some last a day, and others last a week or longer. It's impossible to prove that a site is the largest or most reliable, or the "premier" site. Rely on user feedback and reviews of auction sites for accurate evaluations rather than being swayed by a site's impressive-sounding self-promotion.

If you're looking for a specific car part or 1950s jazz record, you don't need to visit lots of different auction sites. Instead, you can let a program called a search engine do the walking for you. A *search engine* is a program used by a site called a *search service.* You enter search terms (words or phrases) in a text box, and the search engine looks through a database for those terms. The search engine displays a Web page with links to pages containing the desired search terms.

The following sections explain how to choose a search service and how to refine your search.

Table 4-1	Internet Auction Starting Points
If You're Looking For . . .	**Go Here**
Reviews of auction sites	www.auction-guide.com or www.planetclick.com and search for **auctions.**
An extensive list of Internet auctions	BidFind (www.bidfind.com/af/af-list.html)
Antiques	Golden Age Auction (www.goldnage.com)
Beanie Babies	The Collectible Exchange (www.beaniex.com)
Computer-related equipment (bargain, refurbished)	Interactive Auction Online (www.iaoauction.com)
Computer-related equipment (new, high-end)	AuctionGate (www.auctiongate.com) or uBid (www.ubid.com)
Consumer electronics	Encore Auction (www.encoreauction.com)
Guitars	Guitar Auction (www.guitarauction.com) Gibson Musical Instruments (auction.gibson.com)
Movie-related memorabilia, walk-on roles VIP seats	Hollywood Auction (travel.to/Hollywood)
Music (CDs, LPs)	4Tunes.com (www.4tunes.com)
Sewing/stitching supplies	Cross Stitches (www.xstitches.com)
Sporting Goods	The Mountain Zone (auctions.mountainzone.com)
Stamps	Dennis R. Abel Stamps for Collectors (www.drabel.com)
Vacation travel deals	Bid 4 Vacations (www.bid4vacations.com/auction.cfm)
Wine	Wine.com (www.wine.com/bidwineauction.cgi)

Using general search services

You can sometimes find individual auction items listed on the big Internet search services such as AltaVista (www.altavista.com), Excite (www.excite.com), Lycos (www.lycos.com), and NetFind (www.aol.com/netfind).

The problem with using one of these well-known search services is that their databases can't always keep up with auction sites whose listings change constantly. An item listed for a one-day auction isn't likely to turn up on one of these sites. It's far more reliable, given the transitory nature of Internet auctions, to try an auction-specific search utility. See the next section for details.

Using auction search services

Most Internet auction services provide a search utility to help you locate specific items currently offered for sale. Many, like Biddington's (www.biddingtons.com), let you type words in a simple text box on the service's home page (see Figure 4-1).

Just as Internet-wide search services can't keep up with constantly increasing listings, don't expect an individual auction search utility to provide you with a link to an object that just went online an hour ago. It's far more reliable to burrow into a site by clicking category names.

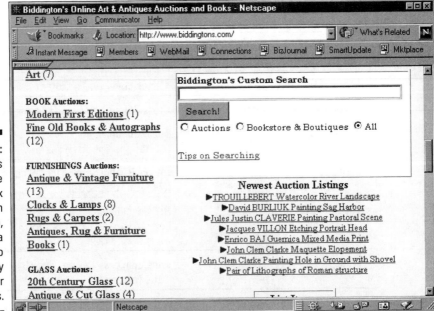

Figure 4-1:
Type words in the search box to begin your search, or click a category to quickly narrow your choices.

The fact that there are so many auction services can work to your advantage: You can use one of the services that lets you search multiple services at the same time. These include BidFind (`www.bidfind.com`) and Auction Connect (`auctionconnect.lycos.com`).

Refining your search

Depending on how a search engine program is written, you can "steer" the engine by using special words and symbols to increase your chances of finding what you want. The actual search terms vary from service to service, so check the site's Help section or click a Search Tips or Search Strategies link if one is available. Here are some things to consider when refining your search:

- ✔ Entering a single search term (for example, **jar** if you're looking for cookie jars), gets you every Web page that contains the word *jar* in the title or description (some services let you distinguish between a title search or a description search). You're likely to end up with many more Web page listings than you want.

- ✔ Entering more than one word as the search criteria (such as **cookie jar**), doesn't necessarily narrow the search. Some search programs respond to this query by finding all listings that contain either *cookie* or *jar*. You end up with twice as many irrelevant listings.

- ✔ Enclosing the search terms in quotation marks is a reliable and useful way to limit searches. However, keep in mind that the program looks for listings that exactly match the search criteria. So, a search for "cookie jars" misses any auctions that contain the terms "jars, cookie."

- ✔ Using the singular form is your best bet. A search for "cookie jar" turns up more sites than a search for the plural "cookie jars."

- ✔ Typing a plus sign (+) before the required word can help narrow your search. Entering **cookie +jar** tells the search program to look for any listings that contain both of these words, not necessarily in the order you typed them. You can also tell the search program to ignore a search term by typing a minus sign (-) before the word. A search for **cookie +jar –elephant** excludes cookie jars advertised as looking like elephants.

Bidding to Win

After you do your homework (see the previous section) and find a site that offers items you may be interested in, you're ready to jump into the auction fray. The following sections walk you through the bidding process, from registering with the auction site to placing a winning bid.

Traditionally, the seller or auction house sets the price on an item, and you bid on it. However, a number of Internet auction services use alternative processes:

- ✔ At TravelBids (www.TravelBids.com) you specify the type of trip you're looking for, and travel agents submit bids to you so you can choose between them.

- ✔ At Sell and Trade (www.sellandtrade.com) you can come up with your own rules for your auction. A buyer can try to trade merchandise rather than purchase an item outright.

- ✔ At Bidnask (www.bidnask.com) the seller lists the lowest price at which he is willing to sell, and buyers list the highest price at which they're willing to buy. The difference is called the *spread.* The goal is for the seller and buyer to reduce the spread until they make a deal.

Register

You register by filling out an online form like the one shown in Figure 4-2. You typically have to provide the auction house with your name, e-mail address, and other personal information so that it knows who you are, where it can ship to, and how to contact you if the need arises. If the auction house accepts credit cards, you may be asked to provide a credit card number. In the course of registering, you're usually asked to choose a username and password to use when you submit bids to the site.

If you're asked for a credit card number, make sure that the site uses a *secure server* — a type of computer that protects sensitive data by encrypting it so that thieves cannot steal it. A lock or similar security icon appears in your Web browser window if you visit a site that uses a secure server. See Chapter 2 for more detailed explanations on encryption and other ways to protect yourself when conducting e-commerce online.

Shop 'til you drop

Virtually all auction houses give you two ways to navigate their contents. You can click through a categorical listing of contents until you find the type of item you want (see Figure 4-3), or you can enter a description of what you're looking for in a search box (refer to Figure 4-1). You then click a button labeled Go or Search or something similar to activate a search of the items currently for sale and return matches. (See "Using auction search services," earlier in this chapter, for more detailed information about searching for specific items on an auction site.)

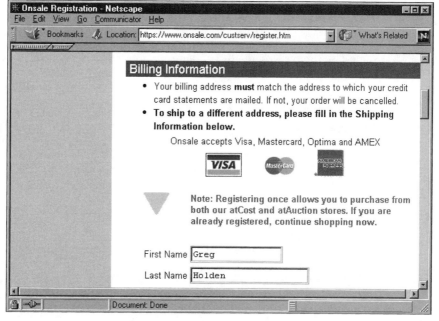

Figure 4-2: You have to register to bid. Enter the required information in each box, and then submit the form to the site.

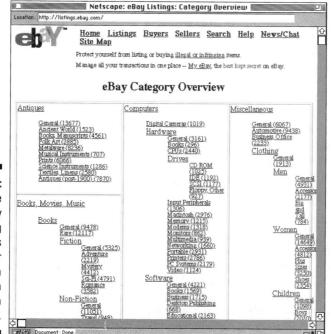

Figure 4-3: Locate items by clicking categories like these or entering a description in a search box.

Formulate a winning bidding strategy

A number of factors contribute to devising a successful bidding strategy, including the type of auction and certain logistical elements. This section offers tips to help you take everything into account.

Making your bids suit the auction

Winning Internet auctions depends in large measure on the type of auction. Before you get your heart set on a particular item and rush into a bid, make sure you understand the rules and procedures of the auction you're getting into. Chapter 1 explains the differences between various auction types in detail, but here's a quick review of some of the most popular auctions and the strategies you might pursue with each.

Reserve price auction

In order for a bidder to win this type of auction, he must not only have the highest bid but also must meet or exceed the reserve price (the lowest price at which the seller is willing to sell the item). The reserve price usually isn't disclosed to bidders, although some sellers actually reveal the reserve price in an item's description. If the high bidder doesn't meet the seller's reserve price, the two can negotiate a compromise price.

Some bidders, knowing that a common reserve price is an even amount such as $50, $100, $200, and so on, bid just over one of these amounts (say, $51 or $101 to see if they meet the reserve. (If they meet the reserve, the auction listing displays a message such as "reserve met" rather than the previous "reserve price not yet met.")

Open reserve auction

The seller places the starting bid to guarantee that he'll get the desired minimum amount — he doesn't have to sell the item for less than the starting bid. In some cases, the seller may choose to lower the starting price to meet a bid before the auction closes. There isn't much strategy you can try here: You can meet the minimum amount if you think the price is fair. You can also bid near the amount and ask the seller if your offer is sufficient.

Yankee auction

The seller posts multiple identical items for sale. Bids are ranked first by price. If two or more bids are for the same price, the bid for the larger quantity takes precedence. If bids are for the same price and quantity, then the earlier initial bid takes precedence. Bid just above the offer that is the lowest current winning bid. For instance, if ten items are offered for $450, and the tenth-highest bid is $451, and the next bid is $500, try bidding $461. A safer bid would be $501. That way you won't be the low bidder and stand a risk of being knocked out of the winning bid group.

Dutch auction

The seller posts multiple identical items for sale and specifies the starting bid (minimum price) and the number of items available. Bidders bid at or above the starting price for the quantity they're interested in purchasing. At the close of the auction, the highest bidders purchase the items at the lowest successful bid.

The strategy for a Dutch auction is basically the same as for a Yankee auction. (See the preceding section.)

Live auction

Bidding takes place in real time rather than over a number of hours or days. Because the action takes place so quickly and competition can be intense, the best strategy is thorough research: Know before the sale starts exactly how much you can afford to bid and what constitutes a good price. Then when the bidding starts, determine not to go beyond that self-imposed limit.

Paying attention to the little things

One of the most exciting parts of auction sales, whether they take place in an auction house, online, or both, is the strategizing involved in coming up with bids. I remember watching a *Masterpiece Theatre* series on TV in which the actress Helen Mirren helped to recover a lost work of art by outbidding more experienced dealers at an auction. Her trump card was her intimidating physical presence — which doesn't help even Arnold Schwarzenegger online.

Internet auctions have their own bidding nuances that are a result, in part, of the technology involved:

- ✔ **Timing.** If you're bidding by computer, timing becomes important. Sometimes it pays to place the first bid; other times it pays to jump in at the last minute.

- ✔ **Vigilance.** You can check bids online on a regular basis, any time of the day or night. Many Internet auction services send an automatic e-mail message to notify you if you're outbid.

- ✔ **Proxy bidding.** You can use *proxy bids* to hold off challengers. In a proxy bid, you bid the maximum you're willing to pay for an item rather than the minimum bid increment. Any competitors have to beat your maximum bid in order to be the high bidder.

It's easy to get carried away by the excitement of finding what you want. Make sure the item you're bidding on really is a good investment. You have days or sometimes even a week to place a bid; think about it, ask your friends, and shop around for comparison prices.

AUCTION LINGO

How proxy bids/automatic bids work

One of the benefits of using Internet auctions is that their high-tech features can save you time and headaches. One feature common to many auction sites is an automatic bidding system. Such a system eliminates the need for you to keep your eye on your current bid to see whether someone has outbid you.

You *can* check in on an auction every few minutes or hours, but your other responsibilities may suffer. If you need to make work or family a priority instead of your bid, make use of an automated bidding system. eBay calls this Proxy Bidding; uBid calls it BidButler. Whatever the name, the operation is similar:

You tell the bid service the maximum amount you're willing to pay for an item. The service monitors current bidding and if someone outbids you, automatically places the smallest incremental bid possible to keep you the high bidder. (Incremental bids vary depending on the merchandise being sold, and may be 50 cents, $1, $5, and so on.)

If the bidding in an auction goes over your maximum bid, the automated bid utility sends an e-mail to let you know. You can then connect to the Web page where the item is offered and place a new bid.

TIP

Try your best not to get carried away in the thrill of the chase. I know this is difficult! Be prepared not to get what you want, too. Make the decision in your mind that you are willing to spend no more than a certain amount on that special something, and then stick to it.

Bid once and let the chips fall

I have a friend named Alex Fan who is a network specialist for a high-tech firm. Alex purchases monitors and other computer equipment at Internet auction houses that specialize in computer equipment. Alex's strategy is to bid low on every item he's interested in. Someone outbids him almost every time — as well they should, because his initial bid is sometimes ridiculously low. But once in a great while, when bidding is slow, no one turns up to outbid him, and Alex ends up with a great bargain.

Bid early and then bid again at the end

Another strategy is to submit one bid early to establish yourself as being in the running for an item. Then, sit back and wait patiently until the auction is almost over before placing a higher bid, rather than continually bidding against others. Patience has its rewards: If you continually place bids while the item is available, you are in essence increasing the price by bidding against yourself.

Many Internet auctions provide prospective buyers with an automatic incremental bid feature. For example, say you specify $100 as your maximum bid on an item. The bid *increment* on this item, specified by the auction house, is $1. That is, you have to bid at least $1 more than the current high bid in order to be considered the current high bidder. Your initial bid is $10. Someone places a bid of $20, thus outbidding you. But wait! Because you specified a maximum bid of $100, you still show up online as the high bidder with a bid of $21. Your competitor bids $22; the system automatically places you as the high bidder at $23, and continues to do so up to your maximum of $100 — all without you having to get anxious and over-stimulated (at least, until the auction ends).

Check out the seller

Always check out the feedback comments on a seller before you place a bid on something that person put on the auction block. Chapter 3 discusses how to research sellers on several auction sites. Pay particular attention to problems that buyers have reported in previous transactions.

If you use Yahoo! Auctions, you can find out about the site's user feedback system at `help.yahoo.com/help/auctions/agen/agen-07.html`. Buyers and sellers receive an e-mail that includes a link to a Web page where you can provide a rating for the buyer or seller. There's nothing to prevent you, on this or other sites, from asking for more details from people who left comments about a user you're thinking of doing business with.

Ask the seller questions about the item

Don't be reluctant to approach the seller and ask questions about the merchandise you're considering before placing any bids. Be sure to ask about flaws, important and desirable features, or about more nuts-and-bolts details like payment options and shipping costs. It's better to get all your questions answered before the sale rather than after.

Submit your bid

After you spot an item you want, you access a Web page form that lets you enter your username and password, how you much you want to bid, or how many objects you want (if more than one is available). You click a button to submit your bid to the site's server. The bid is then registered online.

Watch out for shill bidding

If the bidding suddenly goes up dramatically and the bidder's e-mail address is the same as the seller's, back out immediately. You may be a victim of shill bidding, which occurs when a seller arranges with a friend, family member, or other acquaintance to artificially push up the bidding to make more money than they would otherwise. It's also known as "bid padding."

If a friend bids on your item with the honest intention of purchasing it, then it is certainly allowed. Bidding on your item for the sole purpose of inflating the final bid amount is prohibited.

It isn't always easy to tell if shill bidding is taking place, of course. Relatives are allowed to bid on items for sale like everyone else. For this reason it's better to leave it up to the auction service to determine if there's a problem. They look at factors such as the number of bids made. Another is if the bidder has only placed bids on one seller's auctions and never on any other. A seller cannot bid on his or her item at eBay; this is considered shill bidding.

If someone is found to be guilty of shill bidding, he or she can be suspended, either temporarily or permanently, from registering with the auction service in the future.

Sometimes (for example, on eBay), the bid form is on the same Web page as the auction item itself. On other services, you click a Place a Bid or Bid Now link on the page that contains the object you want. Your browser connects to the form you fill out to specify your bid. The form used by uBid (www.ubid.com) is shown in Figure 4-4.

Track your bid

Choose Edit⇨Refresh or Edit⇨Reload from your browser's menu to revisit the Web page on which the item you bid on is displayed and see whether you've been outbid. Many of the more sophisticated auction sites automatically send you an e-mail message if you're outbid.

Getting help for an auction addiction

Auctions can be addictive. I know of at least one young woman who had to give them up because they were consuming too much of her time and money. Check out the Internet Directory for some Web-based resources that can help if you think your online auction use or other Internet shopping activities are getting out of hand.

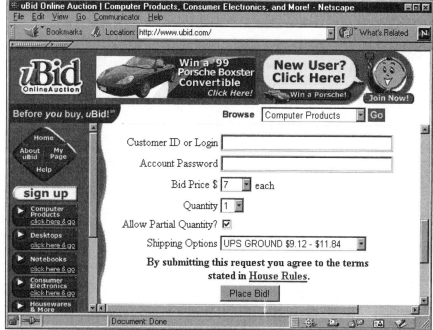

Figure 4-4:
Fill out this
form with
your bid
information
and click
Place Bid!
to submit it.

(Maybe) You win!

If you're the high bidder, you need to work out payment and shipping details with the auction house — or, in the case of a person-to-person auction, the individual seller. See Chapter 5 for more information on getting the goods after an auction ends.

Fads are fleeting

Remember mood rings? Pet rocks? Anything having to do with CB radio? Avoid bidding on "instant" collectibles — objects that have just come on the market and have become super-popular. They may not be popular a month or a year from now. Need some reminders? Visit the Bad Fads Web site (www.adscape.com/badfads) for examples of things that were once considered treasures that quickly fell by the commercial wayside.

Chapter 5

Getting the Goods

● ●

In This Chapter

▶ Using escrow services to make sure you get what you pay for

▶ Ensuring safe and speedy shipments

▶ Choosing a payment method

● ●

*F*or auction buyers, the scariest part of a purchase is the prospect of sending payment for an item that never arrives. You wait anxiously for the mail or delivery truck driver to come up the front steps with your precious package. When your package does arrive, you have to inspect the item to make sure the condition is what you expected — it works, it's not broken, and it wasn't damaged in transit.

My first online purchase was a used laptop computer that I bought through a newsgroup. I remember anxiously wondering if I was really doing the right thing as I put the check in the mail. After the delivery came, I half expected the box to be empty (it wasn't). My next fear was that the device wouldn't function (it worked fine).

Happily, all my bad feelings were for naught. But they begin to resurface whenever I buy something at auction. How can you bid and purchase with confidence, eliminating the doubts and uncertainties? As auctions boom in popularity, new safeguards become available. This chapter describes how to use online resources to seal the deal and get the goods for which you made the qualifying bid.

Don't Get Escrewed — Use an Escrow Service

An *escrow service* is a business that functions as an intermediary between someone who provides goods or services and someone who pays money in exchange for those goods or services. (The word *escrow* refers to a bond or agreement between two parties to do something — usually, *pay* something — in exchange for goods or services; the "something" is usually held by a third party until the goods are delivered or the services are rendered.)

Using an escrow service to fulfill an Internet auction transaction can benefit sellers as well as buyers, although the most obvious benefits are for buyers: If you're paying someone you've never met, you naturally have fears that the person may take your money and never deliver what was promised. By having the escrow service hold your money, you can inspect an item to make sure it's satisfactory. After you notify the escrow service that the shipment is acceptable, the service releases your payment to the seller.

One of the best benefits to buyers is that an escrow service enables you to make purchases with a credit card. You can authorize the escrow service to charge the purchase to your credit card number, thus making it easier to pay sellers who normally only accept checks or money orders.

Escrow services place another bureaucratic "layer" between the seller and buyer, and sellers naturally have concerns about it. But escrow services benefit sellers in a number of ways:

- The seller must usually wait days or weeks after a sale closes before receiving payment and then shipping an item. With the security of an escrow service, the seller can ship the merchandise the same day the auction closes and be confident that she'll receive payment.

- Because the seller must track the packages he sends, he can be absolutely sure that a package will arrive at its destination.

- Escrow companies also make credit card transactions feasible for sellers who don't have merchant accounts. This feature is especially useful for overseas transactions, which can take extra time and involve currency exchanges.

- The buyer commonly pays the escrow charges.

Setting up an escrow transaction

You've done it. You purchased a high-ticket item, something far more expensive than anything you've invested in before. You're worried about payment and you decide to use an escrow service. What do you do? The details vary slightly from service to service, but in general, the procedure is the same. Here are the steps you follow to use one popular service called i-Escrow.

The person who starts the ball rolling by notifying the escrow service about the transaction (and this can be either the buyer or the seller), needs to have the other person's e-mail address. It's especially important to keep in mind that *both buyer and seller need to be registered users of the same escrow company.* If you bid on an item and you know you want to use an escrow service, send an e-mail inquiry to the seller to ask him whether he belongs to the same service, or will register with the service you chose. You can also wait until after the auction is over to bring this up. Generally, registration is free, takes only a few minutes, and doesn't require you to submit sensitive information like phone or credit card numbers. Some sellers don't like using escrow services because they make sealing a deal a little more work, but the benefits work both ways. Follow these steps to use i-Escrow:

1. **Go to the i-Escrow home page at** www.i-Escrow.com. **To register with i-Escrow, click the Free Sign Up! icon. (If you're already registered, enter your username and password in the User Login boxes on the i-Escrow home page, and then click Enter.)**

   The i-Escrow – New User Signup Step 1 of 2 page appears.

2. **Enter your e-mail address, choose a password, and enter your name, birth date, and company name, if applicable, on this page. Also fill in all the fields in the User Identification section of the page. After you're through, click the Continue button on the bottom of the page to go to the i-Escrow – Credit Card Payment page. Enter your address on this page. After you're done, click Continue.**

   The New User Signup Step 2 of 2 page appears.

3. **Enter your address, phone number, and fax number on this page and then click the Submit button.**

   The New User Form page appears.

4. **If you're ready to initiate the payment process for a transaction, click the HERE button next to the To Continue and Start a NEW Transaction button. (If you aren't ready, you can click the Home or FAQ links to move to other parts of the i-Escrow site.)**

   The i-Escrow New Transaction form appears (see Figure 5-1).

5. **Fill out the form by identifying yourself as either the buyer or seller, providing the other person's e-mail address, and entering the purchase and shipping prices. After you're done, click the Create Escrow button at the bottom of the page.**

   The Transaction Detail page appears, with information about your transaction as well as extensive instructions about the buyer's and seller's respective responsibilities in closing the deal. (See Figure 5-2.)

6. **Read through the information, verify that the data pertaining to your arrangement is okay, and click the I Accept button at the bottom of the page.**

   The transaction information is submitted to i-Escrow.

At this point, it's up to the buyer to pay i-Escrow by credit card, check, or wire transfer. i-Escrow automatically charges its own service fee, which is 5 percent of the purchase price or a minimum of $5. The seller is notified that payment has been received and ships the item to the buyer. i-Escrow requires that the merchandise be shipped insured and with a tracking number.

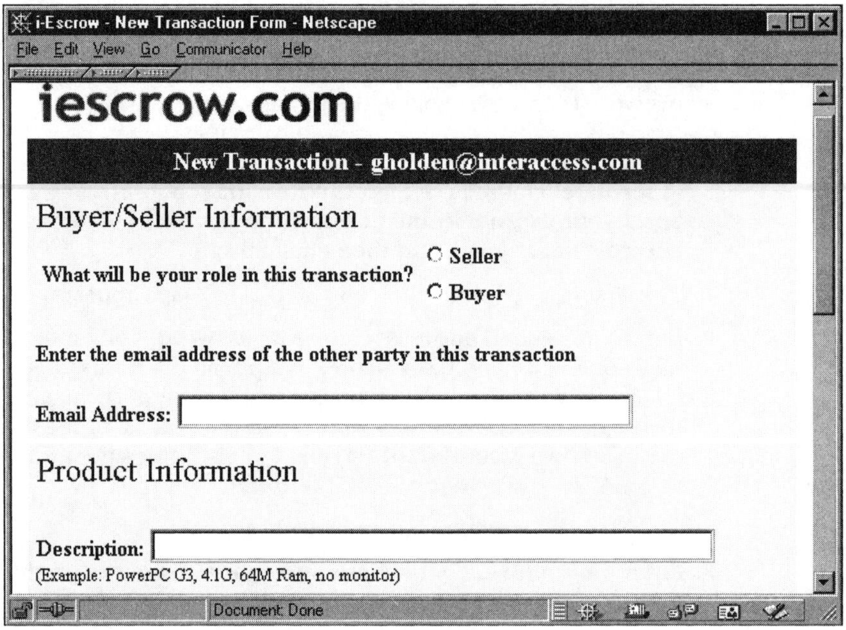

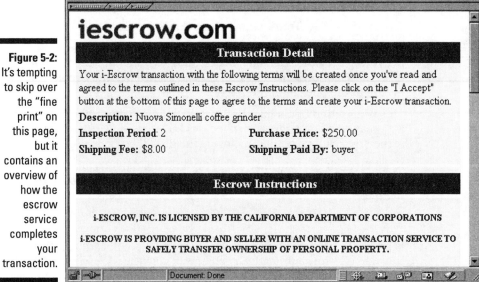

Figure 5-1:
Use this form to send the purchase price, shipping information, and other data about your transaction to the escrow service.

Figure 5-2:
It's tempting to skip over the "fine print" on this page, but it contains an overview of how the escrow service completes your transaction.

i-Escrow suggests a two-day inspection period when the buyer receives the merchandise, but the buyer or seller can adjust this and other aspects of the deal.

After inspecting the merchandise, the buyer either accepts or declines the purchase by notifying the escrow service. If the buyer accepts the item, the escrow service sends a check to the seller, and the transaction is complete. If the buyer declines the item, he must ship the item back to the seller and pay for the additional shipping costs. The original payment is then refunded to the buyer.

All escrow services are not created equal

Escrow services, like auction houses, have their own fees and procedures. It pays to compare prices and requirements to make sure the service fits your needs.

Here are just a few of the differences I noticed between the four escrow companies I found on the Web as I was writing this (see Table 5-1 for URLs, fees, and additional comments about these services):

- **i-Escrow** requires sellers to ship using a package tracking service, including the U.S. Postal Service's tracking options. Other services don't specify this but do require you to use FedEx or United Parcel Service (UPS) but *not* the U.S. Postal Service.

- **Internet Clearing Corporation** requires the buyer to enter sales data; in contrast, i-Escrow lets either the buyer or seller do this. With Internet Clearing Corporation, the seller is paid immediately upon shipping an item rather than having to wait until the buyer inspects and approves it. The buyer can still return the item and get a refund. The service also has a fax service that makes it especially easy to fax sales information to the service, for users who are wary of filling out and submitting data via Web page forms.

- **SecureTrades.com** offers a Merchandise Holding option: The seller ships the merchandise to SecureTrades rather than to the buyer. SecureTrades then ships the goods, so that the buyer can be sure something is being sent. However, SecureTrades accepts only checks or money orders, not credit cards.

- **TradeSafe** suggests a standard inspection period that lasts until midnight of the business day following receipt of the shipment (though this can be modified by buyers or sellers). The company also provides a discount to users who pay by check or wire transfer.

As Internet auctions become more popular, the number of escrow services will grow as well. Take a look at Yahoo's directory of online escrow services at `dir.yahoo.com/Business_and_Economy/Companies/ Retail_Management_Supplies_and_Services/Electronic_Commerce/ Online_Escrow_Services`.

Table 5-1	Internet Escrow Service Fees and Regulations			
Service	**URL**	**Fee for $100***	**Fee for $1,000***	**Remarks**
i-Escrow	www. i-Escrow.com	$5	$50	Either buyer or seller can initiate transaction.
Internet Clearing Corporation	internet clearing.com	$3.50**	$35**	First transaction free for purchases of up to $1,000. Credit card purchases not allowed for trans-actions of $5,000 or more.
Secure-Trades.com	securetrades .com	$5	$50	Merchandise Holding option has higher fees; see Web site for details.
TradeSafe	tradesafe.com	$15 cash, $12.25 credit	$40 cash, $50.50 credit	

*Check Web sites for fee schedules for other amounts
**Fee charged to both buyer and seller

Most auction buyers and sellers who use escrow services end up being glad they did. Don't wait until you have a bad transaction to try these services.

Shipping Shouldn't Be Shocking

Paying for an item is only half of the process of completing an auction sale. The other is making sure the goods arrive safely.

A successful shipment has the following features:

✔ **Speed.** Overnight delivery is great but expensive. The buyer and seller should work out a good system for delivery that meets both of their needs.

✔ **Trackability.** You can track the shipment either with a tracking number, or by knowing with reasonable certainly how long a package should take to get from origin to destination.

✔ **Security.** Don't overlook the question of how the shipment is wrapped and protected; a good shipment is securely wrapped so it isn't damaged by burly package handlers. Along with this physical protection, protecting an item by insuring it is important as well.

This section is about shipping from the buyer's point of view. Find more about shipping for auction sellers in Chapter 8.

In April 1999, eBay, which recognizes the importance of sealing deals successfully through reliable shipping methods, announced an alliance with iShip and Mailboxes Etc. (MBE) to provide an integrated shipping interface for eBay users. By the time you read this, the system may be well in place.

Initial descriptions call for iShip.com to provide information up front to eBay sellers and buyers regarding shipping costs and options, helping reduce the need for frequent e-mails to work out terms of shipping. MBE will offer eBay sellers and buyers supplies, stores, and staff to help with the actual shipping. In addition, eBay and MBE expect to implement a "hold for inspection" program where MBE franchisees will provide a place for delivery and inspection of goods.

Whether or not you use eBay, you might look into using iShip.com (www.iship.com). iShip.com is an Internet shipping services company that lets buyers and sellers choose shipping carriers, check pricing, and track packages.

If you have a tracking number, you don't have to be in suspense while you wait for your purchase to arrive. You can track it online at the shipping company's Web site. Otherwise, you can visit the One-Stop Parcel Tracking site; enter the shipping number for your UPS, FedEx, Airborne Express, Emory Worldwide, DHL, Roadway Express, or U.S. Postal Service package, and you can track it right away (www.teleport.com/~mailman). (See "Tracking your package," later in this chapter, for more information about tracking your shipment.) For more information about the procedures used by individual shipping services, consult their Web sites or call the toll-free numbers listed in your telephone book.

Insuring your investment

If the merchandise you're receiving is especially valuable, ask the seller to insure it. Insurance adds to the eventual purchase price, but for special items, it's worth it for the extra peace of mind.

At this writing, eBay is developing an insurance program with Lloyd's of London for its users. eBay already has a policy in place that is available to all eBay users in good standing. The insurance covers qualified items bought on eBay listed on or after March 1, 1999. Purchases are covered for up to $200, less a $25 deductible, at no cost to users.

Keeping your eyes out for the prize

You may have to wait a long time to get your order — it always takes longer than you want to wait. The remedy is to know when the package was shipped, be able to track it, and keep in touch with the seller. This is where picking a reliable seller who has lots of positive feedback comes in handy (see Chapter 3 for more about using feedback and finding a reliable seller).

I'm not the most patient person. After a few days of waiting, I get tired of checking the mail. I've been known to e-mail sellers with anxious questions. A good seller responds patiently with information about when the shipment was sent and when it should arrive. Most sellers provide you with this information automatically, but not all of them do. Don't be reluctant to ask.

The important thing is to be patient when you make these inquiries. You don't need to assume that your package has been lost or that the seller is misleading you. Information is the key. One of the best services I've seen in this regard is Amazon.com, which sends e-mails at virtually every stage of the shipping process. It notifies you when your order is received by Amazon.com and when your shipment has been sent, for instance.

If your shipment does seem to be overly late, it's often a good idea to set a deadline for receipt with the seller. Whatever you do, don't engage in personal attacks against the seller's character or personality. You only end up damaging your own reputation, or possibly embarrassing yourself if it turns out that the shipping delay was an honest mistake.

Your communications with the seller are effective if you can document everything pertaining to the purchase. In case your computer crashes, your hard disk fails, or your equipment is stolen, you can be extra-careful by printing out hard copies of:

✔ All your e-mail correspondence to and from the seller

✔ The auction listing

✔ Any "End-of-Auction" notices from the auction house

See Chapter 3 for more suggestions about how to avoid trouble, or how to deal with problems such as sellers who won't ship items for which you paid.

Tracking your package

It's to your advantage to have your expected package include some kind of tracking method, so offer to pay an extra dollar or two for this service. (See Chapter 8 for more details.) The following shippers provide tracking services and let you check your shipment's progress online:

- ✔ United States Postal Service at `www.usps.gov/cttgate`
- ✔ United Parcel Service at `www.ups.com/tracking/tracking.html`
- ✔ Federal Express at `www.fedex.com` (Select your country name from the drop-down menu.)
- ✔ Airborne Express at `www.airborne.com/trace`
- ✔ DHL Worldwide Express at `www.dhl.com`
- ✔ Roadway Express, Inc. at `www.roadway.com`
- ✔ Emery Worldwide at `www.emeryworld.com/eww/emeryweb`

You don't have to leave it up to the seller to determine how to ship your package. Tell the seller that you want to use a certain carrier, or that you're willing to pay a few dollars extra to get the package faster or have it tracked, or both.

Citing the 30-day rule

In case you or your deadbeat seller thinks there aren't any laws or regulations obligating the seller to ship the merchandise you purchased within a certain period of time, think again. The Mail or Telephone Order Rule (commonly called the "30-Day Rule") adopted by the U.S. Federal Trade Commission in 1975 states that when you order by mail or phone:

- ✔ You must receive the merchandise when the seller says you will.
- ✔ If no specific delivery period is specified, the seller must ship the merchandise to you no later than 30 days after your order is placed.
- ✔ If you don't receive the item shortly after that 30-day period, you can cancel your order and receive a refund.

If you experience delays in receiving shipment, begin sending e-mails that cite this rule. If this doesn't elicit a response, and if the seller is a credit card merchant, threaten to have the business's merchant credit card status revoked or state that you will report the problem to the Federal Trade Commission.

What to do if you're not a happy camper

All the preparation in the world can't always prevent you from getting taken by someone who is really disreputable. If you are taken by someone, keep after the person and try to maintain a courteous but persistent (even stubborn) demeanor as you badger the individual to keep his word.

If the seller is on eBay and repeated attemptsto resolve the problem are unsuccessful, get eBay's SafeHarbor Investigations service involved (pages.ebay.com/aw/safeharbor-investigates.html). Also notify other users of the problem via the eBay Feedback Forum (pages.ebay.com/aw/feedback.html).

eBay also has a Fraud Reporting System (crs.ebay.com/frs/start.asp) whose staff can try to contact the offender and, if they are unsuccessful, possibly remove the person from the eBay system.

If eBay's fraud resolution services aren't working and you are still in contact with the seller, you can try a professional mediator. At this writing, eBay was developing a program with the Online Ombuds Office of the University of Massachusetts, but the program wasn't up and running yet. Check its status at pages.ebay.com/aw/safeharbor-mediation.html.

If you are using a "company" auction service such as The Sharper Image or Egghead Software and you run into trouble, contact the company's customer support service.

If you are using one of the computer auctions that specialize in sales of computer and other electronic equipment, try the customer support area of the service in question, but these are notorious for slow response and otherwise slow service. You can also try one of the following online resources:

- ✔ If you think you have been victimized by mail fraud, call the U.S. Post Office crime hot line at 1-800-654-8896.

- ✔ The National Fraud Information Center also has a toll-free hotline (Consumers can call the NFIC hotline toll-free at 1-800-876-7060 as well as a Web site (www.fraud.org). It can forward your complaint to the appropriate government agency for action.

- ✔ The Web Police (www.Web-Police.org) will let you file a report and add your information to its database of Internet crime cases.

- ✔ The Alexander Law Firm in San Jose, CA operates the National Consumer Complaint Center (www.alexanderlaw.com/nccc/cb-intro.html) that will communicate your complaint to agencies that are interested in investigating and taking action for consumers.

- ✔ Internet ScamBusters (www.scambusters.org/Scambusters21.html) contains more tips and resources for victims of fraud, including a page titled "What to Do If You Get Scammed."

- ✔ The Better Business Bureau (www.bbb.org) will also let you file a complaint online. The BBB will attempt to facilitate communication between the company and you.

You can order a copy of the Mail or Telephone Order Rule for $28 ($23 plus $5 for handling) from the U.S. Department of Commerce's International Trade and Business Bookstore (tradecenter.ntis.gov/search.htm). Search for publication PB97-190730INP.

Exploring Alternative Payment Options

If you don't want to get into credit card or escrow payments (for example, if the merchandise is only a few dollars in price and it's not worth the trouble) what can you do?

You can ask your seller if personal checks are acceptable, but most won't accept them because of the danger of having the check bounce. It's never a good idea to send cash through the mail, either. The following sections describe some more practical options.

Cashier's checks and money orders

These are the most popular forms of payment on auction sites. After all, cashier's checks and money orders are guaranteed not to bounce. However, they require you to go to a bank or a post office to obtain them, and you usually have to pay a service charge as well.

If you're high bidder on an item being sold overseas, get a money order from a U.S. bank rather than the U.S. Postal Service. Some (though not all) overseas users complain that they can't cash postal money orders, and they have a much easier time with money orders drawn on U.S. banks.

The security of having a tangible, certified piece of paper is hard to beat. However, some online companies are trying to come up with virtual forms of payment that are quick and easy to use, as described in the following sections.

Reaching for your virtual wallet

A term commonly thrown around in the jargon of e-commerce is *wallet.* A wallet is software that, like a real wallet that you keep in your purse or pocket, stores available cash and other records. You can reach into your cyberwallet and withdraw virtual cash in the form of ecash, scrip, or CyberCoins. Security is provided by a form of Internet encryption (see Chapter 2).

A cybershopper who uses wallet software, such as Microsoft Wallet (www.microsoft.com/wallet/default.asp), CyberCoin Wallet (developed by CyberCash), or Instabuy (www.instabuy.com) can pay for items online in a matter of seconds, without having to transfer credit card data. What's more, some wallets can even "remember" your previous purchases and suggest further purchases.

CyberCash

CyberCash is one of the best-known companies providing payment options for online businesses. The fact that CyberCash is well-known should help you if you decide to use one of its many systems, which include:

- ✔ CashRegister helps process credit card transactions.
- ✔ CyberCoin handles small sums called micropayments. (The following section discusses micropayments.)
- ✔ Instabuy is relatively new and was not supported by many retail sites as this book was written. However, it *was* supported by Egghead.com, which has its own online auction service (www.surplusauction.com).
- ✔ PayNow electronic checks enables customers to pay bills online.

You can find out more about CyberCash's options for consumers at www.cybercash.com/cybercash/consumers.

MilliCent

MilliCent (www.millicent.digital.com) is a promising system that was still undergoing trials as this was written. When the system is fully implemented, it will work with a kind of virtual currency known as micropayments. (Other companies, including CyberCash's CyberCoin, offer similar services.)

Micropayments are very small units of currency exchanged by merchants and customers. The amounts involved may range from one-tenth of one cent to only a few dollars. Such small payments enable sites to provide content for sale on a per-click basis. For example, if you want to read an article, listen to music files, or view video clips online, you may be required to pay a few cents or a couple of dollars. These micropayments are automatically subtracted from your account.

How do you do it? First, you install a bit of software called a plug-in, which works along with your Web browser. The MilliCent plug-in is called MilliCent Wallet. Next, you choose a MilliCent broker from a list on the MilliCent Web site and set up an account by depositing money with the broker. The Wallet software automatically contacts the broker when you want to make a purchase from a vendor that supports the MilliCent system. The broker converts the "real" money in your account into MilliCent's form of electronic money, which is called *scrip* and pays the vendor with this scrip, which is sent over the Internet.

The micropayment system is particularly useful if you're a software developer who wants to accept moderate shareware fees for your products, or if you have any kind of content that you want to charge small amounts to give people access to, such as online courses or articles.

If you want to know more about the various forms of digital cash used on the Internet, you can't do much better than a site in England that is chock full of useful links and information: `www.netlink.co.uk/users/abracad/emoney.html`.

Part III
Selling at Internet Auctions

The 5th Wave   By Rich Tennant

"I learned the hard way that you should always use an escrow service when you're the high bidder on the Venus de Milo."

In this part . . .

So you're ready to make some money by banging down the virtual gavel on your own Internet auction sales. Or, maybe you're an online entrepreneur just trying to get rid of Grandma Carol's old jewelry. Either way, this is the part for you.

Here you find all the strategies you need to know to say "Going, going, gone!" to your merchandise, from advice on setting the price to tips on delivering the goods. You can also find hints on how to set terms for your auction and how to present your wares to make them attractive to buyers.

If you're really serious about the moneymaking part of this whole auction thing, this part can really help by providing all the info you need to set up your own sales-boosting Web page and how to provide customer service to the auction fanatics who come to them. I cover everything from how to handle complaints to (more importantly) how to get paid. I even devote a chapter on how to market to overseas bidders. Finally, I discuss the financial and legal considerations you need to be aware of as an auction sales guru so that the IRS doesn't start pounding on your door.

Chapter 6

Assuming the Role of Virtual Auctioneer

In This Chapter

▶ Choosing an item to sell

▶ Finding the right auction site for your item

▶ Preparing an effective auction listing

▶ Sealing the deal

*S*elling at auction is easy — astonishingly easy. You don't have to rent a building and stock it with merchandise like you would if you were running a retail shop. You don't have to apply for space and transport all your possessions like you would if you were selling at a flea market. You don't even have to mark all your items like you would if you were having a garage sale.

Despite the simplicity of Internet auctions, you usually have to go around the auction block a few times before you catch on to some of the tricks of the trade. In this chapter, I tell you step by step how to be a successful auction seller from the get go — whether you plan to sell once a year or once a day. Even if you didn't know an auction from a junction before you picked up this book, this chapter prepares you to compete with individuals who sell online professionally and are well-acquainted with the ins and outs of Internet auctions.

The most important piece of advice I can give if you're just starting out is to have fun. That means that you should try not to take pitfalls too seriously. You aren't making any life-or-death decisions here, after all. Don't become obsessed, anxious, or over-involved with online sales. If you don't make as much money as you expected on one sale, chances are you'll make more than you expected on the next one. Not knowing upfront exactly how things are going to turn out is what makes auctions exciting.

Deciding What to Sell

Most of us have stuff lying around that could be sold at auction. Just make sure that the item you put up for auction is something you're really willing to part with and that it's not near and dear to someone else in your household. This scenario was recently described on a popular TV sitcom. The son sold an old "Beverly Hillbillies" lunchbox he found in the attic for $300 on eBay. The father, however, was so upset at being deprived of one of his childhood icons that the boy had to buy it back for $400.

One person's trash is not always another person's treasure. The best place to find out whether someone will actually bid on the item you want to offer is the Internet itself. Search archives of past auctions to see whether others have attempted to unload items that are similar to yours, and whether the high bids represent what you consider to be the value of your merchandise. Keep in mind, though, that past bids are no indication of future performance. As more and more buyers and sellers frequent online auctions, more bids are placed, and prices tend to go up. You're far more likely to have luck finding purchasers for your treasure now than someone else did six months to a year ago.

After you've made up your reverse shopping list (that is, a list of your items that you want other people to shop for), the fun begins. Which of the many Internet auction sites is the best one to offer your wares? As competition heats up and more and more companies compete for bidders' attention, that question becomes harder to answer. The next section helps you discover which outlet is right for you.

Choosing an Auction Service

Some auction services are better than others, depending on the type of item you're placing on the auction block. eBay (www.ebay.com) is good for almost anything but is particularly good for rare or unusual items that a few avid enthusiasts will bid on.

However, eBay isn't the only auction on the Web, and shopping around pays. Don't use a single service all the time. Other, smaller auction sites are good, too — especially those that trade in a single type of item, such as stamps, coins, books, and so on. See Chapter 4 for some suggestions of "niche" sites that specialize in specific items like these. Also keep in mind that some sites are more likely than others to get clogged up at holiday times.

If you're selling computer equipment, strongly consider selling on one of the auction services that specialize in computers such as uBid (www.ubid.com) or Auction-Warehouse.com (www.auction-warehouse.com). Many buyers go there rather than to all-in-one shopping stops such as eBay or Amazon.com Auctions (auctions.amazon.com).

Joining the Ranks

To become a seller on a person-to-person auction site such as Yahoo! Auctions (auctions.yahoo.com), Global Auction Club (www.globalauctionclub.com), or the sports memorabilia auction site Fan2Fan (www.fan2fan.com), you first need to become a registered user. Usually, this involves providing the site with your real name, street address, phone number, and e-mail address. This information is known only by the auction service. You then pick a username and password by which you are identified to other buyers and sellers on the site.

Most sites, such as The Bidder Network (www.bidder-network.com) don't require you to provide sensitive credit card information at this point (see Figure 6-1). However, making sure that any information that you submit from your computer to a remote site on the Internet remains secure is always a good idea. If you see a checkbox that enables you to use a special security scheme called SSL (Secure Sockets Layer; see Chapter 2) to protect your data, check it. After you register, the site sends you an e-mail message to confirm your identity. You may also receive a User ID number in this message. You then read a user agreement and submit your acceptance to the site to complete your registration.

SSL stands for Secure Sockets Layer and refers to a form of encryption (see Chapter 2 for more information about this secretive stuff) widely used to protect data on the Internet. It's also sometimes called *public key encryption*. In order to use SSL encryption, you need a Web browser that supports SSL. (Most newer versions of Netscape Navigator and Microsoft Internet Explorer do this.) When you connect to a site, like Amazon.com Auctions, that uses SSL, the remote site's Web server sends your computer a bit of data called a *public key* that is used to encrypt the data you send to the server, along with a *certificate* that establishes the site's identity. The remote site's server uses a *private key* to decode the data you send to the site. You can obtain your own certificates, which enable you to encrypt your own e-mail messages and certify your own identify; see Chapter 2 for more information.

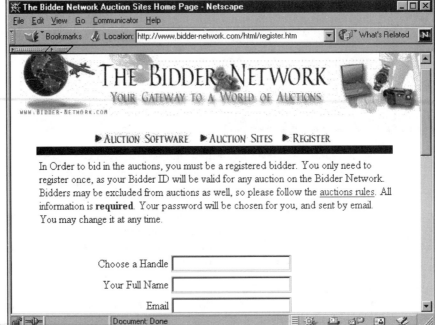

Figure 6-1:
The Bidder
Network
lets you
register for
multiple
auction
sites by fill-
ing out this
online form.

Choosing an Auction Type

The type of auction that's the best for you depends on what you have to sell. Generally speaking, though, your choice is pretty simple: If you have a single item, offer it at a traditional auction where the highest bidder wins. If you have multiple copies of an item to sell, use the Dutch auction format. You can call attention to your merchandise offered in either type of auction by paying extra to "feature" your sale, which means you showcase it by using special formatting or by placing the sale listing in a special location where visitors are more likely to see it. You can also try private auctions. (See Chapter 1 for more information on different types of auctions.)

When to use featured auctions

A *featured auction* is one that's extra easy to find in a sea of similar sales. On eBay, a featured auction can appear on the first page of a crowded category or even on the home page of the well-traveled eBay site itself. On Yahoo! Auctions, you can pay a nominal fee to format an auction listing in boldface or colored type. On The Bidding Post, you can highlight an auction title in bold or with an arrow pointing to it; you can also pay extra to have it featured on the first page of a category. (Find out more at `www.biddingpost.com/ html/sell_tutorial.htm`.)

When should you pay the extra fee to feature your auction? Personally, I'm not sure that featuring your auction helps at all. People who are committed to bidding on the type of item you're selling will find you through an auction service's search engine whether you're in a featured spot or not. Still, if you have an especially valuable or rare item and want to make it stand out from the crowd, spending an extra $15 or so probably can't hurt.

When to use Dutch auctions

If you have lots of copies of a piece of merchandise, consider using a *Dutch auction*. This form of sale is already commonly used by many of the auction houses that deal in electronics and computer equipment, as well as Amazon.com Auctions and The Bidding Post. In a Dutch auction, bidders specify how many items they want to bid on along with the price they want to pay for each. See Chapter 1 for more information.

In a Dutch auction, all winning bidders pay the same price, which is the lowest successful bid. Proxy bidding (in which the auction service automatically places bids for you based on a maximum bid you specify, as explained in Chapter 4) is not used on Dutch auctions.

Creating Listings that Sell

In traditional auctions, such as those held by Sotheby's and Christie's, a good deal of attention is paid to creating an accurate, detailed description of an item appearing in the auction sales catalog. Then, when the sale is actually held, the auctioneer describes the object in glowing terms that encourage bidders to ante up. Don't scrimp when it comes to writing your description. Take some tips from the pros: The more thought and effort you put into your descriptions, the more bids you'll get.

In this section, I tell you what you need to know to create a bidworthy listing.

Access a listing form

In the following sections, I use the example of an item my mom has for sale to fill out eBay's auction listing form (see Figure 6-2). After all, any dutiful son would jump at the chance to help his own mother make a few extra bucks. Right, Mom?

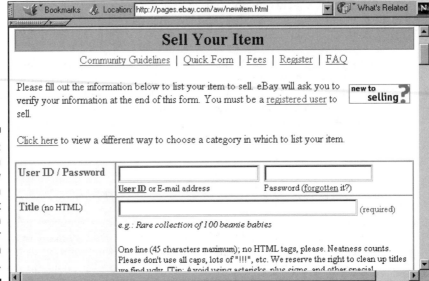

Figure 6-2:
When you're ready to sell on eBay, fill out this form with your auction terms.

eBay, like the IRS, provides sellers with either a "long form" or a "short form" to complete. Figure 6-2 shows the "long form." You can click the Quick Form link at the top of the long form page (`pages.ebay.com/aw/newitem.html`) to access the supposedly easier version, but I don't see a great deal of difference between the two. I suggest that you stick with the long form to make sure that you get all the options and information you need.

Each auction site has its own variations on sellers' forms. You typically find them by clicking a link labeled Seller's Guide (Yahoo! Auctions) or How to Sell (Amazon.com Auctions).

Come up with a titillating title

One of the beauties about a system in which users set up their own auction sales is that you can come up with any kind of title and description you want. In my opinion, this is both a blessing and a curse. Users who don't have experience in writing newspaper-type headings are at a disadvantage. They come up with either confusing titles that don't encourage any mouse clicks or generic titles and descriptions that sound like everyone else's.

Remember that your auction listing title will appear in a long list of auction listing titles, whether your listing appears on eBay or on another service like Haggle Online (`www.haggle.com`) or Yahoo! Auctions (`auctions.yahoo.com`). Your title needs to grab attention while still being to the point. Here are some guidelines:

✔ **Keep it short.** A good title should be six to eight words or less in length.

✔ **Be specific.** Remember that avid collectors who are knowledgeable about brand names and model numbers are looking for specific goodies to fill out their collections. They are scanning your items in the midst of all the competition. Including the model numbers and brand names in your titles is to your advantage.

✔ **Say what's special.** If an item is especially rare or has a desirable feature (it's a solid gold watch rather than a gold-plated one, for example), say so.

✔ **Avoid fluff.** By *fluff,* I mean keyboard characters like @@@ and !!!! that are supposed to draw attention to your listing. After buyers have seen a hundred or so auction titles that are full of these things, the characters lose their impact and do more harm than good. Forget 'em.

For my mother's sale item, I provide the following title:

```
Precious Moments figurine: "The Voice of Spring"
```

You don't need to reinvent the wheel here. Scan past auctions that are similar to yours for examples of good titles and descriptions. There's nothing wrong with borrowing some wording from another listing, as long as you don't copy the whole thing outright.

Provide a complete and accurate description

Often, I see descriptions that are only one or two sentences in length, and titles that are vague and unexciting. Which of the following listings would you take the time to check out?

```
Old Coffee Grinder
```

```
Kitchen Aid Model A-9 Burr Grinder by Hobart in Chrome
```

The more details you provide, the better your chances of getting bids. If you aren't sure exactly what an item does or how much it is worth, consult fellow auction sellers. Just visit newsgroups or bulletin boards of the sort described in Chapter 3.

Don't be reluctant to mention any defects in what you're selling. Such accuracy shows people that you are honest and prevents disputes after the item is shipped. Don't worry — you can write a positive description *and* be honest at the same time. See Chapter 11 for more tips on composing good listings.

Include an image

To sell something online, it's pretty much a given that you have to include some sort of graphic image along with your words. Listings that are text-only are much less attractive than those that include images.

At traditional auctions, buyers are used to being able to inspect the merchandise beforehand. Likewise, online shoppers are used to seeing photos of items for up for sale.

When adding an image to your listing, keep in mind the following guidelines (see Chapter 7 for specifics):

✔ **In order to put an image on the Internet, it must be a computerized or digitized image that exists as a computer file.** (The visual information in a *digitized* image has been saved in the bits and bytes that computers understand.)

✔ **The image must be saved in one of the formats that Web browsers are able to display.** The most popular formats are GIF and JPEG.

✔ **The image file must be hosted by a Web server, a computer that is connected to the Internet all the time.** You then add a link to the location of the image file to your auction description.

Capturing digital images and placing them online is easier than ever. Many photo processing labs will digitize photographic images for you, and many sites exist online solely for the purpose of hosting images for auction sellers and Web page creators. See Chapter 7 for more information.

Set a minimum bid and reserve price

Be sure to do some research into what your item is worth and decide whether you want to guarantee that you get a certain amount by setting a reserve price. Then you can set your price by filling out these fields (Minimum Bid and Reserve Price, respectively) on eBay's New Item form.

Setting the minimum bid

A *minimum bid* tells bidders where you want the bidding to start. Time and again, I see sellers use this feature the wrong way: They specify their ideal price as the minimum bid. This essentially discourages bidders from trying to get a bargain by telling them that you won't take less than a certain amount for an item.

In the case of the Precious Moments figurine I researched for my mother, I saw one that was listed for a minimum bid of $189. That item had received zero bids by the time the auction closed. Take my advice and pick a small starting point, such as $1, for the minimum bid.

Other sellers agree. "My experience has shown in auctioning regular items that the lower you set the minimum bid, the better you do in the end," says Robbin Tungett. "People are more likely to bid on something even if they don't want/need it if the price is low enough. This starts a bidding war, and the next thing you know, someone has paid more for an item than he would have regularly. My advice is start your bid price low and don't use a reserve unless absolutely necessary." (See the next section for tips about setting a reserve price — or not setting one at all.)

Is it ever to your advantage to set a high minimum bid? If you have something you absolutely won't sell for less than a certain amount, you can specify that amount as the minimum bid. Doing this might make sense if you are a retail store, the item you are offering at auction is new, or you absolutely can't sell the item for less than a certain amount because you'll lose money on the deal otherwise. But be aware that you are very likely to discourage bidders by doing so, and don't be surprised if the auction ends without a single bid coming in.

Setting the reserve price

A *reserve price* is the minimum amount for which you're willing to sell an item. Specifying a reserve price gives you a measure of safety in cases where you feel strongly that you don't want to sell an object for less than a certain amount. For example, my mother was reluctant to sell her Precious Moments figurine for less than the $200 she estimated it was worth. In this case, $200 made a sensible reserve price.

However, I took the extra step of checking similar items for sale to see what they were going for. When I searched eBay for Precious Moments, I was stunned to find a whopping 2,300 items currently for sale. I narrowed my search to the specific figurine ("The Voice of Spring") and found two of them already being offered for sale with current bids of $50. I searched through eBay's archive of completed auctions and found that this figurine had sold for only $149 and $133 in recent weeks. At that point, Momsie decided to take her chances with the flea markets she loves to haunt and not list the figurine online. (Oh well, I'll find another way to be nice to my mom. In the meantime, I'll still use her item as an example for this chapter.)

As a longtime buyer, I feel more confident about bidding on items if the seller has made accurate appraisals of their value and set aside reserves that more or less reflect the current market value.

For example, I was recently in the market for an espresso machine. I spotted a nice one on eBay that the seller described as retailing for $300. I took a half-hour or so and dug up some price comparisons that listed the machine at $309 and $299. My findings indicated that the seller had done her homework and that she was probably a good person with whom to do business. (Her feedback rating and positive comments from other buyers helped boost the esteem I had for her, too.)

Before you set your price, do your homework (as described in Chapter 4) so you make a good impression on your prospective buyers. If you aren't sure what an item is worth, go to the local library and look it up in a price guide. Or get an online appraisal from the International Society of Appraisers (www.isa-appraisers.org/search.htm).

Consider leaving the reserve price box blank. By offering an item with no reserve, you guarantee to sellers that it will be sold, and that they may be able to get a bargain. As a result, you're likely to get more bids than you would otherwise, and you may even sell your object for more than you would with a reserve. If things go wrong and no one seems to be bidding anywhere near what you think the item is worth, remember that you can cancel an auction. See the "Ending your auction immediately" sidebar later in this chapter.

Don't keep your hideaway secret

This important part of an auction listing is sometimes overlooked by sellers who enter "joke" or obscure information about where they are located. It's important to let overseas bidders know that they may have to pay extra shipping charges before they make an offer, for example.

Be specific and accurate here and leave the jokes for your descriptions and e-mail messages. For example, don't say you're located in the "Home of the Blues" or "The Windy City." Just declare proudly that you're in my own hometown of Chicago, Illinois.

Set the payment and shipping terms

Providing prospective purchasers with instructions on the types of payment you want to receive and how you plan to ship the item is essential. Providing specific and accurate information up-front eliminates confusion and disagreements after the sale is made.

It seems unreasonable to ask anyone to send cash through the mail, especially when they're trusting you to follow through after the sale is made by shipping the merchandise in a timely manner. The most common forms of payment accepted on Internet auctions are cashier's checks and money orders. If you have a merchant account and can accept credit card payments, you're likely to get more bids. (See Chapter 8 for more information about payment options.)

Some sellers find that cashier's checks slow down the transaction by taking longer to clear than postal money orders. One way to accept credit card payments without actually applying for a merchant account is to work with one of the escrow services such as i-Escrow (www.iescrow.com). See Chapter 5 for more information.

Be sure to include shipping and handling information in your ad description: Tell customers how you plan to ship, how long it should take, and (roughly) how much shipping should cost. Providing this information takes a little extra effort, but remember that shipping charges are something the customer must pay in addition to the purchase price, so revealing all costs upfront helps prevent sticker shock after the auction closes. Also be sure to tell people if you don't want to ship internationally, if you want only local buyers or others who can pick the item up in person, or if you have any other special restrictions.

Find a time frame that's on your side

You're in control when it comes to when your item will appear online and how long people will have to bid on it. eBay lets you specify whether the auction will last for three, five, seven, or ten days. The most common option is a seven-day auction. Some services like Haggle Online (www.haggle.com) have a one-day auction option.

Opinions vary as to the best starting and stopping times for Internet auctions. It seems logical to me that you'll get more attention if the sale ends on a weekend when more users have access to the Internet. But experienced sellers tell me that it doesn't make much difference whether the sale ends on a weekend or a weekday.

Watch out if you offer items at particularly busy times, such as early December. eBay and other Web sites are likely to be overloaded with buyers, so neither bidders nor sellers can access the system to place bids or make offers on sales items. If you plan to hold some holiday sales, be sure to do them well in advance of the holiday rush.

Adding a counter

A *counter* (sometimes called a *hit counter*) is a utility that records the number of visits that are made to a Web page — that is, the counter provides a visual record of how many times the files on a page are accessed.

Counters are commonly added to personal or commercial Web pages. They're a fairly good — though by no means precise — way to measure how many times the page has been viewed by someone with a Web browser.

You *can* add a counter to one of your auction pages, but I don't know why you would want to do this for an auction listing. To me, what counts is the number of bids you receive, not the number of times your merchandise is viewed. I

suppose that you can compare the number of views to the number of bids to judge the effectiveness of a listing, but this is hardly scientific research.

The computer program that makes the counter work usually resides on a computer that's hosted on another Web site; therefore, having the counter on your page can slow down the amount of time it takes your auction listing to appear. Keep this in mind and use a counter only if you really want to.

Honesty Communications (www.honesty.com) provides eBay and other users with counters and instructions for adding counters to auction listings.

Categorize your merchandise

Picking a category for your auction item is important, but doing so isn't as essential as it may seem. When I'm shopping for items on auction services, I use the Search function rather than burrowing through particular categories, which may contain a thousand or more individual selections.

What's a good way to find a category for your object? You could search for similar items and see where they're located. For example, I had no idea where Precious Moments figurines should be listed on eBay, so I scanned the list of major categories on the Item Listing form and found that they typically appear in the category Pottery: Precious Moments.

Many of the options near the end of eBay's New Item Listing Form let you feature the item in one of several special categories. These can make your merchandise easier to find by placing the description at the top of the first page of the selected category, or perhaps even on the eBay home page.

If you think that your merchandise would be an especially good gift, eBay provides you with a special icon that you can add for a minimal extra cost. (See eBay's Gift Icon page at pages.ebay.com/aw/gift-icon.html for more information.) For example, the Mother's Day "Mom" icon shown in Figure 6-3 only cost $1 to add to an auction title at the time this was written.

Figure 6-3:
For a dollar
or two extra,
you can add
an icon to
give your
listing some
extra pizazz.

After you get the hang of this selling thing, you're quite likely to jump into the auction game with both feet and start selling lots of items at once. For those of you who have tons of things to list online, eBay has a utility called Mister Lister that lets you submit as many as 100 listings at the same time. That way, all your auctions can start or end at approximately the same time. You have to have a credit card number on file with eBay before you can use this feature. Find out about Mister Lister at `pages.ebay.com/aw/mr-lister.html`. Some software programs will help you prepare preformatted auction listings and upload multiple listings to eBay at the same time. Check out AuctionPoster 98 (`www.auctionposter.com`) and ListerPro (`www.listerpro.com`).

Submit your listing

After you finish your description, you click a button at the bottom of the New Item form. eBay receives your information and returns a Web page to your browser that displays what you entered in the form. Review your description and verify its accuracy. This page also contains an explanation of how much you have to pay eBay to list the item and the commission you have to pay to sell it. You have to pay the listing fee whether you sell the item or not. You pay the commission only if you sell. (See " Paying the Auction Service to Be Your Piper," later in this chapter, for more details.)

Read the verification information, and if everything seems okay, submit your information to eBay by clicking the Submit Your Listing button at the bottom of the page. You can also click the Click Here to Cancel link to correct your information or to abandon listing the item altogether.

Ending your auction immediately

If you have second thoughts, you can end the auction right away. Amazon.com Auctions makes this easy. Click the Your Account link at the upper right-hand side of any Amazon.com page. On the Your Account page, click the link for the summary page of the auction. When the summary page appears, click the Cancel This Auction button. Keep in mind that you still have to pay listing fees for auctions you cancel. Find out how to cancel auctions on eBay at pages.ebay .com/aw/help/help-t-sll-bids.html and on Yahoo! Auctions at help.yahoo .com/help/auctions/asell/asell-07 .html.

eBay's standard procedure for quitting a sale is to cancel each of the bids that have been made on the item you're offering. See Chapter 13 for a slightly less offensive — although tricky — way of ending a sale by placing the winning bid yourself. On Yahoo! Auctions, you have to first cancel any current bids on your auction before you cancel the sale yourself.

Don't make a habit of backing out of sales. You'll still have to pay a listing fee to the auction house for putting your item online in the first place. And you'll probably receive negative feedback from disgruntled bidders who are unhappy that the sale ended. Such feedback can hurt your reputation for future sales.

During the auction on eBay, you can add to your description, add an image, or change the payment or shipping terms. You can change the description at pages.ebay.com/aw/add-to-item.html. Bidders see the current listing until you submit the revised one. Yahoo! Auctions and Amazon.com Auctions let you edit your listings and don't interrupt the sale in progress or make your description inaccessible.

Providing Good Customer Service

Even though you aren't a corporate retailer, you have to conduct customer service just like the big guys. In fact, you can provide better service than many big stores because you have the immediacy of e-mail and you can provide the personal touch. On one of my auction purchases (an espresso machine) the seller included a small pack of coffee with the machine, for example. More commonly, though, the personal touch means responding quickly and in a friendly way to e-mail inquiries.

Answer questions posed by bidders promptly (within one day). In your listing, be sure to tell buyers whether you plan to be out of town for a certain time period so they'll know when you're unreachable and won't think you're ignoring their questions. Experienced sellers know they need to treat buyers and sellers with respect. Excellent customer service gives you plenty of benefits: You get positive feedback, return business, and referrals.

Processing Payments

When the auction is over, contact your winner(s) promptly — preferrably within the hour, but at least within one day. Along with offering your congratulations to the winners, give them directions for paying you.

When you receive payment (see Chapter 8 for payment options), be sure to send the buyers a quick e-mail acknowledgment that the credit card payment or check was received and let them know when their shipment will be going out. Shipping your item the same day the payment clears your bank is good business, but don't wait any longer than a week.

Paying the Auction Service to Be Your Piper

Before you offer something for sale on eBay, you set up an account with the service so it can bill you. You set up an account by supplying eBay with your credit card number to bill and filling out the form supplied on the Web page at `arribada.ebay.com/aw-secure/cc-update.html`.

eBay immediately charges a non-refundable insertion fee when you list an item. This fee is collected even if your item does not sell. If your item receives bids, you're charged a Final Value Fee based on the closing value of the auction. (eBay calls the commission it levies on sales a Final Value Fee rather than a commission. You can read about the company's fees at `pages.ebay.com/aw/agreement-fees.html`.) This fee is 5 percent of the value for items sold for less than $25, 2.5 percent of the value for items sold for from $25 up to $1,000, and 1.25 percent of the value for items sold for above $1,000.

If you're just starting out online and are squeamish about paying commissions, consider using one of the up-and-coming, small auction services trying to give eBay some competition like Haggle Online (`www.haggle.com`) or The Bidding Post (`www.biddingpost.com`). Often, they let you list for free. A variety of Internet auction sites are listed in this book's Internet Directory.

Delivering the Goods without Delay

Don't wait until the auction is over to box up your item for shipment. Doing a good job takes some time and effort, so you might as well get a head start.

Protect the item thoroughly. Use double boxing, extra bubble wrap, and scraps of cardboard to add extra strength. Good packaging not only protects your item but also protects you from complaints and disputes.

It's also important to insure the item with the carrier for what the buyer paid, if practical. If the carrier loses or damages the item, you don't want to have to make a refund out of your own pocket. Contact the buyer when the item ships and tell him when to expect the item. If you receive a tracking number from the shipper, pass it along to the buyer.

If the buyer has a complaint, handle it gracefully, but don't do anything that's unreasonable. If the buyer claims that the item arrived damaged, leave it up to him or her to handle the carrier claim process after you pass along the information needed. If, however, a buyer claims the item never arrived, it's your job to track down the package with the carrier. Do this quickly and keep the buyer updated on the status of the claim, promptly remitting the payment in full to the buyer if the package can't be located.

After the auction is over, be sure to leave feedback for the buyer. Feedback systems are taken seriously by the online auction community, so you shouldn't overlook this part of the process.

What If Your Sale Fails?

What happens if no one bids on your item? Take stock: Did you place too high of a minimum bid? Is what you have to offer just not desirable enough?

If you want to try again, you can do that. eBay has provisions for resellers. Amazon.com Auctions lets you relist an item for sale for free if you do it within 30 days of the previous sale's close. Yahoo! Auctions goes one step farther and lets you resubmit a listing for free at any time.

For suggestions on writing headings and other ways to resell an item, as well as help when you're selling an item the first time, check out `cgi.ebay.com/aw-cgi/eBayISAPI.dll?BetterSeller`. Also review Yahoo! Auctions' page on resubmitting items at `help.yahoo.com/help/auctions/asell/asell-16.html`.

Chapter 7

Creating Sales-Boosting Web Pages

*P*eople will feel at ease bidding on your goods and, more important, will send payments if they feel that they can trust you. Anything you can do to build goodwill and trust among your prospective customers promotes return business and encourages the positive feedback you need to succeed long-term as an auction seller.

One effective way to promote trust is to create your own Web page. On your page, you can talk about yourself and your qualifications. You can also promote your business if you have one. A Web page can be the glue that links an online business and an auction listing.

You don't *have* to provide a Web page if you plan to sell at auction. For the most part, it makes sense to take this additional step if one of the following applies to you:

✔ You're in a business related to the items you're selling.

✔ You plan to make auction sales a significant part of your income.

✔ You have accumulated a substantial amount of good feedback based on successful transactions with a wide variety of buyers, and you want to present examples of the feedback on a Web page in order to build trust and credibility among people who may want to purchase more of what you have to offer.

A Web *page* is a single document created with HTML (HyperText Markup Language), but a Web *site* is a set of interlinked Web pages that's created by an individual or an organization.

When it comes to creating Web pages, you have a few choices:

✔ You can create a free personal Web page on an auction Web site, such as Yahoo! Auctions or eBay, by filling out a simple form. You don't have to install special software or learn any complicated computer languages for this option. (See "Creating a Personal Page on an Auction Site," later in this chapter.)

✔ You can create a personal Web page on a free Web page hosting service, such as GeoCities. Working with a Web hosting service to create Web pages gives you several advantages. For one thing, you have choices. You have the option of creating a single personal Web page, producing a full-fledged set of Web pages called a Web site, or simply placing your image files online so you can link to them when you create an auction description. On a free site like GeoCities, you can design your page the way you want rather than use one of the formats provided by Yahoo! Auctions or another service. The process of creating the page is easy: You simply fill out an online form with your content, rather than having to install special software or learn HTML. You can also obtain a free e-mail address from a Web host if you need one. (See "Creating Pages on a Free Web Hosting Site," later in this chapter.)

✔ If you're the independent sort and are comfortable with computers, you can use a Web page editor or HTML — that's *HyperText Markup Language,* the set of instructions used to format Web pages — to create a Web page or a full-blown Web site and then post it to your ISP's site. You can include a link to it in each of your auction listings, as shown in Figure 7-1. The advantage of doing this is control: You can design your page by selecting your own colors and page layouts, and by adding as many images as you want. In contrast, a simple Web page feature (such as that offered by eBay) lets you select a basic page layout that may or may not look the way you want. On the other hand, the downside of creating your own Web page and hosting it with an ISP is complexity: You're pretty much on your own when it comes to selecting Web page software and learning how to publish your documents with the ISP. (See "Creating Pages on Your ISP's Site," later in this chapter, for more information about using a Web page editor or HTML.)

In this chapter, I tell you how to create simple Web pages to supplement your auction listings. I give you a few tips on what you can publish online and some instructions on using special auction software that helps you format auction listings.

Figure 7-1:
This eBay
listing
includes a
link that
leads to the
seller's Web
site.

Finding a Host for Your Web Page

The first step in creating your auction Web page is to decide where your page
is going to live online — or, in other words, where your page will be hosted
on a Web server so others can view it. You need to find a host before you do
anything else because where your page is located can affect how you create it
and how it looks.

Lots of companies want to get in on the Web hosting act and provide businesses and individuals with space for their Web pages. Basically, though, the
principle is simple: You find space on a Web server, and you send documents
and graphics there so they can be accessed by someone with a Web browser.

Some Web hosting services are free. They make money by attracting lots of
individuals to their sites and then selling ad space on their Web pages to
businesses. Some Web hosts are also Internet Service Providers: They provide you with a connection to the Internet and also give you space for a
personal Web site. Still others are full-fledged Web hosts: They focus solely
on providing businesses with lots of complex hosting solutions, which range
from database access to serving audio and video files online. I explain your
options in the following sections.

Which service is right for you? That depends on your needs. If you're primarily going online to do auction trading and aren't planning to start a full-fledged Internet business any time soon, consider signing up with a free Web hosting service.

Using an auction service as your host

A growing number of auction services are including the ability to create Web pages among the services they provide to their users. In this case, the auction service itself lets you create a simple individual Web page that enables you to discuss anything you want. Most auction Web pages enable individual buyers and sellers to talk about themselves, provide photos, and include contact information for other users who want to find out more about them. (See "Creating a Personal Page on an Auction Site," later in this chapter, for the particulars.) Examples of auction sites that offer this feature include

- ✔ **eBay.** Each eBay user can create a page about himself that serves as a sort of press release announcing who he is and what he does. Creating an About Me page is fast and easy because you create your document online without having to use special software or learning HTML (HyperText Markup Language, the language in which Web pages are formatted).

- ✔ **Yahoo! Auctions.** Every registered user has a My Listings page where she can include personal information along with links to current sales being offered on the site. An additional Yahoo! Profile page lets users present lots of personal information. This page is automatically created for all users when they register with Yahoo! Auctions and obtain a Yahoo! ID. If your username is gholden, for example, you enter the URL `profiles.yahoo.com/gholden` to access your profile page. You can then edit the page by going to `profiles.yahoo.com` and clicking the Edit My Profile Page link.

- ✔ **The Bidding Post.** Go to the Auction Manager page (`206.151.91.7/biddingpost/auction_manager.htm`) and enter your username and password. The Auction Manager leads you through the process of setting up a Web site with The Bidding Post as your host.

The advantages of using an auction service to host a simple Web page are speed and simplicity. You can create a page by filling out a Web page form that contains the page's contents. You don't have to know HTML, and you don't even have to include a photo of yourself if you don't have one.

Another advantage is credibility: Having a personal Web page on an auction site gives you the appearance of being an active user who wants to participate with the rest of the service's community of users.

Using a free Web hosting service

If you want to create your own full-fledged set of Web pages (otherwise known as a Web site) and possibly get an e-mail address, sign up with one of the organizations that gives people space on a Web server where they can publish their own Web pages. These sites often give members easy-to-use Web page forms that automatically create Web pages for them. Here are some sites to consider:

- ✔ **GeoCities** (`www.geocities.com`). GeoCities is an extremely popular and feature-rich site. Members identify themselves as being part of a "neighborhood" of individuals with similar interests. You can set up Web sites for free and get an e-mail address for free, too.

- ✔ **Tripod** (`www.tripod.com`). Tripod, which is owned by the Internet search service Lycos, also has an active site that hosts lots of individual Web surfer home pages. Members can chat and post messages on message boards.

- ✔ **AOL Hometown** (`hometown.aol.com`). This is America Online's site where individuals can create Web pages. One difference between this and the preceding services is its business orientation. If you want to create a business site, you can locate it in a "neighborhood" within Hometown AOL called Business Park. An area within that area is set up for home-based businesses, too.

One advantage of signing up for an account with one of these organizations is that they are targeted at users who have little or no experience setting up Web pages. Help pages and other instructions lead you through the steps in becoming a Web publisher. Another advantage is that you become part of another community of Web surfers. You can join clubs and interact with other users who also publish their pages on the site.

Using your ISP as your host

An Internet Service Provider (ISP) is a company that gives individuals like you and me access to the Internet. ISPs give customers dialup accounts that let those customers connect to the Internet with their computer modems over conventional phone lines. More exotic and faster connections are available, too (see Chapter 2).

Along with Internet access, most ISPs also let users create personal home pages and publish them on a Web server. The advantage of using an ISP as your host is that it's convenient and free. Most ISP Web servers are fast and reliable. On the downside, you're pretty much on your own when it comes to obtaining software to create your Web pages, and when it comes time to publish those pages by moving them from your computer to the ISP's Web server. The process is hardly as user-friendly as it is on GeoCities, for example. The ISP route is really only for intermediate to advanced users.

Some ISPs (like mine) frown on individual users setting up commercial Web sites with the Web space that comes with a personal account. If you want to set up a business site to supplement your auction sales, you may need to pay extra for a business Web site account. Check with your ISP to see what options are available to you.

The CD accompanying this book includes software that helps you set up an account with a well-known ISP called MindSpring Enterprises (www.mindspring.com). You can also check out lists of ISPs, such as The List (thelist.internet.com) or Providers of Commercial Internet Access (celestin.com/pocia).

Deciding What to Put on Your Web Page

Web pages can be about all sorts of things. You can create pages that talk about your family, your car collection, your company, your club, or your favorite figures in music and cinema — or a hundred other flakier, off-the-wall topics.

In this case, though, you're creating Web pages that talk about you, the auction seller. Your goal is to tell people that you're a reputable person who can be trusted. Your goal is to emphasize that the things you're selling are what you say they are; that your prices are reasonable; and that you will deliver what you promise, promptly and in the physical condition described in your auction listings.

The average page consists of a paragraph or two about the seller: name, occupation, areas of interest, and shipping policies. Just the facts, ma'am. You can easily do better than this. The amount of detail you provide depends on how active a seller you are, how many different kinds of items you sell or collect, and whether your page is about you personally or just about your auction activities.

Whether your page is about yourself or about what you sell at auction, the following are some suggestions on how to get your message across.

Present your qualifications

No one is a World Wide Web old-timer. The Web has only been around since the mid '90s, so everyone is a newcomer. Tell people how long you've been trading online. Provide them with concrete examples of the kinds of things you have sold.

If you're lucky enough to have any honors, awards, or professional affiliations associated with your auction sales, by all means mention them. More likely, though, you should tell visitors how long you've been collecting or selling what you sell and how you got to know what you know about your business. Be sure to tell people why you love what you do and why you're so darn good at it, to boot. You don't have to be modest — just truthful.

Provide quotes from satisfied customers

Feedback is a built-in feature of many auction sites, but there's no reason why you can't single out a quote or two that you're particularly proud of and mention them on your Web page. Amazon.com Auctions lets you create a link to your Participant Page on your auction listings. A Participant Page isn't a personal profile page as such, but lists ratings and feedback you have received from people you've done business with. Other sites like eBay and Yahoo! Auctions let prospective bidders view your feedback easily by clicking the feedback rating number next to your Yahoo! ID.

Include links to other Web sites

To establish yourself as an authority in your field, you can tell people where to find more information about the items you sell. For example, many Web sites include a list of related links to sites featuring more information about a particular subject. If you collect antique paperweights, for example, you can include a series of links to sites that you visit online that have images of beautiful paperweights or discuss their history. Such links can be especially helpful if you buy or sell specific items that aren't easy to find.

Convince with tips and information

Providing useful, practical information about a topic is one of the best ways to market yourself online. After you state who you are and what you do, set aside a paragraph of free advice. What should people look for when shopping for Fiestaware, Edsel station wagons, or early woodworking tools? Share your expertise.

Finding a Home for Your Auction Images

You may not need to create a Web page to help you sell your items. You may only need a place to stash your images. For example, before it started attracting an average 800,000 bids each day, eBay allowed people to store their images on auction site's computers. Now, so many people use the service that eBay requires sellers to host images on other sites. AuctionUniverse also makes sellers store images off-site.

Although eBay and AuctionUniverse don't host photos for you, Yahoo! Auctions does enable users to store photos on its servers. That means if you sign up for an account with Yahoo!, you don't have to find a separate Web host for your images. The feature that enables the photos to be stored is called the Yahoo! Photo album. Go to the Seller's Guide area of Yahoo! Auctions and click the How Do I Add a Photo to My Listing? Link. Scroll down the page (`help.yahoo.com/help/auctions/asell/asell-02.html`) for step-by-step instructions on adding one or more images to the Photo album.

It may sound confusing, but your auction listing may be stored on an auction house's computer while the actual image file is stored elsewhere. Both the image and the description end up appearing on the same page. The idea of linking to an image on another computer is confusing, but it's no mystery. It's part of what makes the Web work. The principle is called *hypertext*. If you include a reference to the URL of an image on a Web page, the image itself will appear on the Web page where the reference is made.

When the description of this item actually appears on the auction site, the words `<Link to image of bike goes here>` don't actually appear on the prospective bidder's computer screen. Rather, the image itself appears.

The steps involved in creating a computer image, saving it in the right format, and sending it to an organization that will host it on the Web so you can create a link to it are all covered in the next section. The important thing to remember for now is that if you're going to sell at auction, you need to find a place to host your images just as you need to find a place to host your Web pages. You send your auction image files to the image storage location and create a link to the image in your auction description, and the image appears along with the description.

Where do you find a host for your Web images? Your first choice should be the site that hosts any Web pages you have published online. This can be the ISP that gives you access to the Internet or a free Web hosting service like GeoCities or Tripod (see the previous section "Finding a Host for Your Web Page"). I suggest that you try one of these options first, because they're free. Sites that specialize in hosting auction images may let you put one or two photos online for free, but after that, they charge a fee.

For example, the PixHost site shown in Figure 7-2 lets you host two images on its site for free; after that trial, hosting images costs 50 cents each for 30 days.

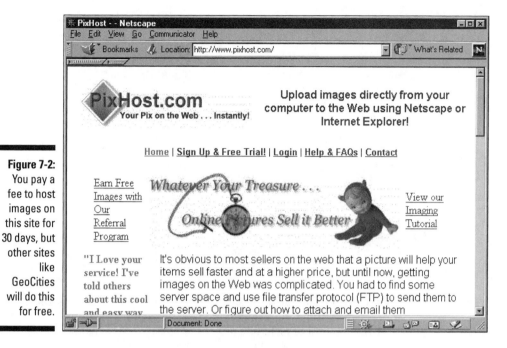

Figure 7-2:
You pay a fee to host images on this site for 30 days, but other sites like GeoCities will do this for free.

Creating Clear Auction Images

Before an image can appear on the Web, it must meet a few technical requirements:

- ✔ **The image must be converted to tiny dots (called *pixels*) that a computer can interpret and display.**

- ✔ **The image must be saved in a file format that a Web browser can display.** Web browsers are set up to display graphic images in one of several formats. The most common are GIF and JPEG. (Find out more about these funny-sounding alphabet soup words later in this chapter.)

- ✔ **The image must be located on a Web server so people can access it.** You can't just save an image on your own computer or a friend's computer and expect people to see it online, even if the computer in question is connected to the Internet all the time. The computer that hosts the image must be equipped with special Web server software that is specially designed to make text and image files available online. After your image is on one of these special Web servers, it is located in a directory on that computer and can be accessed with a URL. You make a reference to the URL for the image file and thus create a link to the file on your auction listing. The link causes the image to be displayed along with your description.

Capturing images

You have lots of options for getting images on your computer and ready for the Web. Not so long ago, the only way you could get a picture on your computer was to draw it. Drawing an item by using a computer graphics program is still an option, but if you're as artistically impaired as I am, this option probably isn't a good idea — unless you're selling stick figures.

Getting an image into your computer is much easier these days — and after it's in your computer, you can transfer the image to one of those Web hosting services I mention in the preceding section.

Here are your best bets for capturing images for the Web:

- ✔ **Scan conventional print or slide photos by using your own scanner or a friend's equipment, or by renting time on one at a photo lab or print shop.** Save the scanned image files to your computer. Using a photo lab or print shop's scanner usually costs only a few dollars for each scan.

- ✔ **Snap conventional print or slide photos of your item and ask the photo processing lab to return the images to you on computer disk or CD-ROM instead of or in addition to conventional prints or slides.** Depending on the photo lab, this may cost as much as $5 per image and can also take from ten days to two weeks to get your images back. Save the files from the disk or CD-ROM to your computer.

- ✔ **Use a digital camera to take photos of what you want to sell and then download the images to your computer by following the instructions that come with the camera.**

Some companies will process your photos and give you the option to have your photos saved in a digital format suitable for the Web. (See "Choosing a graphics format," later in this chapter, for help in choosing the right graphics format if you decide to save your images yourself.) PhotoNet Online (www.photonet.com) is a network of photo dealers that puts your images online for 30 days so you can e-mail them to friends or move them to your Web host. Fujifilm.net (www.fujifilm.net) offers similar services.

Choosing a graphics format

Suppose you drop off your film to be developed at the photo counter and you ask the attendant to return the images to you on disk. The person says, "Do you want those back in GIF or JPEG?" Will you blink your eyes and say, "Huh?"

If you're up to the (small) challenge, take a step beyond "Huh?" and read on to discover just a little bit about the two most popular graphic image formats on the Web.

Critiquing your images

An important part of selling at auction is providing a good image that will attract attention and help people decide whether what you are offering is a good match for what they need. People are more likely to inquire about or bid on something that is illustrated with a good image.

What, exactly, makes a good image? Magazine, newspaper, and book editors, as well as photographers around the world, make their livings by mulling over such questions. However, the fundamental principles are ones that you, too, can understand. And luckily, the requirements for an image on the Web aren't as stringent as those in a printed book because they're only shown on a computer monitor, which has limited display capabilities anyway. A good Web page image

✔ **Is clear and well-lighted, and has good contrast.** *Contrast,* in terms of photographic images, is the degree of difference between light and dark tones. An image that does not have good contrast may look "washed out" or may lack detail. One that has good contrast is clear and has lots of detail.

✔ **Is cropped fairly closely.** The borders of the image should be close to the edges of the object being displayed so there isn't too much wasted space. (Space, after all, is a precious commodity when you're working with Web pages that often appear on 14-inch or 15-inch monitors.)

✔ **Is small in both physical dimensions (height and width) and in file size.**

Generally, file sizes of 20 to 30K or less are optimal. You can determine a file's size on a Windows PC by using Windows Explorer to locate the file. Make sure that you choose View⊃Details from the Windows Explorer menu bar to view not only the filename but also the size and creation date. On a Macintosh, view the file in the Macintosh Finder but choose View⊃By Name to get the filename, size, creation date, and file type.

eBay has a bulletin board page where you can ask questions about adding images to auction listings and get help from other eBay users. Go to the eBay Site Map page at `pages.ebay.com/aw/sitemap.html`, scroll down to the eBay Bulletin Boards section, and click the Help with Images and HTML link. Yahoo! Auctions has a special Help page that includes plenty of tips for adding photos to auction listings (`auctions.yahoo.com/html/help/services/photo_help.html`). Amazon.com Auctions includes a similar page full of image-related instructions (`auctions.amazon.com/exec/varzea/ts/help-no-links/adding-images`). You can also access this page when you're filling out the Sell Your Item form with your auction description and other details. Simply click the Image Tips and Tricks link in the Add a Picture section.

A graphic image *format* is a method of presenting or saving the digital information in a computer file. In the case of GIF and JPEG, the information is compressed in size so the file can be easily transported from one machine to another along the Internet.

When to choose GIF

GIF stands for Graphics Interchange Format, and is pronounced either "Jif" (like the peanut butter) or "Gif" (like "gift" but without the 't' at the end). The GIF format was originally developed by the commercial online provider CompuServe to let customers with different computers send graphics files to one another. The GIF format works best with images that have well-defined edges, such as cartoons, line art, or drawings, although you generally won't go wrong if you save your digitized photos in GIF format as well.

When to beg for JPEG

JPEG stands for Joint Photographic Experts Group, the name of the group that came up with the format, and is pronounced "jay-peg." JPEG compresses an image in a different way than GIF does, but without getting too technical about it, JPEG generally works better with black-and-white or color photos than GIF does. Generally speaking, if you want to create good-quality computerized photos of the items you sell, choose JPEG (although most images will also display correctly if you save them in GIF format).

Tweaking images

You scanned and photographed your images. You or the appropriate technicians saved them in GIF or JPEG format. Now, you can put them on a Web page. Right?

Hold on there, pardner! Simply putting images online without making any adjustments is what many auction participants do. Sometimes, the images come out fine. More often, they end up having the following common problems:

Choosing a JPEG compression level

JPEG lets you choose from a number of different compression levels: Low, Medium, High, and Maximum. You run into these choices if you scan a photo and use graphics software to save the image file in graphics format.

The higher the level of compression, the smaller the image file, which is good because smaller images appear on your prospective buyers' computer screens more quickly than big,

bloated ones. However, with Maximum compression, some information in the image is lost, and the image doesn't appear as sharp as it would with a lower level of compression. Although Low compression makes images bigger in file size, the sharpness and color of the images come out better. When in doubt, try High or Maximum compression.

✔ **The image extends far beyond the width of a monitor, forcing the prospective buyer to scroll to the right to see it in its entirety.** These images may be as much as 8 or 9 inches in width, compared to the typical 7-inch maximum width of most inexpensive computer monitors. You can't depend on fidgety auction customers to scroll left-to-right as well as up-and-down to see an image.

✔ **The image crawls onto the shopper's screen s-l-o-w-l-y.** A shopper sees messages like `Loading image... Loaded 50% of 120K` and so on in the status bar at the bottom of her browser window. You're likely to lose bidders this way.

The smart seller takes extra time to crop and retouch a photographic image to make sure that it appears in the optimal size for most Web pages and that it's bright and clear enough to be seen on all kinds of computer monitors, from ten-year-old 14-inch screens to the new ultra-sleek two-page flat displays.

The following sections provide sellers with some tips for adjusting digital images when they don't look quite right.

Cropping images

Cropping has nothing to do with farming. In photography, *cropping* means that you eliminate unnecessary or distracting parts of an image to concentrate the viewer's eye on the important stuff. In my old-time newspaper days, I used to do this with a marker and a ruler. Today, you can do this on your computer by using a graphics program.

In the case of Web images, cropping serves two especially important purposes:

✔ **It makes the image size smaller so the photo fits better in a Web browser window.**

✔ **It makes the image load on computers faster.** By making the image smaller, you also make the file size smaller. An image that's 12K in size appears on screen much faster than one that's 100K in size. This fact is especially important for people who have pokey modems that are 28.8 Kbps or maybe even slower.

Here are some suggestions for graphics programs you can use to retouch your digital images (all are available in versions for Windows 95/98/NT as well as for Macintosh users; see the Web sites for the latest prices and system requirements):

✔ **DeBabelizer** (`www.equilibrium.com/ProductInfo/solutions.html`). DeBabelizer by Equilibrium enables you to optimize images for use on your Web site. At the company's Web site, you can download a trial version, purchase a registered version for either Windows or Macintosh users, and get technical support.

✔ **ImageReady** (www.adobe.com/prodindex/imageready/main.html). ImageReady by Adobe Systems is a professional Web tool for preparing graphics for use on the Web. You can either purchase the program or download a trial version online.

✔ **ImageStyler** (www.adobe.com/prodindex/imagestyler/main.html). ImageStyler is marketed to the "creative business user" or non-design professional to "instantly add style to your Web site." You can download a trial version or purchase ImageStyler online.

The following example explains the steps involved in cropping an image with Version 4.0 of Paint Shop Pro (an evaluation version of Version 5.*x* of Paint Shop Pro appears on the CD that accompanies this book), but the steps are pretty much the same for both versions of this program as well as for most other graphics programs:

1. **Open Paint Shop Pro.**

   A blank gray window opens, showing Paint Shop Pro's menu options above the window.

2. **Choose File⇨Open.**

   The Open dialog box appears.

3. **Select the image you want to work with from the Look In drop-down menu.**

   You do this by clicking the arrow next to the Look In drop-down menu. When the image's filename appears in the Open dialog box, click the filename.

4. **Click Open.**

   The image appears.

5. **Click the selection rectangle tool button in the toolbar. (This is the rectangle that is constructed of dashes rather than a solid line.) Then draw a box around the part of the image you want to preserve.**

   You do this by clicking just above and to one side of the image. Then, holding down the mouse button, drag the box down and to the other side of the image.

   It's generally a good idea to leave a little space around the person or object in the image you want to preserve so it doesn't look "squished" when you crop it.

   The area contained within the rectangle you just drew is the area that is preserved; everything else will be cropped out (see Figure 7-3). (The crop box will disappear when you do this.) If you didn't draw the cropping area quite right the first time, click somewhere else and draw another box.

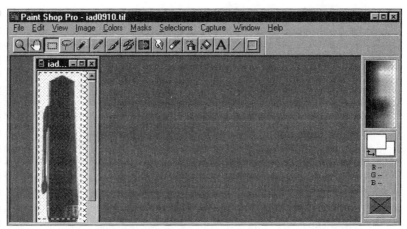

Figure 7-3:
When you
draw a
rectangle
like this one,
be sure to
leave a little
space
around the
object or
person you
want to
focus on.

6. **Choose Image⇨Crop to Selection.**

   The image is instantly cropped. If you aren't satisfied with the result, choose Edit⇨Undo and recrop the image by following the preceding steps.

7. **Choose File⇨Save.**

   The Save As dialog box appears. This is where you select either JPEG or GIF as the image format for this image. Be sure to select either JPEG or GIF from the Save as Type drop-down menu at the bottom of the dialog box. Also, add the extension that corresponds to the file type: .jpg for JPEG or .gif for GIF.

Zooming in for a closeup

You want an image to appear quickly and fit easily in a Web browser window. Yet, for auction purposes, you often need to show prospective buyers the fine details of an object. When should you provide a huge closeup, and when should you provide a simple, small overview of an object?

Think about what buyers want to know. Research your item and determine what is special about it. If a closeup is needed to show a critical feature, provide it. You can take a closeup of an object while still observing the principles of keeping the image's file size and physical size small. By "taking a closeup," I mean capturing a new image of the object after you have already taken an image with which you are dissatisfied. If you're using a scanner to capture a photographic image, re-scan the photo and use your scanner's software to increase the resolution as you do so: Instead of taking a scan at 100 percent of the original, try 105 percent or 110 percent, for example. You can then crop the part of the image you want to focus on as described in the preceding steps.

For example, I love old fountain pens and know them pretty well. Figure 7-4 shows a quite desirable example — in fact, the pen shown is generally considered to be one of the best American fountain pens ever made. The seller has provided no less than three images, each showing an important feature that collectors will want to see. In particular, the medallion at the top of the cap is important to show because it is often missing on pens of this model. The closeup of the pen point (or *nib*, in penspeak) is also important because this model of pen has special wording that is unique to this brand. The seller needs to show that this is the original and correct nib for this type of pen, so a closeup is critical.

Images should be no more than 20 to 30K in size if possible. I get the willies when I try to view an auction item and see a status message indicating that my browser is struggling to load an image that's 90, 100, or 150K in size.

Adjusting contrast and brightness

Another easy way to achieve dramatic improvement in image quality for just a minute or two of effort is to improve its contrast and brightness. (Brightness is also sometimes called *brilliance* and refers to the vibrancy or energy of the colors or shades of color in the image.) This is especially important if your image wasn't captured well in the first place and you aren't able to recapture it. A good graphics program can't make a silk purse out of the proverbial sow's ear, but it can make a poor image a little better.

Most graphics programs include controls for changing the contrast and brightness of an image. In Paint Shop Pro, choose Colors⇨Adjust⇨ Brightness/Contrast. The Brightness/Contrast dialog box appears

Figure 7-4:
Provide closeups and multiple images when needed, while cropping and keeping each image small in size.

(see Figure 7-5). Click the up-pointing arrow next to the %Brightness or %Contrast dialog box to increase the Brightness or Contrast, and click the down-pointing arrows to decrease these qualities. The changes to the image appear in the Preview area.

Figure 7-5:
Paint Shop
Pro lets you
change the
brightness
and contrast
of an image
by adjusting
the settings
in this dialog
box.

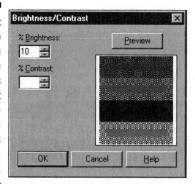

When you scan an image on a scanner, the image is processed by scanning software that also lets you control these two variables. Typically, you move sliding controls up or down to make the adjustment.

Be careful when you play around with retouching settings like contrast and brightness. Sometimes only a little change can produce a dramatic effect. If you don't like what you've done, choose Edit⇨Undo to return to the previous settings.

Creating a Personal Page on an Auction Site

Auction sites like it when you browse. They love it when you sell items, too. But they really like it when you stick around the site long enough to do things like create your own personal Web page to provide supplemental information about you. That's why more and more sites are giving their users space on their Web servers and providing them with easy-to-use Web page forms that can automatically format Web pages based on the personal information users submit.

You, too, can become a Web publisher and create a Web page on an auction site. The following sections explain how.

Using eBay's About Me Web page feature

The auction transactions at eBay, like those at other auction sites, depend to a large extent on trust. But not just blind trust — it's trust backed up by information.

Without getting too philosophical about it, one of the best things about the Internet, in my opinion, is the atmosphere of people helping people and sharing information. By providing some background information about yourself, combined with the feedback you receive from the individuals with whom you do business, you build your reputation. You present your qualifications to prospective bidders. You let them know that they can trust you to keep your part of the bargain by accurately describing your wares and following through on deals.

One of the easiest ways to talk about yourself on eBay (other than by posting messages to chat rooms and bulletin boards, which is discussed in Chapter 3) is to use the About Me Web page feature. eBay allows people to create pages about themselves that serve as a sort of press release announcing who they are and what they do. Creating an About Me page is fast and easy because you create your document online without having to use special software or learning HTML (HyperText Markup Language, the language in which Web pages are formatted).

In the following sections, I walk you through the process of creating your very own About Me page on eBay.

Before you start creating your eBay Web page, you have to log in with a registered User ID and password. If you haven't yet registered with eBay, now is the time to do it; see Chapters 5 and 8 for instructions. Before you log in, however, you should take a few minutes to think about what you're going to say. Write down some biographical notes and have a friend or family member look them over and provide some editorial suggestions. (See "Deciding What to Put on Your Web Page," earlier in this chapter, for some of my content suggestions.)

Perhaps the best way to figure out what to say about yourself is to look at other About Me pages. As you shop around for items on eBay, you'll see a Me icon (see Figure 7-6) next to the seller's name if that individual has created a page. Unfortunately, no single listing of all About Me pages exists, so you can't click through a number of them at a time, at least at the time I write this.

Figure 7-6:
If you spot a Me icon next to the buyer's or seller's name, click the icon to visit that individual's About Me Web page.

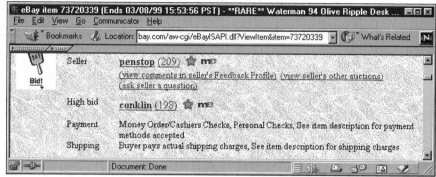

When you're ready to create an About Me page, follow these steps:

1. **Connect to the Internet, launch your Web browser, and go to the About Me Login page** (`members.ebay.com/aw/aboutme-login.html`).

   The page provides some introductory information and preliminary instructions about the About Me feature.

2. **Read the instructions on the About Me Login page and enter your eBay account information in the User ID and Password boxes at the bottom of the page. Then click the Create and Edit Your Page button.**

   The Choose an About Me Layout Template page appears.

3. **Review the available Web page layouts and click the button next to the arrangement you prefer: Two column layout, Newspaper layout, or Centered layout.**

   Choose the two column layout if you want to present a variety of general subjects to talk about (such as Me, My Family, My Collection, and so on). Choose the newspaper format if you have a lot of different tidbits of information about the same general topic — for example, the different categories in which you sell on eBay. Choose the centered arrangement if your Web page content, such as your personal biography, is short and sweet.

   Figure 7-7 shows the Two column and Newspaper layouts.

   The Select Template Elements page appears.

4. **Choose a title for your page and add personal information in the boxes. You can specify the URL for a single photo to include on your page. Also select an option that indicates how many eBay feedback comments you want to include. When you're done, click Preview Your Page to view your page as others will see it in a Web browser.**

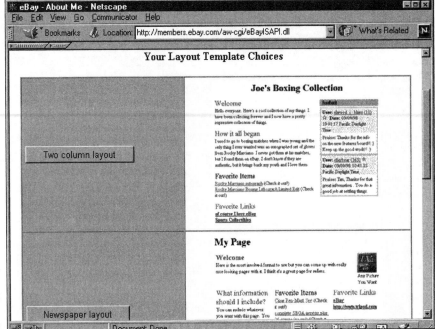

Figure 7-7:
Your About
Me page
can have a
lively multi-
column
layout that
addresses
different
topics.

Click Choose New Layout if you want to try a different layout before you
even preview this one. You return to the About Me Styles page, where
you can select a new page layout. If you don't like the layout you see,
click the Start Over button at the bottom of your preview page. A
Confirm Your Selection page appears, asking you to confirm that you
really want to delete the page you just created and start over with a new
page. Click Delete and start over. You return to the About Me Styles
page, where you can select a new page layout.

If you click Preview Your Page, your page appears so you can evaluate it
and make revisions (see Figure 7-8).

5. **Depending on what you want to do next, click Edit Some More, Save
My Page, Edit Using HTML, or Start Over.**

Edit Some More returns you to the Select Template Elements page,
where you can edit what you've written. Edit Using HTML opens a confirmation page that asks whether you're sure you want to edit your page
by using HTML commands. Click Edit Using HTML on the confirmation
page to view the Edit Your About Me Page page. Your About Me page
text is displayed in a single large text box on this page. You can enter
HTML commands to words or phrases to format them. (In order to use
this option, you need to know HTML.) Clicking Save My Page posts your
About Me page on the eBay Web site so everyone can see it, so only
click Save My Page when you are satisfied that any changes you've made
are what you want.

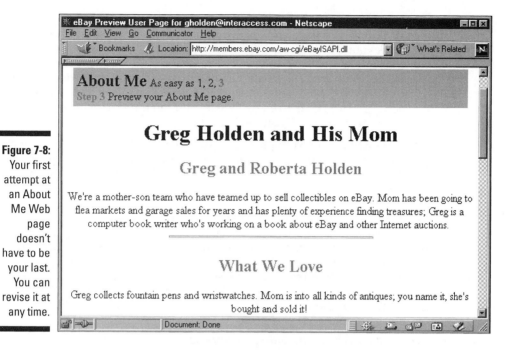

Figure 7-8:
Your first attempt at an About Me Web page doesn't have to be your last. You can revise it at any time.

6. When you're satisfied, click Save My Page.

After you click Save My Page, the Me icon is added to your listings.

Don't expect your new Me icon to appear instantly. It may take a while for eBay's computers to communicate with one another and make sure that your About Me page is attached to your name. When the Me icon does appear, be sure to click it so you can test your page to make sure that it looks the way you want. If you don't like your page, you can edit it later by returning to the About Me Login page (members.ebay.com/aw/aboutme-login.html). Enter your User ID and password on this page, and then click the Create button or the Your Page button. Your existing About Me page appears. You can also access your About Me page at members.ebay.com/aboutme/[YOUR USER ID].

Posting profile information on Yahoo! Auctions

Yahoo! Auctions users can post personal information about themselves in two different places on the Yahoo! Web site:

✔ **An About the Seller area that appears at the top of the Yahoo! Auctions Web page and lists your current items for sale.** When people click your Yahoo! ID on a Yahoo! Auctions page, they view this page, and your About the Seller information appears at the top. This is not a full-fledged Web page, however; you don't have the option of adding images. You only add a few sentences about yourself and what you buy or sell at auction. This is a convenient and fast option for users who don't have the time to create a "real" Web page.

✔ **A Yahoo! Profile Web page.** This is a full-fledged Web page that you can furnish with headings and images. It serves as your profile page not only for the Yahoo! Auctions area of the Yahoo! Web site, but for other areas as well.

The following two sections describe how to create each of these profiles. It's a good idea to at least provide your information for the About the Seller area because that's what other Yahoo! Auctions users see immediately when they click your Yahoo! ID to find out more about you. If you're very active on Yahoo! and want to provide more information about yourself than what you trade at auction, create your Yahoo! Profile page in addition to your About the Seller description.

Creating an About the Seller description

You can create an About the Seller description at any time. You can do it when you first register with Yahoo! Auctions or after you have posted some items for sale. Follow these steps:

1. **Connect to the Yahoo! Auctions Web site (`auctions.yahoo.com`). Start with any Yahoo! Auctions page on screen, whether it's one of your own sales listings or someone else's. Click the Customize link at the top of the page.**

   This link, along with three others (Yahoo!, Sign In, and Help), appears at the top of virtually every Yahoo! Web page.

   If you haven't already registered, click the Sign Me Up! link and fill out the registration form.

   A Contact Information page appears.

2. **Scroll down to the About Me text box near the bottom of the Contact Information page (see Figure 7-9).**

3. **Click the Update button under the About Me text box.**

   Your About the Seller information is transmitted to the Web site, but you don't see it on your browser window right away. Rather, the Yahoo! Auctions home page appears. It takes some time for your About the Seller information to appear. You may have to wait a few hours because the Yahoo! site is so busy.

4. **To view your About the Seller description, go to one of your own auction pages and click your Yahoo! ID.**

   A Web page that contains a list of auctions in which you are the seller appears. Your About the Seller text appears near the top of the page.

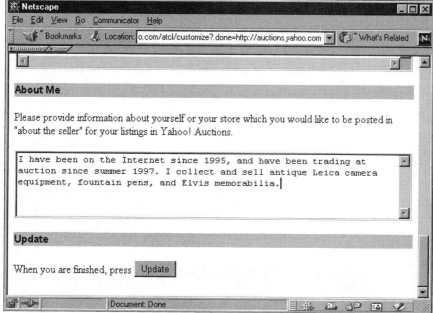

Figure 7-9:
Whenever you want to create or edit your About the Seller information, click Customize and enter text in this box.

If you ever want to change your About the Seller information, click Customize. Your profile page appears. Scroll down to the About Me text box to see the About the Seller information you entered earlier. (The Yahoo! site remembers who you are and doesn't require you to enter your Yahoo! ID and password.) Edit your About the Seller description and click the Update button, and your new information appears in the About the Seller area on the Web page that lists your current auctions.

Creating a Yahoo! Profile page

Yahoo! Auctions buyers and sellers can use their Yahoo! Profile page to provide personal information that supplements their sales information on the site. In order to buy and sell by using Yahoo! Auctions, you need to be a registered Yahoo! user and have a Yahoo! ID.

I'm talking about your Yahoo! ID for the entire Yahoo! Web site/empire here, not just Yahoo! Auctions. The ID and Profile page you create for Yahoo! is the same one you use for Yahoo! Auctions. If you obtained a Yahoo! ID already when you were using some other area of the Yahoo! Web site, you don't need to create a special one for auction buying or selling.

When you first sign up for a Yahoo! ID and password, you have the chance to create your own Yahoo! Profile Web page. Follow these steps:

1. **After you fill out the form to select your Yahoo! ID and password and then submit your information to Yahoo!, a Welcome to Yahoo! Web page appears.**

2. **Scroll down the page and click the Create Your Public Profile link.**

   A Public Profiles for [your Yahoo! ID] page appears.

3. **Click the Create New Public Profile button.**

   The Yahoo! Profiles page shown in Figure 7-10 appears.

4. **Fill out the fields in the form:**

   • The Name Your New Profile box should include a descriptive title for your page. It doesn't necessarily have to be your own name. However, it must be a single word with no blank spaces.

   • In the Expand Your Public Profile section of the form, enter any personal information you want to provide: your name, occupation, marital status, and interests. Also delete any information that Yahoo! has already entered in the form for you if you don't want it to appear online (such as your age or where you live).

Figure 7-10:
Fill out the form on this page to create a Yahoo! Profile page that other Yahoo! Auctions users can see.

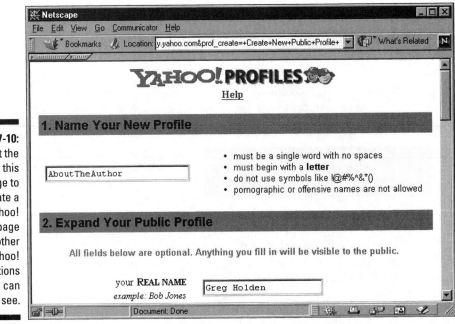

- Don't overlook the Advanced Profile Editing area at the bottom of the profile form. This area contains several text boxes in which you enter the URLs for your home page (if you have one on another Web site that you want people to visit); the URLs of favorite Web sites you want to point out to visitors (these may be related to the types of merchandise you trade at auction); and last but not least, the URL for an image file if you have one. You may need to find a host for your image (as explained in the section "Finding a Home for Your Auction Images," earlier in this chapter).

5. **After you fill out all the fields, click the Click Here When Done button.**

   Your information is submitted to the Yahoo! site. However, you don't see any visible evidence that this has been done. The same Web page form you just filled out appears on screen. You can create a second profile if you want to by changing the title and other information and then submitting it to Yahoo!.

6. **To view your Web page, go to** `profiles.yahoo.com/[yourYahooID]`.

   Don't be surprised if your page isn't yet available when you try to do this, and you see a profile page with the bare information you gave Yahoo! when you first registered with the site. You may have to wait up to 24 hours for your full profile information to be added to the busy Yahoo! site.

If you create such a page, other auction buyers and sellers can access it by clicking your username to display the Yahoo! Auctions page, which presents any current sales you have on the site. The user then clicks the Yahoo! Profile link at the top of this page to view your Web page.

 You don't have to create your Yahoo! Profile page when you first sign up. You can do it later on by going to `profiles.yahoo.com` and clicking EDIT MY PROFILE. Click the Edit link next to the name of the profile that you want to add. Scroll down and check the Add This Profile to Yahoo!'s Searchable Member Directory box to add it your profile. Uncheck the box to remove your profile from Yahoo!'s site, which effectively deletes your profile from the Internet if you want to remove it. Click the Finished button to put your change into effect. Your profile will be added or removed within 24 hours.

Creating Pages on a Free Web Hosting Site

Every penny you save is a penny you can put toward Internet connection fees or auction fees. When you're looking for an online home for your Web pages or images, checking out some resources that will host your auction (and other) content for free only makes sense.

As long as you have access to an Internet connection and a Web browser, you can create a single personal Web page, produce a full-fledged set of Web pages called a Web site, or simply place your image files online so you can link to them when you create an auction description. All of this doesn't cost you a cent when you use a free Web hosting service.

Going with a free Web host is a great deal — not only for you, but for the business that does the hosting. One of the best ways for a commercial enterprise to make money on the Web is to attract a lot of visitors. The more visitors a free Web hosting service gets, the more money it can solicit from advertisers. The free sites have plenty of ads crowding their pages, and you must include them on your personal pages whether you want to or not. If you ever get tired of seeing them, remember that those ads help you store your words and images online for free.

GeoCities (www.geocities.com) is one of the oldest and most successful of the free online services. It not only provides users with a place on the Web for their personal home pages but also supplies users with easy-to-use Web page forms that format the Web pages for them, as well as programs that transfer (or, in technospeak, *upload*) the files from their home computers to GeoCities. Advanced users can use the site's own Advanced HTML Editor to format pages exactly the way they want.

You can also get your own e-mail address by signing up with GeoCities. Rememver that e-mail is essential for submitting bids, receiving confirmations, and communicating with buyers and sellers. If you live in a household where many family members use the computer but only one person has an e-mail address, you can go to GeoCities and sign up for a unique e-mail address that you can use for your auctioning.

Signing up for free services on GeoCities

GeoCities is just one of the many options you have for hosting your images and text online. See the *Internet Auctions For Dummies* Internet Directory for descriptions of more Web page hosts you can try.

The following steps explain how to sign up for the free services on GeoCities:

1. **Connect to the Internet, launch your Web browser, and go to the GeoCities home page (www.geocities.com). Click the Your Free Home Page is Waiting...Join Now link, as shown in Figure 7-11.**

   You're taken to the GeoCities Personal Home Page Program page.

Figure 7-11:
GeoCities
lets you
become a
"home-
steader" on
its site by
providing a
place for
your pages
on the Web.

2. **Follow the instructions on this and subsequent pages to sign up for an account, locate a "home page home" on a GeoCities computer, and obtain an e-mail address if you need one.**

One of the best things about GeoCities is that you're allocated a whopping 11MB of Web space, which is plenty of room for everything from a few Web pages to a full-fledged e-commerce site.

Creating a home page on GeoCities

A point-and-click tool called GeoBuilder helps you create your home page quickly on GeoCities. Other software is available to move your images and text from your home or office computer to your new home as well. Check out the tools available to GeoCities customers at
www.geocities.com/main/build.html.

If you have signed up for a member account with GeoCities and are ready to begin building your own home page, follow these steps:

1. **Go to (www.geocities.com/members/tools/editor/inter.html).**

The GeoCities – GeoBuilder Web page appears.

2. **Read the system requirements for GeoBuilder to make sure that you have enough memory (16MB of RAM), the right type of operating system (Windows 95, 98, or NT 4.0), and other software you need (Version 4.0 or later of Microsoft Internet Explorer or Netscape Navigator).**

3. **Scroll down the page to the section titled The Fastest, Easiest Way to Build Your Website. Click one of the predesigned Web page templates included in the list beneath this heading, or click the Blank Page link if you want to start building your Web page from scratch.**

   A *template* is a Web page that is already supplied with graphics and headings; you only need to fill in your content to finish creating the page. Auction users, for example, may want to click the Shopping template.

   When you click Shopping, a Enter Network Password dialog box appears.

4. **Enter your GeoCities user name and password and click OK.**

   The Shopping template opens, as shown in Figure 7-12.

5. **Edit your Web page by replacing the content that's already present with your own.**

Figure 7-12: GeoBuilder is a Web page editor that works within your Web browser window to create pages on GeoCities.

For detailed instructions on how to do this, choose Help➪Editor Help from the menu at the top of the template window (not at the top of your browser window). A separate GeoBuilder Help Topics window opens on top of the template you just opened. Scroll through the topics (Choosing a Template, Adding or Editing Text, and so on) to find out how to create your own personalized page.

GeoCities isn't the only place on the Web where you can sign up for a free Web page and/or e-mail address. Other resources include Tripod (www.tripod.com), XOOM.COM (xoom.com/home), and Angelfire (www.angelfire.com).

Creating Pages on Your ISP's Site

In fact, it's only natural to turn to your own ISP first to ask about its Web hosting policies for its customers. If you already go online with AOL, for example, it makes sense to try out its Web hosting facilities. If you install the software provided by MindSpring Enterprises (www.mindspring.com) that's included on this book's CD and sign up for an Internet access account with that company, by all means consider MindSpring as a Web host for your business site.

What should you look for in an ISP Web hosting account, and what constitutes a "good deal"? MindSpring's setup is pretty good, but many ISPs charge only $19.95 per month for unlimited access (perhaps $12 per month if you sign up for an entire year at once). They also give you free use of up to 10MB of Web site space besides. You don't necessarily need to go with a provider that gives you a free Web editor, either. You can easily download and install the editor of your choice.

In this section, I tell you how to create Web pages on your ISP by using a Web page editor or HTML. I don't go into every detail about creating a Web page in this section. If you need more information than my brief overview provides, check out *Creating Web Pages For Dummies* by Bud Smith and Arthur Bebak (published by IDG Books Worldwide, Inc.).

Using a Web page editor

Most auction listings consist of black text on a white background, but just because they all look more or less similar, that doesn't mean that the other personal Web pages you create need to be boring.

When you post pages on an ISP's Web server, you can use a special software tool called a *Web page editor* to liven up your text. You specify the purpose you want a word, phrase, sentence, or paragraph to serve on a Web page by simply clicking familiar computer software features like toolbar buttons and menu options. Instead of typing a techy-looking series of symbols to make a word bold, for example, you click a button with a bold letter or choose a menu item called Bold. All you do is click buttons and select menu items to format text and images on a Web page. Good Web page editors do more than just save you time. They allow you to create documents that are as good as those created by professionals, some of whom enter the HTML instructions by hand. (See "Using HTML," later in this chapter, to find out more about HTML.)

Some features are common to virtually all Web page editors:

- **Formatting.** An assortment of menus and toolbar buttons enables you to format selected text as bold, italic, or another style.

- **Previewing.** Most Web page creation software lets you preview your work so you can see what it will look like in a Web browser.

- **Linking.** Web page editors let you create both *internal links* (links that move from one part of a single document to another part of that same document) and *external links* (links that take you from one page to another on a single Web site, or to another Web site altogether).

Web page editors can differ in one respect, however: Some keep the HTML commands transparent; others make them visible on-screen as you work with the document. If you're an HTML-phobe at all (test your courage by reading the next section), try one of the transparent programs.

If you're shopping for a Web page editor that keeps the HTML hidden, check out one of these:

- **Microsoft FrontPage.** A popular and powerful Web page creator and Web site organizer that comes with utilities called *wizards* that help you create forms, discussion group pages, and more. You have to purchase FrontPage through an online store like PCConnection (www.pcconnection.com). You can find out more about the program at www.microsoft.com/frontpage.

- **Adobe PageMill.** You can download a trial version for Windows 95/NT 4.0 or later and for the Mac from the Adobe Systems Incorporated Web site (www.adobe.com/prodindex/pagemill/main.html).

- **Netscape Composer.** Netscape Composer is part of the standard version of Netscape Communicator, which you can download from Netscape's Web site (www.netscape.com/computing/download/index.html).

- **Macromedia Dreamweaver.** Dreamweaver is a feature-rich, professional piece of software that excels in producing Dynamic HTML, which makes Web pages more interactive through scripts, and HTML style sheets. This Web page editor is a little complex for beginning users, but if you're at all comfortable with Web pages or HTML, you can do practically anything you want with this program. Dreamweaver is available for Windows 95/98/NT 4.0 or later and for the Mac. Find out more at Macromedia's Web site (www.macromedia.com/software/ dreamweaver).

Using HTML

HTML (short for HyperText Markup Language) is a standardized way of coding documents so that all computers (Macs, PCs, laptops, palmtops, whatever) can read them, whether they're on one network within a single building or on a giant series *(web)* of networks like the Internet.

Web browsers are computer programs that were invented to recognize and display the instructions in HTML documents. Standard HTML instructions are known as *tags*. These instructions work in the background, like an architect directing a construction crew, telling a browser things like, "This phrase is a level 1 heading," This phrase is italic," or "Put this image here." You never see the instructions unless you choose View⇨Source in your browser's menu bar.

Table 7-1 shows some of the most essential HTML tags used on almost all Web pages. Often, tags come in pairs that enclose the text they're supposed to format. The first tag is called the *start tag;* the second one begins with a forward-slash (/) and is called the *end tag.*

Table 7-1	Common HTML Tags
Tag(s)	*What Tag(s) Do*
<Title> </Title>	Encloses Web page title, which appears in the title bar of the browser window.
<H*n*> </H*n*>	Encloses a Web page heading; *n* is a number from 1-6.
<B> </B>	Encloses text to be formatted in bold.
<I> </I>	Encloses text to be formatted in italic.
<BODY> </BODY>	Encloses the body of a Web page, the contents that you see on screen.
<P>	Begins a paragraph. Browsers typically insert a blank line space between it and the preceding paragraph.
 	Breaks a line without inserting a blank line space.

For example, here are the HTML instructions for a simple Web page that contains a heading, some text, an image, and a single hypertext link:

```
<html>
<head>
    <title>Greg Holden</title>
</head>
<body>

<h1>Greg Holden</h1>

<p>Here is an image of the author taken several years (and
            several pounds ago).</p>

<p><img SRC="Greg.gif" height=199 width=159></p>

<p>Feel free to contact me with questions at
            <a href="mailto:gholden@interaccess.com">
            gholden@interaccess.com</a>
</body>
</html>
```

A Web browser interprets these commands and presents the contents of this HTML document as the Web page shown in Figure 7-13.

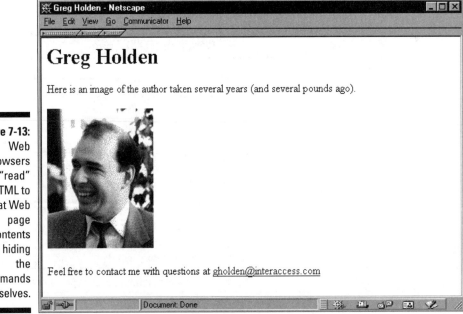

Figure 7-13: Web browsers "read" HTML to format Web page contents while hiding the commands themselves.

You can find more detailed explanations of how HTML works in *HTML 4 For Dummies* by Ed Tittel and Steve James, published by IDG Books Worldwide.

Uploading your pages to a server

Uploading is a fancy way of saying that after you create your Web pages, you need to place your files on a *Web server,* a computer that's connected to the Internet all the time.

Special software transfers your files from your computer to the Web server. Sometimes this software is built into the same program that you use to edit your Web pages; sometimes you have to use a special program that does the transfer by using a special set of instructions called File Transfer Protocol (FTP). Usually, your ISP gives you FTP software that does the moving for you. Ask your ISP for more information.

Using Software to Track Bids and Jazz Up Your Auction Web Pages

Suppose that you want to go beyond creating a simple background page on an auction site, such as Yahoo! Auctions or eBay. You may want to create more than one page about yourself, include images, or link your page to listings that you've posted on other auction service sites. You need to use a special program to format text and images for presentation on the Web. This section mentions several options for enhancing and adding functionality to your Web pages.

Listing and tracking items on eBay by using AuctionAssistant

AuctionAssistant automates many of the processes involved in selling items through eBay. (It works only with eBay, not other auction services.) If you're the type who prefers to maintain control over your Web content and do all your file transfers manually, this program isn't for you. But it can help save time required to keep track if you have many items to sell at the same time. Suppose, for example, that you have a dozen or even more items for sale on eBay at any one time. You can track them all easily through AuctionAssistant.

Before you can start listing items with AuctionAssistant, you have to list your item with eBay and get an item number for it (see Chapter 8). You then enter the number in the eBayID field in the AuctionAssistant window.

A shareware version of AuctionAssistant appears on this book's CD-ROM. You can also download a trial version of the program from the Blackthorne Software Web site and then register the program for $59.95. The evaluation copy of AuctionAssistant enables you to track only two auctions at a time. The program works with Windows 95/98/NT.

Follow these steps to use AuctionAssistant:

1. **Connect to the Internet, launch your Web browser, and go to the Blackthorne Software Download Web page** (www.blackthornesw.com/bthome/download.htm)

   The Customer Support - Download page appears.

2. **Scroll down the page and click the link for the evaluation version of AuctionAssistant.**

   The AuctionAssistant file is downloaded to your computer. This can take a while; the version of the file that I downloaded was more than 7.5MB in size. The file you download has a name like aa22xx.exe, depending on the version that is available when you download it.

3. **When downloading is complete, double-click the aa21xx.exe file.**

   The AuctionAssistant Setup program opens. Follow the steps shown in the Setup windows to install the application.

4. **When installation is complete, restart your computer. When the computer has restarted, double-click the application file or choose Start⇨Programs⇨AuctionAssistant⇨AuctionAssistant 2 to open the program.**

   When you start the program for the first time, the User Registration window opens.

5. **Enter your serial number if you purchased a registered copy of the software; if you're using an evaluation copy, enter Evaluation in the text field near the bottom of the User Registration window. Click Ok.**

   The Licensing Agreement window opens.

6. **Read the licensing agreement and click I Agree.**

   The AuctionAssistant window opens.

7. **If you need detailed instructions about how to use the program at any time, choose Help⇨User's Guide, or click the big yellow question mark icon in the toolbar.**

   The AuctionAssistant User's Guide opens in your Web browser window.

8. **AuctionAssistant will upload your image files to your Web hosting service and perform other automated functions; but first, you need to identify your host and provide the Uniform Resource Locator (URL) for the directory where your files are located. You do this by choosing File⇨Options.**

   The Options dialog box opens.

9. **Enter the information for your account on a Web hosting service. (AuctionAssistant refers to this as your Internet Service Provider, but this doesn't have to be your ISP; rather, you enter the URL for your Web host directory.) You also enter information for the directories where you host your Web images and your Web pages.**

   Optionally, you can also enter e-mail information so the program can send you e-mail notifications automatically when someone bids on an item or can send a Payment Received message when someone transfers money to you.

10. **Click OK.**

    The Options dialog box closes.

11. **After you enter your ISP and e-mail address information, enter your eBay item name, description, and price information in the appropriate fields in the AuctionAssistant window, as shown in Figure 7-14.**

12. **To add an image, click the Find button next to the Picture 1 field.**

    An Open dialog box appears.

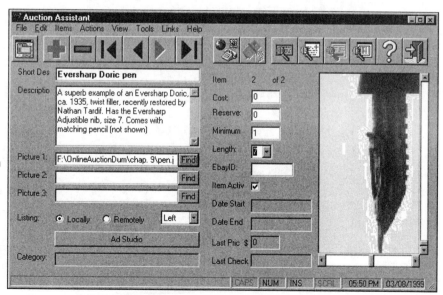

Figure 7-14:
A preview of your image appears in the Auction-Assistant window.

13. **Locate the image you want to add and click it, and then click Open.**

    The image appears in the window in the right half of the AuctionAssistant window.

14. **Click the Preview the Listing Before Adding to Ebay button in the AuctionAssistant toolbar if you want to view your listing in a Web browser window. (When you pass your mouse arrow over the button, a Preview the Listing item Windows Screen tip pops up.)**

    A preview example is shown in Figure 7-15.

15. **If you haven't obtained a user ID for the item you want to auction, connect to the Internet, launch your Web browser, and click the Go to eBay's Add Auction Panel button in the AuctionAssistant toolbar. (This is the button with the magnifying glass and the small green plus sign on it.)**

    The Loading Web Page dialog appears and presents a series of status messages as your Web browser copies eBay's New Item page to your computer so you can fill it out.

16. **When you're ready to start selling, choose Actions⇨EBay's Start Auction Screen.**

    AuctionAssistant launches your Web browser and displays eBay's New Item (Quick Form) page, automatically filled with your sales information. Start the auction by following the steps on the Start Auction page.

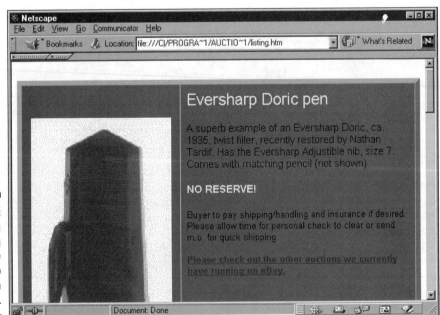

Figure 7-15:
Previewing
your listing
before
sending it to
eBay is a
good idea.

With the AuctionAssistant window open, click the AdStudio button on the left side of the AuctionAssistant window just above the Category field at the bottom of the window. Clicking this button starts AdStudio, another application that comes with AuctionAssistant. This program helps you prepare formatted auction listings. I describe another program that formats your listings, Auction Ad Pro, later in this chapter.

Tracking bids on eBay by using Auction Ticker

Stockbrokers do it. Sports fans do it. Why shouldn't you track the up-to-the-minute action in your auctions, too? You can do it with a program called AuctionTicker that, like AuctionAssistant, is produced by Blackthorne Software (www.blackthornesw.com).

AuctionTicker automatically checks all your auctions throughout the day and works the same whether you want to track bids on items you're selling or items you're bidding on. The program keeps you informed through a scrolling ticker that appears in your browser window.

AuctionTicker is available as shareware. You can download a trial version of the program from the Blackthorne Software Web site (www.blackthornesw.com) and then register the program for $19.95. The evaluation version only lets you keep an eye on one item at a time; the registered version sets no limit on the number of sales you can monitor. The program works with Windows 95/98/NT and requires 2.6MB of hard disk space.

One of the nice things about the program is that sellers can integrate it with AuctionAssistant: You can create a listing and post it on eBay by using AuctionAssistant, and then you can track the high bidders by using AuctionTicker. AuctionTicker works in the background: You can surf Web sites while AuctionTicker periodically visits auctions you have selected and reports on them.

Jazzing up listings and images by using Virtual Auction Ad Pro

Virtual Auction Ad Pro is a program that enables you to add some color and formatting to auction listings not only on eBay but on any online auction that accepts HTML code in item descriptions. Virtual Auction Ad Pro is part of a larger suite of software called Auction Aid.

TIP

Virtual Auction Ad Pro and the rest of Auction Aid are produced by Virtual Notions, Inc. (firstdesign.com). Auction Aid includes a nice shareware program called LView Pro that you can register for $40 if you decide to keep it, as well as a text editor, auction templates, and instructions for using eBay. Virtual Auction Ad Pro works with Windows 95, 98, and NT. The program must be purchased for $9.99.

Like AuctionAssistant, Virtual Auction Ad Pro lets you format a listing and add an image by typing text and then pressing toolbar buttons in a user window. Typically, the formatted auction listing is presented with a border around it and a background whose color you can customize. An example is shown in Figure 7-16.

To find out more about the program, go to the Virtual Notions, Inc., site and click the Virtual Auction Ad Pro link in the right column.

SELLER'S EDGE

Yahoo! Auctions also lets you add special formatting, such as bold or colored text, to an auction listing. However, you have to know some rudimentary HTML to do this. To make the phrase My Item bold, for example, you need to enclose it with two HTML commands called tags: <B>My Item</B>. Rendering text in a color is a little more involved, however.

Figure 7-16:
Virtual
Auction Ad
Pro can
arrange
your ad and
image in
different
ways, but
this two-
column
arrange-
ment is
popular.

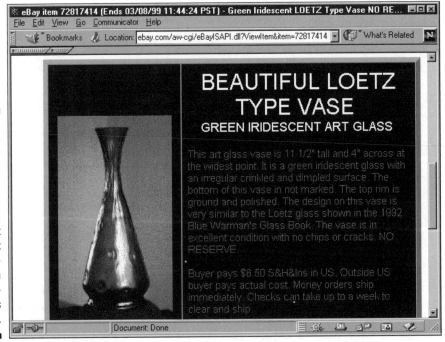

On Amazon.com Auctions, you have to pay $2 per auction to give your auction title boldface formatting. You can also feature your auction in a special category. Find out about the details at `auctions.amazon.com/exec/varzea/ts/help/optional-display-features/002-8675200-8656629.`

Chapter 8

Sold! Now What?

· ·

· ·

Congratulations! You experienced the excitement of seeing your auction merchandise listed on the Internet; you gasped as people actually bid on your item; you cheered as the final few bids came in at the deadline, and you banged a virtual gavel and toasted the final bid.

Now what? At this point, your priority is to seal the deal and receive payment.

This chapter discusses how to get from that final gavel to your ultimate end result — which, you may be surprised to hear, is not receiving payment. Rather, the *real* goal is to receive a positive feedback message from your satisfied customer. Only when you are both happy and your reputation as an auction seller has been enhanced a bit can you truly rest on your laurels. (If you're a high bidder wondering what to do now that the auction is over, see Chapter 5.)

Your work doesn't end when the auction ends. If the bidder didn't meet your reserve price, you have to decide whether to sell the item at a lower price than you originally wanted or withdraw the item so you can sell it another time.

If you and the high bidder reach an agreement, you then have to decide what form the payment will take. When you sell at a flea market or a traditional auction, the transaction is pretty simple: You hold out your hand, and the buyer fills it with the required amount of cold, hard cash. When the transaction occurs online, things get more complicated. You and the buyer may be hundreds or even thousands of miles apart; you may even be in different countries and use different currencies. These differences make things more complex, but if you use common sense and are clear about what you want, you shouldn't have a problem getting paid. This chapter shows you how to protect your interests and deal with the many types of customer interactions that can occur after the sale.

eBay maintains a good page with suggestions for negotiations, payments, and shipping options that occur after the auction (`pages.ebay.com/aw/postauction.html`). Whether you sell on eBay or another service, the tips are general enough to be useful to any auction seller.

Getting What's Coming to You

After the auction ends, take a deep breath and assess the situation. Did your high bidder meet your reserve price? Is the high bidder someone you know, or someone who has successfully bid on other auctions?

On the upside, as the seller you're in the driver's seat. Many more pitfalls await the buyer at this point, because she must commit the money that she just bid. The overwhelming number of complaints about auction transactions involve buyers who either pay for merchandise they don't receive, or receive something that's unacceptable in some way.

On the other hand, you want to protect yourself, too. In particular, you need to prepare for two potential pitfalls:

- A deadbeat bidder who doesn't follow through with the deal
- A check that bounces or payment that fails in some other way

I explain how to deal with these and other problems in the following sections.

You're involved in a business transaction, so don't take it personally if something goes wrong with closing the deal or you and the winning bidder have a dispute of some sort. Handle yourself in a businesslike manner. Don't lose your cool! Think about your reputation and feedback and the many other transactions that will go smoothly rather than getting bogged down by the difficult sale that, by the law of averages, is bound to occur sooner or later.

Tracking down your high bidder

Sometimes the problem with sealing the deal is simply getting in touch with the high bidder (or, if you're the buyer, getting in touch with the seller). It might seem strange that someone who wins at auction wouldn't be eager to get back to you immediately, but it can happen. Don't panic if you're unable to contact someone within a matter of hours after the auction ends, or even if a day or two goes by.

If, after a lengthy amount of time (the exact "comfort zone" depends on your level of patience), you have tried to reach someone by e-mail without success, submit a query to the auction house, which should provide you with more detailed contact information.

If you're on eBay, you can go to the User Information page and get contact information at `pages.ebay.com/aw/user-query.html`. If you're on Yahoo! Auctions and the e-mail address of the high bidder that you receive from Yahoo! doesn't turn up anyone, contact the auction house.

Checking the Internet white pages

What can you do if the high bidder fails to contact you, and the information supplied by the auction service doesn't do the trick? Before you give up, take a few minutes to search one of the Web sites that provide the Internet's own version of the white pages in your telephone directory.

One such service is called Switchboard (`www.switchboard.com`). Go to the service's home page and click the Find a Person link. Enter the name and/or address of the person in the required fields and then click the Search button. You get a list of individuals around the country who match your search criteria, complete with addresses and phone numbers (see Figure 8-1).

If at first you don't succeed with a Switchboard search, try, try again. Enter less specific information. For example, if you previously entered the complete city and state, delete the city in case the person has moved or you spelled the city name incorrectly. Keep subtracting information until you get some results.

Figure 8-1: A Switchboard search can turn up plenty of individuals around the world, whether they're on the Internet or not.

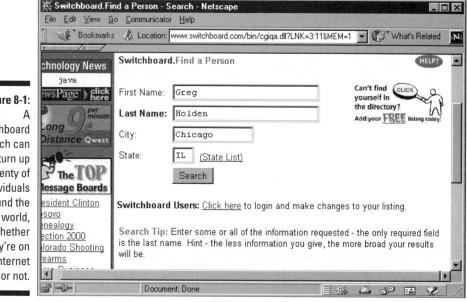

Searching around the world

Switchboard isn't the only online phone directory around. In fact, it's a little eerie how many people now have their personal contact information on the Internet, not only in the United States, but internationally.

For example, if you're looking for a bidder in Lebanon (the country in the Middle East, that is, not the town in Illinois), you can check out the index of white pages services around the world on Yahoo! (`dir.yahoo.com/Reference/Phone_Numbers_and_Addresses/Email_Addresses/Individuals/Regional`). You can find pages of e-mail addresses for people in Bosnia, China, and many more places.

You can also go to `dir.yahoo.com/Regional/Countries` and click the name of the country you want to search. When you get to the Web page for the country in question, click the Computers and Internet link. Chances are you'll find a white pages or people finder directory for that country.

Finally, if you're really determined to find the individual (this can turn into a quest; don't let yourself get carried away, now), go to one of the versions of Yahoo! that covers another part of the world. On the main Yahoo! page (`www.yahoo.com`), you can see a World Yahoo!s list near the bottom of the page. Click the country or region that's closest to the area you want to search. When you connect to the main Web page for the regional Yahoo!, either click the People Search link near the top of the page or follow the links for Society_and_Culture/People. Figure 8-2 shows the list of personal Web pages for Singapore residents.

Dealing with deadbeat bidders

Probably the most common problem that can confront an auction seller is the deadbeat bidder: the individual who doesn't follow through on her high bid, leaving you with an unsold item.

Sometimes, the winning competitor gets back to you and indicates payment is on the way, only to fall silent afterwards. Other unreliables never turn up in the first place. Deadbeat bidders erode the trust necessary for online auctions to work. They also hurt themselves: They start to develop a bad reputation and, if they bail out several times (three, according to the eBay Deadbeat Bidder Policy), they can be suspended from further activity.

Sometimes, you have to give the bidder the benefit of the doubt. She may be ill or experiencing technical problems.

If you truly can't find the bidder, take action, not only to protect yourself and get your money back, but to keep others from getting burned, too:

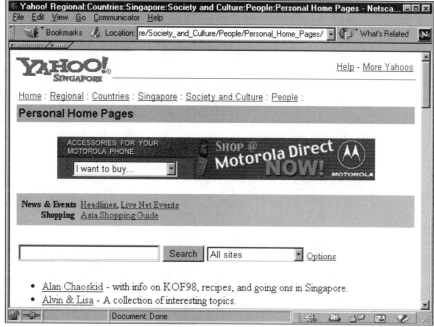

Figure 8-2:
The regional varieties of Yahoo! help you locate individuals in many locations around the world.

✔ Submit a request to eBay for a Final Value Fee Credit.

✔ Send negative feedback.

✔ Send an e-mail message to the bidder notifying him that the auction transaction is canceled and his bids won't be permitted on your items in the future.

✔ Re-list the item.

You don't necessarily have to complain to eBay directly to report your dead-beat bidder. The company says in its documentation that when you ask for a credit of your Final Value Fee, the system automatically identifies the high bidder involved.

On both eBay and Yahoo! Auctions, if you encounter a bidder who has been a deadbeat in the past or who can't be reached, you can cancel that individual's bid in a subsequent auction if the person bids on something else you're selling. See the Yahoo! Auctions page at `help.yahoo.com/help/auctions/asell/asell-03.html` for more information.

Not your reserve price? Now what?

An entirely different situation occurs when your auction ends and the reserve price has not been met for the item you want to sell. At this point you have a choice: You and the prospective buyer can decide whether you want to negotiate an alternate sale price and complete the transaction. But you don't have to. The rules of eBay, for example, state: "If an auction ends and the reserve price has not been met, both the seller and the high bidder are released from any further obligation to complete the transaction."

Here, too, you don't have to be an expert negotiator; you don't have to provide a long "sob story" about how valuable the object in question is to you and how you need the money to put braces on Little Susie's crooked teeth. Acting in a businesslike fashion, tell the high bidder either:

- ✔ "Sorry, since the reserve price wasn't met, I want to cancel the sale and try to sell at another time."
- ✔ "I see that the high bid didn't meet my reserve price. Would you be willing to pay [fill in the amount]?"

If the buyer continues to bargain and wants something less than you are asking, remember that you are under no obligation to sell. Don't be reluctant to say no rather than giving in and accepting a lower amount than you really want.

In my experience as a buyer, bidders are more understanding if the seller explains that he or she paid a certain amount to purchase the item in the first place or has invested money in the item for repairs, and the reserve is needed to protect her investment.

As the check bounces

Many auction sellers request payment in cashier's check or postal money order to guard against the other big problem that can occur with completing a transaction — the buyer's check bouncing. Holding delivery of your auction item until the buyer's check clears the bank is always a good idea in case the check comes back marked NSF (non-sufficient funds).

If an NSF check does come back to you, the first step is to immediately notify the buyer and to request payment in the form of cashier's check or money order. Be sure to hold on to the NSF check; you may need it in case of trouble.

If you still don't receive payment from the buyer, tell the auction house what happened. Also leave feedback about the buyer.

Don't let disputes get you down

If you get into a dispute with a high bidder, what should you do? In most cases, contacting the auction service doesn't do any good. That option is reserved for when a party commits some type of fraud. If fraud or other misuse is involved, eBay has its own service called SafeHarbor (see Figure 8-3) that can investigate.

Often, professional mediation can help resolve disputes. Because your disagreement is occurring online, consulting an online arbitrator makes sense. Check out the arbitration services listed on Yahoo! at `www.yahoo.com/ Business_and_Economy/Companies/Law/Arbitration_and_Mediation/`.

Providing Good Customer Service

Most of your online auction encounters are bound to be positive rather than negative. The atmosphere of trust and cooperation that helped make the Internet popular in the first place is still alive on eBay, Yahoo! Auctions, Amazon.com Auctions, WebAuction, and other auction sites. This section explains how you can provide good customer service to enhance your reputation and encourage repeat customers.

Figure 8-3: eBay's SafeHarbor can investigate fraud, but won't resolve disagreements for you.

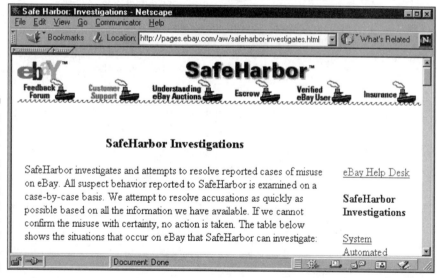

As a buyer (whether online or at the corner grocery store), you know all about good customer service but probably take it for granted. Mostly, you pay attention to customer service when you *don't* get it — when you need to return an item and have to complain; when you have a problem with something you bought and need instructions on how to use it.

Ensuring successful transactions

Tessa Hebert, who runs the Book Dealers mail-order book business with her partner Bill Fulkerson, provides a Web page full of tips (www.mindspring.com/~bookdealers/nopay.html) for eBay auction sellers who run into deadbeat bidders and other problems. Tessa and Bill have been selling online since 1995 at eBay and other locations, including their Web page (bookdealers.home.mindspring.com). Here's how she and Bill deal with problems sealing the deal:

"Most of our transactions on eBay have been very pleasant and smooth," Tessa says. We've had a few deadbeat winning-bidders, maybe six in the last year. Sometimes, the winning bidder e-mails that he/she will send payment, and we never hear from the person again, even after repeated e-mail attempts. Once a woman who had a positive feedback total of 226 wrote to say she was sending payment, then never sent payment and would not respond to our requests. We've also had a few very-late payers, who forget to send their payments for about a month.

"My best advice to sellers is to always keep constant e-mail contact with the buyer. Almost all problems can be resolved by friendly and courteous communication. Send out requests for payment immediately after the auction ends. Respond to all e-mail from buyers or potential buyers who have questions about the auction, being friendly and helpful.

"When someone really turns out to be a deadbeat, we always leave negative feedback, contact eBay for a refund of the Final Value Fee, and re-list our item after notifying the winning-bidder that we are canceling the transaction and will not allow them to bid on our auctions again (and will report them to eBay for suspension if they do).

"When we do receive payment, we notify the buyer when the book is mailed so the person knows when to expect delivery; we also ask the buyer to notify us when the book arrives. Finally, after you know the buyer has received the item and is satisfied with the transaction, leave positive feedback and notify the buyer that you are doing so.

"We will ship by any method the buyer requests and pays for, but we prefer the U.S. Postal Service because it's convenient, reliable, and inexpensive, and we've never had a book damaged during USPS delivery.

"We do pride ourselves on how well we wrap our books for delivery. We want a book to arrive in the same condition it left in. We wrap the books first in brown paper with a mailing label/delivery receipt (which references the eBay auction number, price, and shipping costs; gives our user ID and e-mail address; and requests that the buyer notify us on receipt). Then we wrap the book in bubble wrap (padding the corners well) and place it in a padded envelope.

"We always insure our packages, after one disastrous non-arrival of a very expensive book (which we replaced when it was not found after the post office completed a Lost Mail Claim). That was the only "lost package" we've ever had, and we believe the broker and the buyer scammed us. I always advise sellers to use the U.S. Postal Service and buy insurance, because very few people will attempt to scam a seller once the post office begins a Lost Mail Claim investigation."

The same sorts of customer service issues arise in Internet auctions, but on a smaller scale. For the most part, the problems you encounter are easily handled, as long as you are clear, detailed, courteous, and patient in your response. If you can keep your customers happy, you'll get the good feedback you need.

Managing your e-mail

The most important tool for anyone buying or selling online is electronic mail. E-mail is the way you communicate not only with auction houses but also with buyers and sellers. You don't have to be a technical genius to be an effective e-mail communicator, but some basic knowledge can help when you're trying to build good customer relations, which, in turn, will help you get paid for what you sell. The following sections provide some tips for successfully managing your e-mail.

Don't let your mail grow stale

E-mail, like a delicate plant, wilts if not tended regularly. Among the best and easiest business strategies are these:

- ✔ Check your e-mail as often as possible.
- ✔ Respond to e-mail inquiries immediately.

Again and again, I've found that the most successful businesspeople are also the ones who respond to e-mail inquiries promptly, despite being busy people. *Coincidence?* You decide.

Noting by quoting

Responding to a series of questions is easy when you use the feature available in almost every e-mail program that lets you quote from the message to which you're replying. Quoting is particularly useful, of course, when you're responding to a mailing list or newsgroup message because it indicates what topic is being discussed.

How do you tell the difference between the text being quoted and the reply? Usually, a ">" character (right-angle bracket) appears in the left margin, next to each line of the quoted material.

When you tell your e-mail software to quote the original message before you type your reply, it usually quotes the entire message. To save space, you can snip (delete) the part that isn't relevant. However, it's then polite to type the word **<snip>** to show that something has been cut. Begin your message, like this:

```
Greg Holden wrote:
>I wonder if I could get some info on <snip>
>those little plastic thingies that used to go in the center
         hole of 45 RPM records...
Hi Greg.
Yours is the first request we have received in the last twelve
years for our premium "spindle-spanners." You can place an
order online or call our toll-free number, 1-800-SPINDLE.
```

If you're responding to a series of questions about what you're selling, quote each question and type an answer beneath it so your response takes on a question-answer format. That way, bidders don't have to spend time remembering their original queries; they can devote their energy to placing bids.

Attachment etiquette

A quick and convenient way to transmit information is to attach a file to an e-mail message. In fact, it's one of the most useful things you can do with e-mail. *Attaching,* which means that you send a document or file as part of an e-mail message, allows you to include material from any file on your hard disk. Attached files appear as separate documents that recipients can download to their computers.

Sellers sometimes use attachments to send additional images of an item to a prospective buyer, preferring to ask buyers to e-mail a request for an image rather than posting their images online for buyers to see.

In general, it's better not to put buyers through this extra work. However, there is one instance where you would want to do this: to e-mail a high-quality version of an image where detail is really important. The GIF or JPEG image you post online may be a small-scale, not-very-detailed image of your item. You can tell buyers to e-mail you for a large, detailed image saved in a format such as TIFF (Tagged Image File Format), which provides better detail than GIF and JPEG but can't be viewed directly on the Web.

Many e-mail clients allow users to attach files by clicking a button or using another simple command. Compressing a lengthy series of attachments using software such as StuffIt for the Mac or PC (www.symantec.com) or WinZip for the PC (www.winzip.com) conserves bandwidth.

Leaving your mark with signature files

One of the easiest and most useful tools for marketing with e-mail on the Internet is a *signature file,* a text file that is automatically appended to the bottom of your e-mail messages and newsgroup postings to tell the recipients something about you. You can include information such as where you work and how to contact you.

Creating a signature file is easy. Just follow these steps:

1. **Open a text editing program.**

   This example uses Notepad, which comes with Windows. If you're a Macintosh user, you can use SimpleText.

   A new blank document opens.

2. **Press the hyphen or equals sign key (=) to create a dividing line to separate your signature from the body of your message.**

3. **Type information about yourself, such as your name, the name of your business if you have one, and your e-mail address. Be sure to include your Web site URL if you have one. Press Return or Enter after each line.**

   A signature is typically three or four lines long. If you're feeling ambitious at this point, you can press the spacebar to arrange your text in two columns, but a simple one-column layout works fine, too, as shown in Figure 8-4.

4. **Choose File⇨Save.**

   A dialog box opens, enabling you to name the file and save it in a folder on your hard disk.

5. **Enter a name for your file that ends in the .txt filename extension. This identifies your file as a plain text document so you can locate it more easily. Then click Save.**

   Your text file is saved on your computer's hard disk.

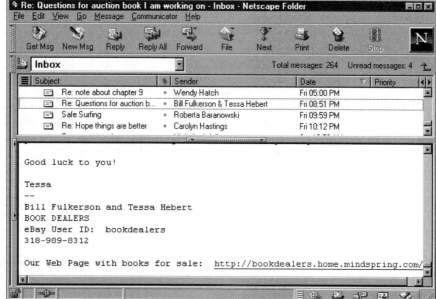

Figure 8-4: A signature file tells busy auction bidders who you are and how to reach you.

Congratulations! You created a plain-text version of your electronic signature. The next step is to identify that file to the computer programs that you use to send and receive e-mail and newsgroup messages so that the signature (or *sig*) file automatically appears at the bottom of your messages. The procedure for attaching a sig file varies from program to program; check your e-mail software's Help file for specific instructions.

Practicing positive public relations

What's all this talk about "public relations," you ask? You're selling some stuff at auction; you're not working for some big corporation. True, you don't have to issue press releases or talk to the media when you become an auction seller, but you *are* in business, whether you realize it or not. Part of being in business means communicating in a positive way with your customers. I tell you how to put your best foot forward in the following sections.

Helping others can help you

Even though you're "only" auctioning off a few sales items, you need to promote yourself online. On the Internet, an excellent way to build credibility is to share your experience and participate in online discussions. Without too much of a stretch, you can establish yourself as an expert and a good person with whom to do business.

Consider making a link to your online resume, either in your e-mail signature file or in your auction listings. A resume can show people how long you've been in your field and how you got to know what you know about your business.

Visit places like eBay's Café and bulletin boards to help answer questions about auction items and share your experiences (both can be found at `pages.ebay.com/aw/newschat.html`). Also join mailing lists (see Chapter 3 for more on these discussion forums).

The number of groups you join and how often you participate in them is up to you. The important thing is to regard every one-to-one-personal contact as a seed that may sprout into a sale, a referral, an order, a contract, or a bit of useful advice that can help your budding business bloom.

You got a problem with that?

The flip side of customer service is dealing with irate customers. What happens when someone isn't happy with what they receive? What happens when a customer claims that she didn't get what you advertised?

Because of the free-form nature of online auctions, I can't give you any rules for dealing with this other than advising you to use plain old common sense.

The best way to deal with the problem of customer dissatisfaction, of course, is to keep it from happening in the first place. You can prevent a lot of trouble by:

- ✔ Being upfront and complete in your auction descriptions
- ✔ Being clear about shipping and other policies
- ✔ Insuring anything you ship, and having a way to track a package if it gets lost

Of course, it's easy to say these things; following through on them is another matter. Even then, you can still run into winning bidders who seem intent on raising trouble. Remember to be as courteous and businesslike as you can: Keep your own reputation and feedback ratings in mind.

What do you do if someone wants her money back? This depends on how hard-nosed you want to be. If you provided a good description and photo of the item and you think the customer understood what she was getting, you aren't obligated to make a return. On the other hand, you can develop a return policy ("we promise to return any item purchased if you are not satis-fied") to your advantage as a way of building business credibility. Make the customer pay for shipping the item back to you, and also make sure that you get the goods back before you return the money.

If you offer the item for auction again, tell bidders that the item was offered earlier, but the deal fell through. This takes into account that some regular visitors to the auction site may remember the item being there. You don't have to go into detail about what happened. (You can find more information about reselling auction items in Chapter 6.)

Keeping secrets safe with Internet encryption

Radio and TV childhood heroes used to give out secret decoder rings to their young audience members. They then broadcast coded messages that only the lucky ring bearers could decipher.

Computers use a similar process of encoding and decoding to protect infor-mation they exchange on the Internet. The schemes used online are far more complex and subtle than the ones used by kids, however. (See Chapter 2 for the details.)

How can encryption help your auction transactions go smoothly? You can use it to certify your identity so people can be sure you are who you say you are. This is a special concern when it comes to auctions. It's not unheard of for unscrupulous sellers to swindle customers, get negative feedback, and then sign on again with new usernames. One way of ensuring your identity online is through obtaining a personal certificate. This is explained in Chapter 2.

Making sure the package arrives safely

What if the high bidder on your item lives in another country? Shipping to this person may cost more than you anticipated. Be sure to include a note in your listing noting that "additional shipping charges to overseas customers will apply." Don't get too specific; the cost will vary by country, and you should only have to calculate that after the auction is closed.

If you don't want to ship an item a particular way or to a particular location, explain this in your auction listings. Technically, you don't *have* to state your shipping policy and you don't *have* to ship to a particular faraway location if you don't want to, but being courteous and helpful can enhance your online reputation and help you avoid negative feedback.

If you need to purchase a lot of U.S. postage and are operating on a tight budget, you can actually save money by buying collectible postage (that is, postage stamps that were issued years ago but are still usable) at less than face value. Find out more at the Henry Gitler Philatelists, Inc. Web site (www.hgitner.com/postage.html).

Safe shipping depends on the company you keep. Make sure you pick a shipper you're comfortable with. The following sections provide some suggestions for features to keep in mind when making the selection.

Choosing a ship-shape shipper

Rather than simply picking the best-known shipping service, use these tips that can save you some money and make things progress more smoothly:

- ✔ **Compare shipping costs.** Use an online service like InterShipper's Universal Shipping Calculator (www.intershipper.net), which allows you to submit, via a Web page form, the origin, destination, weight, and dimensions of a package that you want to ship, and returns the cheapest shipping alternatives. This is a truly convenient and user-friendly Web utility: When I entered a few figures and did a test, in only a matter of seconds InterShipper returned a Web page with comparative costs from Federal Express, United Parcel Service, the U.S. Postal Service, RPS Inc., DHL Worldwide Express, and Airborne Express.

- ✔ **Make sure that you can track the package.** Pick a service that lets you track your package's shipping status.

✔ **Make sure that you can confirm receipt.** If you use the U.S. Postal Service, ship the package Return Receipt Requested because tracking is not available with some services like First Class Mail. Otherwise use the new Delivery Confirmation Service available for Priority Mail and Standard Mail packages.

Federal Express gained a lot of attention, as well as huge numbers of visitors to its Web site (www.fedex.com), when it instituted package tracking a few years ago. The other big shipping services have followed FedEx's lead and created their own online tracking systems. You can link to these sites, too:

✔ United Parcel Service (www.ups.com)

✔ The U.S. Postal Service's Express Mail (www.usps.gov)

✔ Airborne Express (www.airborne.com)

Need suggestions on how to ship an unusual item? Put eBay's extensive search capabilities to use. Search for items that are like yours, and see how the sellers ship them. Try doing a "search" for large items (like tables, beds, etc.) and see how the sellers ship them. Other sites such as Yahoo! Auctions (auctions.yahoo.com) and Haggle Online (www.haggle.com) let you search for sales items, but don't include all of eBay's options such as locating completed auctions.

Insurance for rainy days

You should insure the items you send. If you sell an item for more than $25 to a buyer who doesn't have negative feedback, eBay will insure you as long as the item doesn't violate the service's User Agreement. (Go to pages.ebay.com/aw/help/help-faq-insure.html to see the FAQ on insurance.)

In order to use eBay's insurance scheme, you have to be a registered user in good standing, and you can only make a certain number of claims. For the first six months, the service was free; by now, eBay may charge for the service, but it's probably worth the money. You get a maximum coverage of $200, minus a $25 deductible.

For items more than $200, use one of the escrow services examined in Chapter 5.

The U.S. Postal Service recently began a confirmation service that allows you to track the delivery of any item by calling a toll-free number or using the Internet. On top of the normal shipping fees for Priority Mail or Standard Mail, you can pay an extra fee (35 cents for Priority Mail and 60 cents for Standard Mail) for the confirmation service. You can find out more about the program by going to the U.S. Postal Service Web site at www.usps.gov and searching for Publication 91, Delivery Confirmation Technical Guide.

Offering convenient payment options

Luckily for those of us who live in the U.S., the almighty dollar is the unofficial currency of choice on eBay, Yahoo! Auctions, and most, if not all, of the other big auction houses.

If you're bidding from outside the U.S. on eBay auction sales held in the U.S., you have to deal in U.S. currency, unless your seller takes a major credit card. This can be inconvenient and inexpensive. You'll probably have to pay a fee to obtain a U.S. Money Order, and you may have to wait days or weeks to obtain one. However, eBay now has international sites where users from the same country can find one another and use their common currency. At this writing, there's a version of eBay for Canadian users at www.ebay.com/canada and one for users in the United Kingdom at www.ebay.com/uk.

Some eBay users have reported on bulletin boards such as the one for International Trade that it can be helpful, if you plan to do a substantial amount of business with American customers, to open a bank account in U.S. dollars at your own bank or to open an account with a branch of a U.S. bank in your area if you have one.

The following sections discuss some time-saving alternatives to the usual cashier's check/money order options. (See Chapter 5 for an explanation of those common monetary transfer methods.)

Digital payments

As an alternative to requiring checks or money orders, you can receive electronic checks from customers. This is easier than you think. Go to firstdesign.com/checker to find out more.

Another convenient and safe way to transfer funds on the Internet is to use one of the escrow services described in Chapter 5.

Yes! I accept credit cards

Lots of auction listings have credit card icons or notices that tell buyers that credit card payment is accepted (see Figure 8-5).

Although credit cards are easy for shoppers to use, they make life as an online merchant more complicated. I don't want to discourage you from becoming credit card-ready by any means, but you need to be aware of the steps (and the expenses) involved, many of which probably don't occur to you when you're just starting out. For example, you may not be aware of the following:

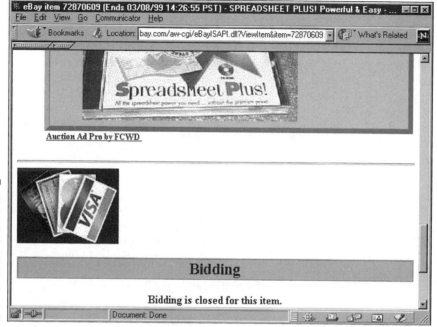

Figure 8-5:
Credit card acceptance can offer speed and security to both buyers and sellers.

✔ You have to apply for a special bank account called a *merchant account* in order for a bank to process credit card orders you receive.

✔ In addition to the bank's merchant application fee ($300 to $800), you pay the bank a usage fee, deceptively called a *discount rate.* Typically, this fee ranges from 1 to 3.5 percent of each transaction. Plus, you pay a monthly premium charge of perhaps $30 to $70 to the bank.

Reach for your wallet!

One of the terms commonly thrown around in the jargon of e-commerce is *wallet.* A wallet is software that, like a real wallet that you keep in your purse or pocket, stores available cash and other records. You reach into the cyberwallet and withdraw virtual cash such as ecash, scrip, or CyberCoins.

A cybershopper who uses wallet software, such as Microsoft Wallet (www.microsoft.com/wallet/default.asp) or CyberCoin Wallet, is able to pay for items online in a matter of sec-

onds, without having to transfer credit card data. What's more, some wallets can even "remember" previous purchases you have made and suggest further purchases. As wallet software becomes more widespread online, you might consider getting an account so you can provide this as a payment option for your bidders. Find out more about CyberCoin at the CyberCash Web site, www.cybercash.com, and Microsoft Wallet at the URL given above. You can also consult Chapter 5.

✔ You need software or hardware that allows you process the transactions and transmit the data to the banking system. The hardware involved is a terminal or phone line, which you can lease for $25 to $50 per month.

The good news is that it's getting easier to get merchant status, as more banks accept the notion that businesses don't need to have a physical storefront in order to be successful. The bad news is that it still takes a long time to get a merchant account approved, and some hefty fees are involved as well. Banks look more favorably on companies that have been in business for several years and have a proven track record. What's an entrepreneur just starting out to do?

You can find a long list of businesses that provide merchant accounts for online businesses at one of Yahoo!'s index pages (`dir.yahoo.com/Business _and_Economy/Companies/Financial_Services/Transaction_Clearing /Credit_Card_Merchant_Services`). The list is so long that it's difficult to know which company to choose. I recommend visiting Wells Fargo Bank (`www.wellsfargo.com`), which has been operating online for several years and is well-established. The Wells Fargo Web site provides you with a good overview of what's required to obtain a merchant account.

Fighting credit card fraud

Unfortunately, the world is full of bad people who try to use credit card numbers that don't belong to them. The very convenience and immediacy of the Web can facilitate fraudulent orders, just as it can benefit legitimate orders.

In *Starting an Online Business For Dummies,* I interviewed a small business owner named Dave Hagan, Jr., who is president of both York Internet Services, a Web site design company, and General Tool & Repair, Inc., a tool supplier based in York, Pennsylvania. Dave pointed out to me that his business receives fraudulent credit card orders "all the time," and that he is able to stop them by checking the shipping address that the purchaser provides against the address registered to the card's owner. If the two addresses are wildly different (the shipping address is in Brazil, but the owner lives in Pennsylvania, for example), Dave knows something is fishy and calls the card's owner to verify the transaction.

Protecting yourself against credit card fraud is essential. Always check the billing address against the shipping address. If the two addresses are thousands of miles apart, e-mail the owner to verify that the transaction is legit. Even if it is, the owner will appreciate your taking the time to verify the transaction. Dave Hagan uses a program called Authorizer (`www.atomic-software.com`) to compare the billing and shipping addresses. Companies such as CheckFree Corporation (`www. checkfree.com`) can also do this for you, for a fee.

Processing credit card payments

Although accepting credit card payments is convenient for both buyers and sellers, credit cards do make things more complicated for sellers. Someone must process the electronic credit card data so the bank receives it and you get paid. In addition, you need to check the buyer's address against the one that is associated with the credit card to help reduce the risk of credit card fraud. Although software solutions are available to help make this easier, you're probably going to have to process the payments.

Be sure to ask about the discount rate that the bank charges for Internet-based transactions before you apply. Compare the rate for online transactions to the rate for conventional "card-swipe" purchases. Some banks charge 1 to 2 extra percentage points for online sales.

If you plan to receive credit card payments, find a Web hosting service that will protect the area of your online business that serves as the online store. This is called a secure server.

A *secure server* is a program that uses some form of encryption to protect data that you receive over the Internet. Customers know that they've entered a secure area when the security key or lock icon at the bottom of the browser window is locked shut and a blue security band appears at the top of the browser window.

Do-it-yourself processing

To submit credit card information to your bank, you need POS (point-of-sale) hardware or software. The hardware, which you either purchase or lease from your bank, is a *terminal* — a gray box of the sort you see at many local retailers. The software is a program that contacts the bank through a modem.

The terminal or software is programmed to authorize the sale and transmit the data to the bank. (You don't have to have an actual credit card to swipe in order to use the terminal, so it works for Internet transactions in which the customer supplies you with credit card information over the phone, by e-mail, or by filling out a Web page form.) The bank then credits your business or personal checking account, usually within two or three business days. The bank also deducts the discount rate from your account, either weekly, monthly, or with each transaction.

A payment processing program called Authorizer is available for Windows or DOS computers. You can download a demo version from the Atomic Software Web site (www.atomic-software.com). A version of Authorizer for Windows that supports 1 to 4 users is available for $349. A version for 1 to 24 users costs $549.

Automatic processing

You can hire a company to automatically process credit card orders for you. These companies compare the shipping and billing addresses to help make sure that the purchaser is the person who actually owns the card, and not someone trying to use a stolen credit card number. If everything checks out, the company transmits the data directly to the bank.

Look into the different options provided by VeriFone, Inc. (www.verifone.com) for such services. If you sign up for an account with a business Web hosting service called QuickSite (primecom.net/quicksite), you can select two options that automatically process credit card purchases for you; one of the two options also handles credit card verification.

Chapter 9

Marketing Around the Block and Around the World

*F*or people who want to sell at auction, faraway places with strange-sounding names are as close as the corner grocery store. International marketing and advertising isn't restricted to business Web sites. You, too, can use some free tricks of the Internet trade to help put your sale items before the eyes of the individuals most likely to bid on them.

I speak from personal experience here. I first found out about eBay not from the Web or from the media, but from reading listings in a specialized online discussion group (called a *newsgroup*) especially for people who collect antique pens and pencils. I noticed that, along with the usual queries and comments about specific pens and upcoming collectors' shows, a few newsgroup participants were either selling pens or advertising pens they were selling on eBay. I clicked the link for the eBay listing supplied in the newsgroup posting I happened to be reading, and my Web browser connected to eBay's site and displayed the pen being sold. I was hooked.

When you begin actively marketing your auction sales, you encounter potential buyers from all over the world. You start to realize the Internet's power to reach across national boundaries. Along with that power, though, comes additional responsibility: You need to be aware of language, time-zone, and other differences that apply when you deal with a worldwide auction audience. Understanding customs and other requirements you may need to observe when shipping your goods internationally is also a good idea, so I discuss those considerations in this chapter, too.

Telling Who Wants It That You Gots It

Someday, some enterprising auction seller will break new ground by taking out gaudy banner ads for his or her sales on popular Web sites like Yahoo!, or perhaps even eBay itself. (A *banner ad* is the Internet equivalent of a traditional rectangular advertisement in a newspaper or magazine, but with one big difference: If a user clicks on a banner ad, his browser usually connects to the advertiser's Web site.)

Until such ads become practical (that is, affordable), sellers have to use cost-effective, and in many ways more efficient, strategies for publicizing the merchandise they offer: the Web and the lively discussion groups on Usenet and America Online.

Advertising on your Web site

If you have your own Web site — whether that site is for your personal use or for a business if you have one — you can increase the number of visits to that site by means of an auction site. If, like many auction sellers, you have a business, and a Web site for that business, you can try selling a few items through a co-marketing arrangement with one of the online auction houses. Lots of auction listings include a link to the seller's Web site, and the Web site, in turn, provides a link back to the seller's current Internet auctions (see Figure 9-1).

Figure 9-1:
Your business Web site and auction listings can work in tandem to promote one another.

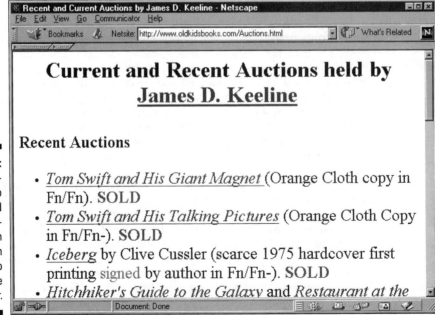

> **Recent and Current Auctions by James D. Keeline - Netscape**
> File Edit View Go Communicator Help
> Bookmarks   Netsite: http://www.oldkidsbooks.com/Auctions.html   What's Related
>
> # Current and Recent Auctions held by James D. Keeline
>
> ## Recent Auctions
>
> - *Tom Swift and His Giant Magnet* (Orange Cloth copy in Fn/Fn). SOLD
> - *Tom Swift and His Talking Pictures* (Orange Cloth Copy in Fn/Fn-). SOLD
> - *Iceberg* by Clive Cussler (scarce 1975 hardcover first printing signed by author in Fn/Fn-). SOLD
> - *Hitchhiker's Guide to the Galaxy* and *Restaurant at the*
>
> Document: Done

It's important not to regard auctions as just a dumpster for your overstock. Instead, think of auctions as an important vehicle that helps you reach new customers and market your business online. Your auction listings are, in essence, ongoing advertisements that can pull more visitors to your Web site, and possibly result in more inquiries and purchases for your business.

Conducting exit polls: They aren't just for elections anymore

Should you be an advertising pioneer and buy huge banner ads for your auction items on Web sites with high "hit" numbers? Not necessarily. Aside from the cost, it's the targeting. This kind of traditional advertising, called *broadcasting*, is designed to deliver short bits of information to huge numbers of people — basically, anyone who happens to surf by and see the ad. But the Internet really excels at a more narrowly targeted type of advertising that focuses directly on individuals, delivering your message on a one-to-one basis to people who want to hear it.

By all means, research where your bidders hang out on the Web. After you complete an online sale, conduct a sort of "exit poll" of your high bidder:

- Ask where he usually shops for the type of thing you just sold.
- Ask about any discussion groups your buyer participates in — maybe he visits one you haven't tried yet.
- Ask whether you could have provided more information that would have been helpful or attracted more bids.

If you have a collection of rare Beanie Babies, you'll have no problem finding any number of Web sites run by people who are pretty much gaga over the little stuffed critters.

In fact, Beanies are the reason the Collectible Exchange began: Collectors visited Web pages called bulletin boards where they talked about and occasionally traded Beanies. One of the Beanie forums is shown in Figure 9-2.

Whether you sell watches, toys, or other desirable goodies, don't expect buyers to magically find your auction site. Actively seek out your niche in the market to find people who are even more eager to find you than you are to find them.

Yahoo! maintains a Web page index of collector's clubs and publicizes it right on the front page of Yahoo! Auctions. You can check it out at `clubs.yahoo.com/Hobbies_Crafts`.

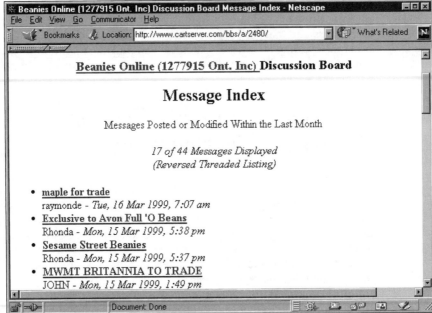

Figure 9-2:
Dull-looking
Web pages
full of mes-
sages about
specialized
topics are
exactly the
right places
to locate
potential
bidders.

Helping bidders find you via BidFind

BidFind (www.bidfind.com) is a search service specializing in Internet auction sites. (A *search service* is a Web site that indexes the contents of Web
pages so users can search for specific contents contained on those pages.) If
you run your own Web page auction, you can use BidFind to help attract business to your site. Search services like BidFind follow the model started in the
Web's infancy by Yahoo! They work like this:

✔ You make sure that your site is listed on BidFind (see "Using your headings
   to get listed" and "Creating a megalist page" to find out how to do this).

✔ The search service makes use of a special computer program sometimes
   mischievously referred to as a *spider, robot,* or *agent.* Whatever it's
   called, the program automatically travels from Web site to Web site,
   recording the contents of Web pages.

✔ Exactly what the program records differs from service to service, but
   the differences are important to understand. Some sites index the first
   50 or so words on each Web page. Others make note of key headings.
   BidFind indicates that the "quality of the keywords in your item titles" is
   especially important.

You can increase your chances of having your auction Web page listed on BidFind by making sure that your item is listed on one of the auction sites that BidFind indexes regularly. It also helps if you have as many specific item names in your listing title as possible and avoid abbreviations. For example, "1966 Ford Galaxie 500 with 304 V-8 and air-conditioning" is better than "66 Ford Gal. 500, 304 V-8, a-c."

✔ All the data that the program gathered is indexed and stored on one or more powerful computers. A visitor to the search service's Web site enters search terms in a Web page form and submits them to the site, where another computer program scours the index for Web pages that contain the terms you are seeking.

Your job as Internet auction seller is to make sure that people find your sales when they search on BidFind. The BidFind Services page (`www.bidfind.com/af/af-spon.html`) includes some tips, and I go through some of the more important tips in the following sections.

If you're selling a few items at eBay or another auction house, skip to the "Create a megalist page" section later in this chapter. BidFind is primarily designed to keep track of full-fledged auction businesses, although these can include the individual who conducts his own specialized auction on a Web page.

Use your head (ings) to get listed

Here are some suggestions for increasing your chances of getting listed on BidFind — thus increasing traffic to your auction listings:

✔ **You have to have an auction site.** (And your site can't deal in X-rated material.)

✔ **List a lot of items.** The more listings you have, the more exposure you get.

✔ **Use effective keywords.** Remember that the indexing is performed by a robot, not a human being; use nouns that clearly denote what you're selling.

✔ **Use high-level headings.** Search programs often look for headings formatted as Heading 1 in the HTML (HyperText Markup Language, the set of instructions used to format Web pages) category. Use these rather than snappy GIF (Graphics Interchange Format, a graphic image format used on the Web) images for your headings. (See Chapter 7 for explanations of HTML and image formats.) Don't use many levels of subheadings, like this:

```
Pez Dispensers (Heading 1)
Cartoon Character Pez Dispensers (Heading 2)
Daffy Duck in Pez (Heading 3)
Mickey Mouse in Pez (Heading 3)
```

These levels look well-organized, but they force the visitor to move from one section or Web page to another to find individual auction listings. To maximize your chances of being listed on BidFind, use the standard categories BidFind lists at www.bidfind.com/af/af-catlist.html.

Create a megalist page

BidFind wants your listings. What's your first clue? It provides auction sellers with a Web page template called a "megalist." You can use this template to create your own "megalist" of items you have for sale. Unfortunately, once you create the list, you can't rush over to BidFind and tell them to include your index. You can't e-mail the list to BidFind, either. All you can do is post the list online and wait for BidFind to index it.

For example, say you have ten items for sale at a Web page located at www.myauction.com/~mystuff.html. How do you create a megalist that maximizes their chances of being listed on BidFind? Follow these steps:

The following example takes a big step over the boundary between User-Friendly Stuff into the land of Serious Geek Material. It definitely helps if you are comfortable with HyperText Markup Language (HTML). If you aren't, check out one of the many books on the subject, such as *HTML For Dummies* 3rd Edition, by Ed Tittel and Stephen N. James, published by IDG Books Worldwide, Inc.

1. **Create a simple text-only document. In Windows, the obvious text-editor choice is Notepad; on the Mac, use SimpleText.**

   A new blank text editing window opens.

2. **Insert the *Internet Auctions For Dummies* CD-ROM into your disk drive.**

3. **Choose File⇨Open from your text editor's menu bar.**

   The Open dialog box appears.

4. **Locate your CD-ROM drive. (Drive D: on most Windows computers.)**

   If you're using Notepad, click the arrow next to the Look In drop-down list box near the top of the Open dialog box and select D: from the list of disk drives and other resources. Then click Open.

   On the Mac, choose File⇨Open. When the Finder dialog box appears, click the Desktop button. Select your CD-ROM drive and then click the Open button.

   A list of files on the CD-ROM appears in the Open dialog box (or, on the Mac, the Finder's dialog box).

5. **Open the MEGALIST.TXT file, which should be on the top level of the CD-ROM.**

The contents of the file open in your text editor window and look like this:

```
<HTML>
<HEAD>
<TITLE>BidFind MegaList for My Stuff</TITLE>
</HEAD>
<BODY>
<A HREF="MySite.com/ItemId=1001">ITEM
          NAME</A><PRICE>$XXX<CAT>CATEGORY<ENDS>END DATE
          here<BR>
<A HREF="MySite.com/ItemId=1002">ITEM
          NAME</A><PRICE>$XXX<CAT>CATEGORY<ENDS>END DATE<BR>
<A HREF="MySite.com/ItemId=1003">ITEM
          NAME</A><PRICE>$XXX<CAT>CATEGORY<ENDS>END DATE<BR>
</BODY>
</HTML>
```

Does this look like gobbledygook to you? Don't be frightened — it's only HTML, the markup language you've been using all along to locate information on the World Wide Web, probably without even realizing it. I provide you with the text for three separate items. Just don't change any of the HTML commands, like <HTML>, <HEAD>, and so on. You need only replace my "placeholder" text with your own listing information, as shown in the following steps.

6. **In the line that begins with** `<TITLE>`, **replace** `"My Stuff"` **with your own site's name, such as "Bert's Auction House" or "Meg's Beanie Babies."**

7. **In the first line that begins with** `<A HREF`, **replace** `"MySite.com"` **with the URL for the Web page containing the auction item you describe on this line. Also replace the ItemID, ITEM NAME, PRICE, CATEGORY, and END DATE with your own information.**

Use one of the categories included on BidFind's list. For example, if your first item is a Ming Dynasty Vase selling for $1,000 until 10/21 and is located at http://www.myauction.com/mystuff.html, use BidFind's Antiques:Ancient category so that this line reads as follows:

```
<A HREF=" http://www.myauction.com/mystuff.html /ItemId=1001">
          Ming Dynasty Vase</A><PRICE>$1,000<CAT>ANTIQUES:
          ANCIENT<ENDS>10/21<BR>
```

Note that there are no spaces before or after the colon in ANTIQUES:ANCIENT, and enter the entire URL for your Web page, including the prefix http://.

8. **Change each line in turn. If you need more lines, copy one and paste it into your document, but make sure that you paste it before the HTML command </BODY>.**

9. **Choose File⇨Save As.**

   The Save As dialog box opens.

10. **Save your file with a filename ending in HTML, such as megalist.html. Then click Save.**

11. **Post your file on your Web site.**

   See Chapter 7 for more information about creating a Web site and posting files on it.

It takes time to get your listings indexed and listed on BidFind. If your auction items are going to be up for sale for only a week, or perhaps just a few days, there's a danger that BidFind will list them long after your sales are over. If you create a megalist, make sure you update it by removing the "old" items promptly and replacing them with new sales items as they go online.

Keep BidFind coming back for more

After you put your megalist file online, you can take an additional step and apply to make your site one of those visited regularly by BidFind. You do this by visiting the Getting Your Site Listed on BidFind page (`www.bidfind.com/af/af-geton.html`) and filling out the form shown in Figure 9-3.

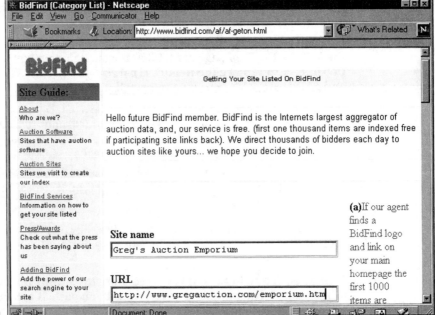

Figure 9-3: If you have an auction site, make sure you list it with BidFind so that your site is included in the BidFind index.

Reaching fanatics on newsgroups

Are you the nerdy techie type? You have plenty of soul mates on the Internet. But some people are surprised that however they define themselves, they feel at home on the Web in no time. The Internet is, in many ways, a community like any other, providing lots of places for auction hounds with similar interests to compare notes and make friends. (See Chapter 3 to find ways you can join the online auction community.)

Those same sorts of online gathering places — bulletin boards, chat rooms, and discussion groups — are some of the best places to advertise stuff to sell. Although you may not find Officer Friendly patrolling his beat, you still must follow some rules when you approach newsgroup users with a sales pitch.

Desperately seeking newsgroups

The first thing you should understand about newsgroups is that they aren't part of the Web. They're on a part of the Internet called Usenet, short for the User's Network, which predates the Web and has its own addressing scheme.

Here, as in my discussions about other areas of Internet technology, I provide only a brief overview. For the detailed ins and outs of Usenet, newsgroups, and other online discussion forums, check out books such as *The Internet For Dummies,* 6th Edition, by John R. Levine, Carol Baroudi, and Margaret Levine Young, published by IDG Books Worldwide.

Newsgroups on Usenet are arranged in hierarchical fashion. Look under the `alt.collecting` tree for groups such as these:

```
alt.collecting.barbie
alt.collecting.beanie-babies
alt.collecting.stamps
rec.antiques
rec.collecting
```

If your newsgroup software gives you the ability to search for a group by name, enter a part of the name. If you do a search for the term "forsale," for example, you come up with a lengthy list of groups that exist solely to advertise computer equipment or other things that individuals are looking to sell. Here are just a few examples:

```
misc.forsale.computers.monitors
alt.ads.forsale.computers
aus.ads.forsale.computers.used
ott.forsale.computing
seattle.forsale.computers
```

One program that lets you search through discussion groups is Netscape Collabra, part of Netscape Communicator's Web browser suite. The following steps show you how to search for a group on your own news server using Collabra.

A *news server* is a computer that provides the many thousands of different Usenet newsgroups to users on a network, using news server software that recognizes Network News Transfer Protocol (NNTP). Virtually all Internet providers have a news server that collects messages and posts them so that individual users like you can access groups and read messages using a news-group client. Not all news servers provide all available newsgroups: Some don't allow any of the .alt groups because they can get silly, childish, and inappropriate.

Follow these steps to use Collabra to search for a group on your news server:

1. **With your modem connected to the Internet and Netscape Communicator running, choose <u>C</u>ommunicator⇨<u>N</u>ewsgroup from the Communicator menu bar.**

   The [news server name] - Netscape Newsgroup window opens. (Instead of [news server name], you actually see the address of your news server. In my case, it's nntp.interaccess.com.)

2. **Click the arrow next to the address of your news server.**

   A list of the newsgroups you currently subscribe to appears. My list is shown in Figure 9-4.

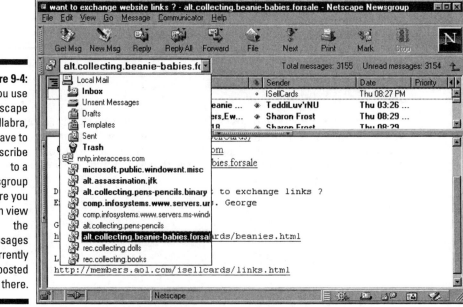

Figure 9-4: If you use Netscape Collabra, you have to subscribe to a newsgroup before you can view the messages currently posted there.

3. Subscribe to the newsgroups you're interested in.

The exact method for subscribing varies from browser to browser: In Communicator, choose File➪Subscribe from any Communicator window (Navigator, Messenger, or other applications).

The Communicator: Subscribe to Newsgroups dialog box appears. For several seconds (perhaps longer, depending on the speed of your Internet connection) nothing seems to happen. Be patient. Collabra is retrieving the list of available newsgroups from your news server. The list is likely to be long (thousands of newsgroups exist). The status bar at the bottom of the Subscribe dialog box shows the progress of the retrieval. When the list is complete, it appears in the Subscribe dialog box (see Figure 9-5).

4. Scroll through the list and, when you see a group to which you want to subscribe, click the dot in the Subscribe column (or, alternately, click the Subscribe button).

The dot turns into a checkmark to indicate that you are subscribed to the selected group (refer to Figure 9-5).

5. Continue to subscribe to other groups (you can subscribe to more than one at a time). When you're done, click OK.

The Subscribe dialog box closes, and you return to the Collabra window. The names of groups to which you just subscribed are displayed when you click the arrow next to the box displaying the address of your news server.

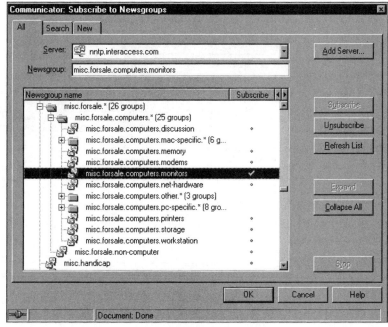

Figure 9-5:
After your browser retrieves the list of available news-groups, you can select the ones to which you want to subscribe.

6. To read a newsgroup posting, select the group from the list. Then select a message from the list of newsgroup messages.

It's a good idea to look for messages that already do what you want to do: advertise auction listings in a newsgroup posting. The message shown in Figure 9-6 does this pretty well.

Read the section "Linking to your auction pages in newsgroup postings" to find out how to link to your auction pages in postings to your newsgroups.

Posting a message to a newsgroup

Discussion group participation is a two-way street. After you get used to reading messages, you can post one of your own. Newsgroup software such as Collabra and Outlook Express gives you the choice of responding to someone else's messages and thus contributing to the series of messages called a *thread*, or posting a new message to start your own thread.

In Collabra, you reply to a message by clicking the message title in the message area of the Collabra window to select it and then clicking the Reply button in the toolbar. To post a new message, click the New Msg toolbar button. In either case, the Message Composition window opens pre-addressed to the group. Enter a title and the content of your message and then click the Send button to distribute the message to the group's members.

Linking to your auction pages in newsgroup postings

Most newsgroup programs, such as the ones built into Netscape Communicator and Microsoft Internet Explorer, are "smart" enough to know what's a Web page address and what's not. When you enter the URL

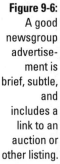

Figure 9-6:
A good newsgroup advertisement is brief, subtle, and includes a link to an auction or other listing.

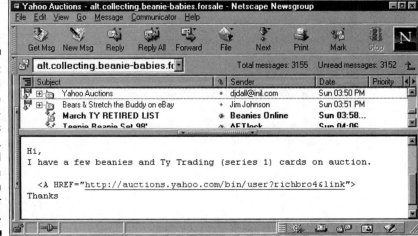

(address) for your auction Web page in a newsgroup message and include the prefix http://, the program knows to display the URL as a clickable hypertext link. A person reading your posting can click the link, and your auction Web page (or any Web page whose URL you enter) appears in his Web browser window.

If you're an eBay user and want to add a link to a newsgroup posting, just use the eBay Search Page and bring up the results you want:

- ✔ Scroll down to the Search by Seller section of the eBay Classifieds Search page and enter your own name in the box next to the Seller Search title. Click Search. A Web page appears with all the auction listings you have online currently. Copy the URL for this page from the Location box (if you use Netscape Navigator) or the Address box (Microsoft Internet Explorer). Paste the URL into your newsgroup message.

- ✔ Scroll down to the Item Lookup section of the eBay Classifieds Search page if you only need to display a link to a single auction listing. Enter the eBay item number in the Item # box. Click Search. A page appears displaying your item for sale. Copy the URL of the item and paste it into your newsgroup message.

It's a good idea to include your signature file with your newsgroup message; see Chapter 8 for instructions on how to create one.

Searching AOL's Collectibles message boards

When it comes to discussion groups for people who are passionately interested in things, don't forget America Online (AOL). This place is teeming with chat groups and message boards devoted to single topics. Often, the action on AOL is far superior to what you find in Usenet because AOL is a closed world. In other words, the people who take part in AOL discussions have to be AOL users to join, and they have to go through the effort of finding the group themselves, so they're sure to have mostly people who share their interests and not a lot of outsiders.

If you have an AOL account, you, too, can find these groups. (That doesn't mean you should spam them — that is, send unwanted advertising about your items for sale.) To find groups, follow these steps:

1. **Connect to America Online.**

   The Channels window appears.

2. **Click Interests.**

   The AOL Interests window appears.

3. **Click the Genealogy, Collecting, and eBay link.**

   The Hobbies window appears.

4. **Click the Collector's Corner link.**

   The Collecting window (Keyword:Collecting) appears. Scroll through the list of topics in the lower-left corner of the Collecting window.

5. **Double-click a topic you want to explore. When a new list appears, double-click a more specific topic. Eventually, double-click a Message Board list item (such as Beanbag Collectibles Message Board).**

   A Message Board window (see Figure 9-7) opens for the topic. At this point the interface is pretty much the same as it is for Usenet newsgroups: You can read messages, post new messages, or reply to a currently posted message.

You can find many resources for collectors and hobbyists on America Online. The preceding steps show only one way to find enthusiasts who might want to bid on your auction items. Also check out Keyword:Antiques or Keyword:Hobbies for other resources.

Reaching collectors via mailing lists

A *mailing list* is made up of a group of Internet users with similar interests. Members subscribe to a list in order to join it. They can then receive and read e-mail messages sent by other list members. Every e-mail message sent to the list is forwarded to all of its members, any of whom can send e-mail replies that can develop into text-based discussions.

Figure 9-7:
America
Online is a
lively and
rich source
for discus-
sion on
collecting
as well as
trading
many kinds
of items.

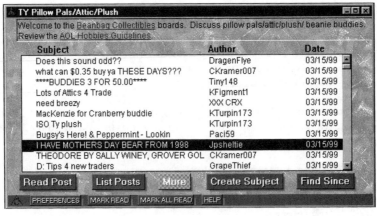

Mailing list discussions tend to be more focused than newsgroup postings because the number of subscribers is much smaller. Two types of mailing lists exist:

- **Discussion lists** are the most common mailing lists on the Internet. Members exchange messages and develop *threads*, a series of replies and counter-replies on a subject.

- **Announcement lists** provide only one-way communication: The list owner sends out news and updates about his organization.

Mailing lists are different than other resources on the Web because — well, because they aren't on the Web at all. You may see mailing lists on a Web site, discussions of especially popular groups may show up on the Web, but mailing lists are e-mail discussion groups. In order to participate, you subscribe to a group and then receive messages by e-mail.

Where, then, can you find mailing lists for collectors, such as the devoted enthusiasts who might bid on your auction items? Check out Liszt, the mailing list directory on the Web that keeps track of mailing lists and lets you search for ones that pertain to your interests (see Figure 9-8).

Figure 9-8: Lots of potential bidders: A search for "collect" on Liszt.com turns up 70 mailing lists.

Avoiding flames: Proper newsgroup and mailing list etiquette

Whether you're trying to reach potential bidders for your auctions on newsgroups or mailing lists, the same common courtesies apply.

Be sure to read the FAQ (a list of frequently asked questions) of the group or mailing list. Newsgroup FAQs are usually published somewhere in the list of currently displayed messages. Most mailing lists include instructions on how to find their FAQ when you subscribe. Became familiar with the goals and procedures of the group before you start trying to communicate. It's also a good idea to "lurk" (stay in the background, reading exchanges but not participating) for a while to get a feeling for what users like to discuss, what topics get negative responses, and who the members are.

When you're ready to start participating, consider responding to a question, rather than dropping an unsolicited announcement about your sales items. You can generate goodwill and develop a good name for yourself by providing a helpful answer. At the end of the message, your signature file can include your name, e-mail address, the items you specialize in, your Web site's URL, or even the URL of an auction item or two.

Making the World Your Oyster

Every businessperson wants to attract a wide range of customers. As an auction seller, you aren't limited to finding customers on the street where you live. In fact, you have a tremendous advantage when it comes to how far your business reaches. Although the *Inter* in the word *Internet* doesn't stand for *international,* the effect is the same. Your customer base stretches across the globe. Networks, computers, and Web browsers eliminate the restrictions of language barriers, political borders, and time zones to create a truly worldwide marketplace.

In fact, one of the most exciting moments for many online merchants occurs when they receive their first order from overseas. That's when a host of new concerns pops up, too: How do I ship this order to Australia, Norway, Mexico, or Japan? How do I accept payment? This section examines some answers to those questions.

When you're looking for places to publicize your auction items, don't forget to research auctions in other countries. If you're fluent in a foreign language and are into auctions, check out the foreign auction sites listed in this book's Internet Directory.

Don't let language be a barrier

A communication gap exists between more than adults and teenagers. Bidders who speak a different language won't understand what you're selling. It's up to you to make your auction descriptions accessible to all your potential customers.

Using slang or a local dialect may have your customers from your own hometown or region in stitches, but it can leave many more people scratching their heads and clicking on to the next site. (Consider what a translation of "putting someone in stitches" might look like!) The first rule in making your site accessible to a worldwide audience is to keep your language simple so people from all walks of life can understand you.

Your ability to make use of those auction services in Germany or other countries is greatly enhanced if you can understand exactly what those sellers are selling. Don't ask, "Why don't they provide alternate descriptions in English?" Instead, do the translation yourself. One particularly easy to use — and, by the way, free — translation utility is available from the AltaVista search service. Follow these steps to get your own instant translation:

1. **Connect to the Internet, launch your Web browser, and go to** `babelfish.altavista.com`.

   The AltaVista Translations Web page appears.

2. **If you have a specific bit of text to translate, click the text box on this page and either type or paste the text. To have the service translate an entire Web page, enter the URL in the text box. Be sure to include the first part of the URL (for example, `http://www.mysite.com` rather than just `mysite.com`).**

   The shorter and simpler the text, the better your results.

3. **Choose the translation path (that is, *from* what language *to* what language) from the Translate From drop-down menu.**

   Your selected option appears on the drop-down menu. At this writing, only English, French, Spanish, German, Italian, and Portuguese are covered by the service.

4. **Click the Translate button.**

   Almost as fast as you can say, "Welcome to the new Tower of Babel," a new Web page appears onscreen with the translated version of your text, as shown in Figure 9-9. (If you selected a Web page to translate, the Web page appears in the new language, except for the title of the page, which remains in the original language.)

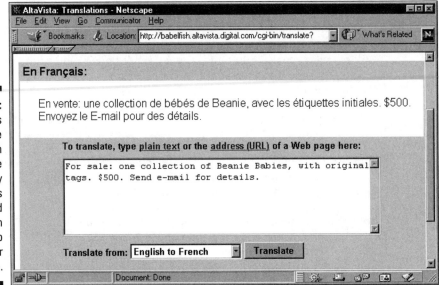

AltaVista: Translations - Netscape
File Edit View Go Communicator Help
Bookmarks   Location: http://babelfish.altavista.digital.com/cgi-bin/translate?   What's Related

En Français:

En vente: une collection de bébés de Beanie, avec les étiquettes initiales. $500.
Envoyez le E-mail pour des détails.

To translate, type plain text or the address (URL) of a Web page here:

For sale: one collection of Beanie Babies, with original
tags. $500. Send e-mail for details.

Translate from: English to French   Translate

Document: Done

Figure 9-9:
AltaVista's
online
translation
service
instantly
translates
selected
text or an
entire Web
page for
free.

Don't play hide and go seek

Web addresses don't say anything about where you come from. Although
eBay tells you where a seller is located, not all auctions do this. Be sure to
specify clearly where you are, geographically, especially if you provide sales
items on your own do-it-yourself auction Web page. That way, overseas
buyers know exactly what they're getting into: They should know, based on
the information you provide, what kinds of payments you accept, and
whether they need to send payment in U.S. dollars or send you a U.S. money
order, for example.

If you don't want to ship an item out of state or out of the country because
it's especially heavy and you want a local bidder to pick it up in person, by all
means specify this in your description.

Observe time-zone etiquette

Got the time? If you want to attract bidders from around the world, try to
schedule your auction so that it ends at a time when the largest number of
potential bidders are available. Although reserve price auctions make it
unnecessary for bidders to be present at the end, the last hour or two of an
auction sees the most action. For other kinds of sales, such as Dutch auctions
or the one-hour Express Auctions held on Onsale atAuction, bidders need to
stick around to the end to make sure they place a winning bid.

I once had to schedule a chat event so that the largest number of participants around the globe would be able to participate easily. The company that provided the chat software suggested Saturday around 2 p.m. Central Standard Time as an optimal time for the event. That way, in Europe, it's Saturday evening, while on the West Coast and as far west as Hawaii, people can still participate without having to stay up until the "wee hours."

Accepting payment: Bucks are best

The safest strategy is to request payment in U.S. dollars and to ask for the money in advance. This approach prevents any collection problems and gets you your money right away.

You can ask the high bidder to send you a personal check — or, better yet, a cashier's check — but it's up to the buyer to convert the local currency to U.S. dollars. Suggest that he obtain an International Money Order from a U.S. bank that has a branch in his area or from the post office, and specify that the money order is payable in U.S. dollars. Suggest that your customers use an online currency conversion utility like the Bloomberg Currency Calculator (www.bloomberg.com/markets/currency/currcalc.cgi) to perform the calculation.

Insurance and escrow aren't dirty words

Wherever you ship your items, make sure that you insure them for their full value. Tell your customers about any additional insurance charges up front. Finally, check that your insurance company is able to respond quickly to claims made from your own country and from your customer's country as well.

Escrow services can provide overseas buyers and sellers with an extra degree of security and reliability. The process of handling overseas transactions is basically the same as domestic sales. See Chapter 5 for more about how escrow services work.

If you're going to do a lot of business overseas, consider getting export insurance to protect yourself. Export insurance protects overseas shipments against loss due to damage or delay in transit. Policies are available from the Export-Import Bank of the United States (www.exim.gov) or from other private firms that offer export insurance.

Packaging for the long haul

If your package is going overseas, it's almost certainly going on an airplane. It'll be traveling not in a plush first-class reclining seat with a cocktail on its tray table, but in a crowded cargo hold, buffeted by lots of luggage. It may get wet and battered before it reaches its destination.

Be sure to prepare your package accordingly. Even letters should be wrapped in a cardboard mailer. Use strong tape and put it over the address to protect it from moisture. Duct tape — or do you say "duck tape"? — is not out of place here. Be sure to write the complete address in big bold letters.

To be extra careful (and get appreciative feedback from buyers) you might even want to write the address on a separate piece of paper and place it inside the package in case the outer covering is damaged and the address can no longer be read. Also be sure to put some paper or bubble wrap around items to keep them from being damaged.

Living with export restrictions

Rules aren't just for the other person, and not being aware of them doesn't make you immune to the consequences of breaking them. So, take a few minutes to check them out. If you're in the business of creating computer software or hardware, you need to be aware of restrictions that the U.S. government imposes on the export of some computer-related products.

You also can't export to certain people and places. In fact, you may incur a fine of more than $100,000 from the U.S. Treasury Department and the U.S. State Department for exporting to a Denied Person, Specially Designated National, or Restricted Country. The list of these people and countries changes frequently. Look for links to the current ones at `www.bxa.doc.gov`.

Customs that aren't just local

The good news is that you've made a big sale. The teensy little complication is that, with packages over several hundred dollars in value, customs and other regulations come into play. A visit to the Airborne Express International Documentation Requirements page (`www.airborne.com/intl/docs.htm`) indicates some of the papers that need to be filed. Here are a few examples:

 ✔ An International Express Package with a declared value requires a Commercial Invoice (four copies).

✔ A Canadian Shipment of $20 to $1,600 Canadian dollars in value requires a Value Supportive Document (three copies).

✔ A Canadian Shipment of more than $1,600 Canadian dollars in value requires a Commercial Invoice (three copies) or a Canadian Customs Invoice.

What, exactly, is a Commercial Invoice? The easy answer is that it's the form the shipping company you use has you fill out if the item you're shipping is bigger than a document and going overseas. The shipping company OCS America, Inc., has a good page on the subject with a sample of a Commercial Invoice that you can view. Go to `www.shipocs.com/howtoship/default` `.htm` and click the The Commercial Invoice link in the page's left frame.

If the item you're planning to ship overseas by mail is valued at more than $500 (or, for items that are to be shipped by other means, more than $2,500), the United States requires you to fill out and submit a Shipper's Export Declaration (SED) and submit it to a U.S. customs agent. The SED requires you to provide your name, address, and either your Social Security number or Internal Revenue Service Employer Identification Number (EIN) if you have one. You also have to describe what's being sent and where it is being sent from, and identify the ultimate destination. You can obtain an SED from your local U.S. customs office or purchase one from the Government Printing office by calling (202)783-3238. You can find detailed instructions on how to fill out the SED on the U.S. Census Bureau's Web site (`www.census.gov/` `foreign-trade/ www/correct.way.html`).

Chapter 10

Laws, Dollars, and Sense

● ●

In This Chapter

▶ Using simple accounting techniques to track your bottom line

▶ Finding user-friendly accounting software for your Internet auction business

▶ Steering clear of legal trouble

▶ Addressing privacy issues

● ●

*S*elling at auction may not seem like a "real" business. You don't have to dress for success and punch the clock. Instead, you can work in your pajamas, and the only thing that you have to punch is your mouse (so to speak).

You don't have a supervisor presenting you with a list of "things to do today" and making helpful comments about "areas where your performance could stand improvement." Rather, you're a lone adventurer surfing the seas of cyberspace, with no one looking over your shoulder and telling you what to do. Right?

Not exactly. When you sell regularly at auction, you're running an online business, and you do have to report to some Big Brother types.

If you sell a couple of family heirlooms a year and make a couple hundred bucks, will you get caught if you don't report your earnings to the IRS? No comment. On the other hand, if you post a hundred items at a given time and take in a thousand dollars or more each month, you need to keep track of your income and expenses. Uncle Sam, after all, has been known to give with one hand as he takes away with the other. Not only do you not want to get into trouble for tax evasion, but you also want to make sure you get all the tax deductions that are coming to you.

 Internet auctions themselves are by no means against the law, but some objects that have been traded on online auctions in the past (such as firearms or bootleg software) can get you into legal trouble if you try to sell them. And if you lift a cool-looking image from the Disney Web site (disney.go.com) and

Speak financial-ese like an accountant

Many people who are in business for themselves pass the torch to a professional when it comes to keeping track of financial data. Whether you decide to do it yourself or work with an accountant, here are some definitions that you should know:

✔ **Assets:** These are resources that you use to generate revenue, such as a digital camera and a computer.

✔ **Equity:** These are your remaining assets after you pay your creditors — in other words, your profits, which you retain for business purposes.

✔ **Revenue:** This is the green stuff that flows into your checking account as a result of sales.

use it to sell Mickey Mouse collectibles at auction, you could be sued for copyright infringement. This chapter discusses how you can benefit by reporting your activities to the IRS and steer clear of legal quagmires.

Debits and Credits and Ledgers, Oh My!

Capturing images of your wares, setting prices, preparing descriptions, finalizing sales, shipping items, answering questions . . . Hey, selling at auction is work enough! I know that the last thing you want to do is balance the books, but keeping careful records and setting up an accounting system can keep your auction business organized so that you can focus on selling items rather than looking for a receipt for that 600-yard-long roll of bubble wrap you bought last month.

This section points out some of the types of records you need to keep and some of the important accounting decisions you need to make if your auction hobby turns into an online business. Most of the financial information that follows applies to international auction traders as well as U.S. residents, but check with an accountant if you have a specific problem or concern.

Recording the important stuff

When you run your own business, it pays to be meticulous about recording everything pertaining to your commercial activities. The more you understand what you have to record, the more accurate your records will be — and the more tax deductions you can take, too. (You gotta love those deductions!)

Income can be gross

You need to keep careful track of your income (or, as it is sometimes called, your *gross receipts*). Not all the income you receive is taxable. What you receive as a result of sales is taxable, but loans that you receive are not. Be sure to separate the two and pay tax only on the sales income. But if you cannot accurately report the source of income that you didn't pay taxes on, the IRS will label it *unreported income,* and you will have to pay taxes and possibly fines and penalties on it.

Just how should you record your revenue? For each item, write down a brief informal statement. This is a personal record that might be on a slip of paper or even on the back of a cancelled check. Make sure you include the following:

✔ Amount you received

✔ Type of payment (credit card, electronic cash, or check)

✔ Date of the transaction

✔ Name of the winning auction bidder

✔ Goods you provided in exchange for the payment

Keeping all your check stubs and revenue statements in a folder labeled Income will help you find them easily at tax time.

Assessing your assets

Any equipment you have that contributes to your auction activities constitutes your assets. Equipment that has a life span of more than a year is expected to help you generate income over its useful life and, therefore, the "portion" of the equipment that you use in a particular year needs to have the original cost spread out (or in other words, *expensed)* over its life span. For this reason, if you purchase a computer that costs $3,000 and you expect to use it for five years, $600 of the cost is expensed each year. Expensing the cost of an asset over the period of its useful life is called *depreciation.* To depreciate an item, you estimate how many years you're going to use it and then divide the original cost by the number of years. The result is the amount that you report in any given year.

The trick is that you probably use your computer for many things other than auction sales. Legally, you need to reduce the amount you depreciate by a corresponding amount. If you use the computer mentioned in the previous example 30 percent of the time for auctions and 70 percent of the time for fun and games, for example, reduce your depreciation to $200 per year.

You need to keep records of your assets that include the following information:

✔ Name, model number, and description

✔ Purchase date

✔ Purchase price, including fees

✔ Date the item went into service

✔ Amount of time the item is put to personal (as opposed to business) use

File these records away in a safe location such as a filing cabinet along with your other tax-related information so you can have them not only at tax time but also in the future, in case you are audited.

Checking your list of expenses

In general, business expenses include travel, equipment, and other costs that you incur in order to *produce revenue.* This is in contrast to instances when you're just exchanging one asset (cash) for another (a printer or modem, for example). That is not an expense. The difference is that in the second case, the act of spending the money does not directly result in more revenue for you — even though the equipment being purchased will *eventually* help you produce revenue.

What is an expense? Some examples would be gas and other travel costs (you have to get to flea markets and garage sales and transport the treasures you purchase, don't you?), as well as postage. Get a big folder and use it to hold any receipts, contracts, canceled checks, credit card statements, or invoices that represent expenses.

An online businessperson needs to pay an ISP and perhaps a Web host. If you take on partners or employees, things get more complicated. But in general, you need to record all payments such as these in detail:

✔ Date the expense occurred

✔ Name of the person or company that received payment from you

✔ Type of expense incurred (equipment, utilities, supplies, and so on)

Recalling exactly what some receipts were for is often difficult after a year has gone by, or even just a month after the fact. Be sure to jot down a quick note on all canceled checks and copies of receipts to remind you of what the expense involved.

Choosing a method for this madness

Accepting that you have to keep track of your business's accounting is only half the battle. You also have to choose an accounting method. The point at which you make note of each transaction in your books, and the period of time over which you record the data either electronically or by hand, make a difference not only to your accountant but also to agencies like the Internal Revenue Service. Even if you hire someone to keep the books for you, it's good to know what options are open to you.

Cash-basis versus accrual-basis: Who's accounting?

Don't be intimidated by these terms. They're simply two methods of totaling income and expenses:

- **Cash-basis accounting:** You report income when you actually receive it and write off expenses when you pay them. This is the easy way to report income and expenses, and probably the way most small-business owners do it.

- **Accrual-basis accounting:** This method is more complicated than the cash-basis method, but if your online business maintains an inventory, you must use the accrual method. You report income when you actually receive the payment, and you write down expenses when services are rendered. Cash payment may not have been received or paid out yet. In other words, you may record an expense before the check actually goes out. For instance, if a payment is due on December 1 but you don't send the check out until December 8, you record the bill as being paid on December 1, when the payment was originally due. Accrual-basis accounting creates a more accurate picture of a business's financial situation.

Choosing to account . . . period

The other choice you need to make when it comes to deciding how to keep your books is the accounting period you're going to use. Here, again, you have two choices:

- **Calendar year:** Under this common accounting period, the fiscal year ends on the same date as the calendar year: December 31. This is the period with which you're probably most familiar, and the one most small or home-based businesses choose, because it's the easiest to work with.

- **Fiscal year:** In this case, the business picks a date other than December 31 to function as the end of the fiscal year. Many large organizations pick a date that coincides with the end of their business cycle. Some choose March 31 as the end, others June 30, and still others September 30, though you can choose whatever end date you want.

 If you use the fiscal-year method of accounting, you must file your tax return three and a half months after the end of the fiscal year. If the fiscal year ends on June 30, for example, you must file by October 15. If you use the calendar-year method, you must file by April 15.

Accounting Software Makes It Easy

What's that? You took Accounting 101 in high school 20 years ago? You already know everything there is to know about recording debits and credits in a ledger and depreciating equipment?

Well, yeah, but times have changed. The difference is that some neat tools are now available to make the job easier. You can use your computer to record your income as well as calculate deductions for the expenses needed to generate that income. You can go online to get instructions on what you need to record. You can also use some cool software tools that crunch numbers for you as fast as a financial cookie monster.

Financial dummies like you and me can get plenty of helpful hints from other Dummies books, including *Taxes For Dummies 1999* by Eric Tyson and David J. Silverman, *Law For Dummies* by John Ventura, and *Small Business Kit For Dummies* by Richard Harroch and Jerome S. Engel, all published by IDG Books Worldwide. Well-known commercial accounting packages such as QuickBooks and MYOB let you prepare statements and reports, and even tie into a tax preparation system. Stick with these programs if you like setting up systems such as databases on your computer. Otherwise, go for a simpler method, and hire an accountant to help you.

Whatever program you choose, make sure that you're able to do the following:

- ✔ Keep accurate books.
- ✔ Set up privacy schemes that prevent your kids, roommates, or pets from zapping your business records.

Nothing's wrong with keeping the books by buying an old-fashioned ledger or journal and recording the data by hand. Doing your bookkeeping the low-tech way may seem simpler. But high-tech programs can help you in the long term.

The big commercial bean counters

A good software package can cut down on the time you spend on accounting and tax preparation for your small businesses. The well-known packages described in this section have plenty of helpful features and add-ons. Programs like Microsoft Money and Quicken, for example, let you create customizable Web pages that you can configure to provide up-to-the minute reports on your stock holdings. They also help you with financial planning. All let you record income and expenses and prepare business reports.

Be sure to shop around to get the best package for your individual needs. Although some users like to buy a reliable commercial program right off the bat, others like to try out inexpensive shareware accounting programs that you can download from the Web. Two of them, Simple Business Invoicing & Inventory and Simple Business Accounting by OWL Software, are included on this book's CD-ROM.

Simple software for small-scale businesses

Two well-known software packages from Microsoft and Intuit are easy to use but are mainly suitable for financial planning, checkbook balancing, and stock watching. If you have a small-scale business and need to manage a simple set of income and expenses, these programs may be just right for you:

- **Microsoft Money 99 Financial Suite** (www.microsoft.com/products/prodref/699_ov.htm). One of Microsoft Money's distinguishing features is its level of integration with the Internet. You can get automatic updates on stock prices and other information. The program has a list price of $64.95.

- **Quicken Home and Business 99** (www.quicken99.com). This program is available for Windows 95 or 98. (A separate program, Quicken 98, is available for Macintosh users at www.intuit.com/quicken98.) The business features that come with the program include invoicing, business reports, and basic accounts payable and receivable. The list price is $89.95.

More powerful software for businesses with inventory

Although the programs in the prevous section are primarily personal checkbook managers, the following three programs are more useful if your needs include managing an inventory.

Often, these programs require you to fill out simple business forms. After you enter the data, the software assumes the role of accountant and crunches numbers in the background in order to prepare reports of your business activities.

You can find an in-depth comparison of ten accounting packages at www.smalloffice.com/expert/archive/tebuyer79.htm.

- **QuickBooks 99** (www.quickbooks.com). This program, which is available for Windows 95/989/NT users, is frequently praised as being one of the simplest and easiest-to-learn accounting programs, especially for those with no prior accounting experience (see Figure 10-1). QuickBooks 99 is available for $119.95 on the Intuit, Inc. Web site.

- **MYOB Accounting Plus** (http://www.myob.com/us/home1.htm). This program, by MYOB US Inc., comes in versions for the Mac and Windows. It is intuitive and uses flowcharts rather than forms to help you organize data. The program's estimated retail price is $179 for the Windows version and $199 for the Macintosh version. You can order a trial CD-ROM version that you can use for 25 sessions only. You can view the system requirements for all versions at http://www.myob.com/ us/products/plus/myob_sysreqs.htm.

✔ **Peachtree Office Accounting** (www.peachtree.com). This powerful program offers very strong features for a complex business operation. Sole proprietors who are afraid of accounting and looking for the simplest possible interface may find that Peachtree has more features than they need; on the other hand, this is a $99 program that you and your business can grow into.

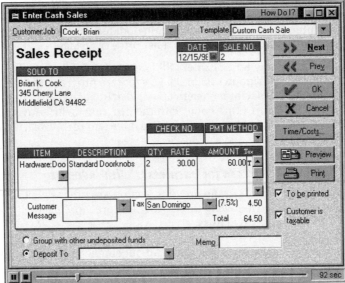

Figure 10-1:
The trial versions of QuickBooks on this book's CD can help you record personal or business transactions.

Shareware programs on the cheap

Many of the commercial accounting packages listed in the previous section aren't available in trial versions. You can't always go to a Web site, download the program, and try it out. (A CD-ROM-based trial version of MYOB is available, but you have to wait for it to come in the mail.) If you're in a hurry and are looking for an accounting program that you can set up right now, look no further than the programs included on this book's CD-ROM, including Owl Simple Business Accounting.

Simple Business Accounting by Owl Software (www.owlsoftware.com) really lives up to its name. It's so simple that even a financially impaired person like yours truly can pick it up quickly. Owl Simple Business Accounting (SBA) is designed to let people with no prior accounting experience keep track of income and expenses. The main Owl Simple Business Accounting window is shown in Figure 10-2.

After entering some data, you can select the Report Generation tab, run each of the reports provided by SBA, and examine the output. SBA can generate: Expense Reports, Income Reports, Profit Reports, and a General Ledger Report. When running the reports, be sure to select a reporting period (calendar year or fiscal year, as explained in the section "Choosing to account . . . period," earlier in this chapter).

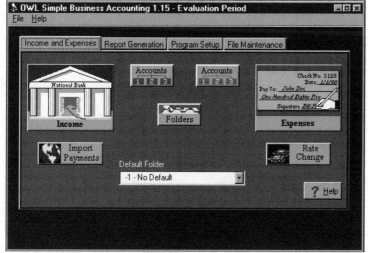

Figure 10-2:
Owl Simple Business Accounting uses folders to contain income and expense data that you report.

Accounting help online

In a 1998 American Express survey of 300 small-business owners, nearly 75 percent of all participants reported that they pass tax work on to professional accountants. You may decide to secure professional help, too, so you can concentrate on obtaining stock and selling it at auction.

Keep in mind, however, that anyone you hire to keep your books or prepare your tax returns will have access to virtually all of your financial information. If you're reluctant to entrust someone with that level of responsibility, look for some free instruction and support on the Web itself. Here are a few sites you can visit for some good starter information for budding cyber-accountants:

- **Entrepreneur's Help Page.** This Web site, which is full of useful information for online entrepreneurs, includes a Financial Records page (www.tannedfeet.com/html/financial_records.htm) that discusses the basics of accounting for lone entrepreneurs like yourself.

- **Accounting Over Easy.** A CPA created this Web site (www.ezaccounting.com) devoted to making accounting easy to learn for small-business owners. He charges a one-time fee of $9.95 for access to most of the content. You can view a preview page for free, however.

Should you hire an accountant?

Hiring someone at least to help you with your taxes and advise you from time to time on financial planning may be a good idea. Enlisting the help of an accountant can be particularly helpful if you're self-employed and don't have sources of financial advice through your place of employment.

How do you find an accountant? I found mine through a personal recommendation, which is always a good way to find professionals. Here are some things to look for:

✔ **Look for a CPA.** Of the two groups of accountants — Public Accountants and Certified Public Accountants (CPAs) — CPAs are the best-qualified candidates.

✔ **Try a small accounting firm rather than going to a big corporate firm.** The small players probably have more experience with small-business concerns, and they tend to charge lower fees, too.

✔ **Get recommendations.** If you can't find a personal recommendation, ask your state CPA society for a list of accountants in your area.

When you interview accountants, ask whether they work with any Internet-based clients.

Taxing Concerns for Auction Sellers

The point of all your recordkeeping is, in part, to get some tax breaks. A little preparation up front can save you lots of headaches down the road. But as a hard-working entrepreneur, time is your biggest obstacle.

In an American Express survey, 26 percent of small-business owners reported that they wait until the last minute to start preparing their taxes, and 13.9 percent said that they usually ask for an extension. Yet advance planning is really important for taxes. In fact, Internal Revenue Code Section 6001 mandates that businesses must keep records appropriate to their trade or business. The IRS has the right to view these records if it wants to audit your business's (or your personal) tax return. If your records aren't to the IRS's satisfaction, the penalties can be serious.

One good piece of news is that in October 1998, Congress passed and the president signed into law a tax package that includes a three-year freeze on new taxes on Internet access and e-commerce. You can read the text of the law at www.house.gov/chriscox/nettax/lawsums.html. Your legislators are trying to help you; your job is to educate yourself about the new laws so you can help yourself come tax time.

Rendering to Caesar at federal and state levels

Although operating a business does complicate your tax return, you can handle the complication if your business is a simple one-person operation, if you are willing to expend the time, and, finally, if you have kept the proper business records.

The following information applies only to U.S. readers; readers from other countries should consult their financial advisors for more information.

Federal taxes

If you have a sole proprietorship (in other words, you're in business for yourself and don't have a corporation), you need to file Schedule C along with your regular form 1040 tax return. If your sole proprietorship has net income, you're also required to file Schedule SE to determine any Social Security and FICA taxes that are due.

State taxes

State taxes vary depending on where you live. You most likely need to file forms for both sales tax you collect and income tax you have paid (or have to pay). If you have employees, you also need to pay employee withholding tax. Contact a local accountant in order to find out what you have to file, or contact the state tax department yourself. Most state tax offices provide guidebooks to help you understand state tax requirements.

A page full of links to state tax agencies is available at www.tannedfeet.com/html/state_tax_agencies.htm.

Deducing your deductions

One of the benefits of going into business for yourself, even if the business isn't profitable in the beginning, is the opportunity to take business deductions and reduce your tax payments. Always keep receipts from any purchases or expenses associated with your auction activities and make sure that you take all the deductions for which you are eligible. I mention some of these deductions in the following sections.

Your home office can pay off

If you work at home (and I'm assuming that, as an entrepreneur, you probably do), set aside some space for a home office. This isn't just a territorial thing. It can result in some nifty business deductions, too.

Making quarterly tax payments

When you start making money for yourself independently rather than depending on a regular paycheck from an employer, you have to start doing something you've probably never done before, but that's an important part of meeting your tax obligations as a self-employed person. That is, you have to start estimating the tax you will have to pay based on the income from your own business. You're required to pay this tax on a quarterly basis to both the IRS and your state taxing agency.

The IRS and your state taxing office provide you with instructions for calculating how much tax you will have to pay. (If you have an accountant, that person will help you determine how much to pay.) You file a 1040-ES form and send a check for the required amount every quarter. You have to do the same on the state level, but the required forms vary by state. Check out IRS publication 505 (www.irs.ustreas.gov/prod/forms_pubs/pubs/p5050205.htm) for the official word on the subject.

Taking a home-office deduction used to be difficult, because a 1993 Supreme Court decision stated that, unless you met with clients, customers, or patients on a regular basis in your home office, you couldn't claim the home-office deduction. However, the 1997 tax law eliminates the client requirement and requires only that the office be used "regularly and exclusively" for business. You can read more about the change at www.dtonline.com/promises/chap8.htm.

What you deduct depends on the amount of space in your home that is used for your business. If your office is one room in a four-room house, you can deduct 25 percent of your utilities, for example. If you have a separate phone line that is solely for business use, you are able to deduct 100 percent of that expense.

Counting on your computer equipment

Computer equipment is probably the biggest expense related to your auction activities, but taking tax deductions can help offset the cost substantially. The key is showing the IRS (by reporting your income from auction sales on your tax return) that your PC and related items, such as modems or printers, were used for business purposes.

In case you're ever audited, be sure to keep some sort of record detailing all the ways in which you have put your computer equipment to use for business purposes. If less than half of your computer use is for your business, consider depreciating its cost over several years.

Tiptoe through tax tips online

The best place on the Internet for tax information (and one of the best resources online) is the IRS's own Web site. The home page is at www.irs.ustreas.gov, but check out its index of pages specifically for businesses (www.irs.ustreas.gov/prod/bus_info/index.html).

Here are some other tax-resource sites you can visit:

✔ **1040.com** (www.1040.com). This site, operated by Drake Software, contains some resources that you won't find on the IRS's Web site, including a tax-related bulletin board, a database of tax preparers, and links to state tax agencies.

✔ **Tax News and Views** (www.dtonline.com/tnv/tnv.htm). If a question arises about the latest tax provisions and you need to look up the answer quickly, try this publication, which is produced by Deloitte & Touche LLP.

Other smart deductions

Many of the business-related expenses that you can deduct are listed on IRS form Schedule C. The following is a brief list of some of the deductions you can look for:

✔ **Internet access charges.** You may be able to deduct monthly fees you pay to your ISP or Web host.

✔ **Computer supplies.** All the equipment you use to operate your online business counts.

✔ **Shipping and delivery.** You can deduct any costs associated with shipping and postage.

✔ **Auction transaction fees.** You can deduct costs required to sell items at auction, such as escrow service fees and auction services' fees for listing items.

✔ **Office supplies.** Your paper, toner or ink cartridges, paper clips, and other costs can be deducted.

✔ **Utilities.** You can deduct the light, electricity, and telephone costs that pertain to your home office.

✔ **Accountants' fees.** Any fees you pay to the person who adds up your deductions are themselves deductible, too.

Do you have a license for that?

You may not have Corp. or Inc. after your business name. Maybe you don't even have a business name. You and I also know that, behind the doors of many residences in your city or town, many individuals run successful home-based businesses.

Nevertheless, it's my job to make you aware of everything that can come your way in terms of legal requirements and potential trouble. For one thing, you should at least be aware of any local licensing requirements that apply to people who make money from their homes. For example, in my county in the state of Illinois, I had to pay a $10 fee to register my company as a sole pro-prietorship. In return, I received a nice certificate that made everything feel official.

Other localities may have more stringent requirements. Check with city, county, and state licensing and/or zoning offices. If you fail to apply for a permit or license, you may find yourself paying substantial fines.

The kinds of local regulations to which a small business may be susceptible include:

- **Zoning.** Your city or town government may have *zoning ordinances* that prevent you from conducting a business in an area that is zoned for resi-dential use or that require you to pay a fee to operate a business out of your home. Check with your local zoning department.

- **Doing Business As.** If your business name is different from your own name, you may have to file a Doing Business As (DBA) certificate and publish a notice of the filing in the local newspaper. Check with your city or county clerk's office for more information.

- **Taxes.** Some cities and states levy taxes on small businesses, and some even levy property tax on business assets such as office furniture and (uh-oh) computer equipment.

Don't be fenced in by trade restrictions

If you're planning to sell your goods and services overseas, which is certainly a realistic possibility for auction sellers whose wares appeal to collectors or enthusiasts with a connection to the Internet, you need to be aware of any trade restrictions that may apply to your business. In particular, you need to be careful if any of the following apply:

- You trade in edible food or agricultural products.

- You sell software that uses some form of encryption (see Chapter 2 for more on this form of Internet security).

> ✔ Your clients live in countries with which your home country has imposed trade restrictions. (To find out about such restrictions for U.S. sellers, click the Trade Policy Measures on the Arent Fox Web link on the site mentioned in the following paragraph.)

The Arent Fox Web site, which is run by a Washington, D.C. -based law firm, has lots of good legal information for people who want to do business online. Of particular interest is its International Trade Legislation Monitor (www.arentfox.com/features/tradeleg/home.html), which publishes recent trade legislation and has links to past articles about trade-related issues.

All That's Fair with Copyrights

You don't want to learn for the first time about copyright law or the concept of intellectual property when you're in the midst of a dispute. This section gives you a heads-up on legal issues you need to know about as an online businessperson so you can head off trouble before it occurs.

Understanding copyright law basics

Copyright is a legal device that gives the creator of a work the right to control how the work is to be used. Copyright law covers the creator's ownership of creative works that are considered to be *intellectual property,* such as writing, art, software, video, or cinema. It provides the owner with redress in case someone copies the works without the owner's permission. But copyright laws don't protect names, titles, or short phrases. To protect yourself, you must assert copyright over your intellectual property.

Copyright notices typically identify the author or owner of what you're reading (or the software you're using) and then spell out the terms by which the owner gives you the right (or the license) to copy his work to your computer and read it (or use it).

For example, at the bottom of every eBay Web page, you see the copyright notice shown in Figure 10-3.

However, everything you see on the Net is copyrighted, whether or not a notice actually appears. For example, plenty of art is available for the taking on the Web, but look before you grab. Unless an image on the Web is specified as being copyright-free, you violate copyright law if you take it. HTML tags themselves aren't copyrighted, but the content of the HTML-formatted page is. General techniques for designing Web pages, such as a page that uses tables or one that uses frames, aren't copyrighted, but certain elements (such as logos) are.

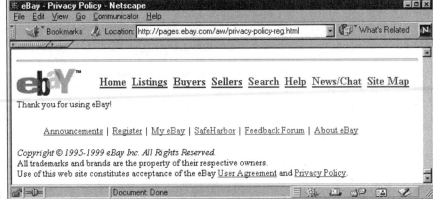

Figure 10-3:
eBay's
copyright
notice
appears on
all of its
pages.

Use policies: Are they acceptable?

Copyright law doesn't cover everything. One of the major limitations is the doctrine of "fair use," which is described in Section 107 of the U.S. Copyright Act. The law states that "fair use" of a work is use that does not infringe copyright "for purposes such as criticism, comment, news reporting, teaching (including multiple copies for classroom use), scholarship, or research."

You can't copy text from online magazines or newsletters and call the use "fair use" because the text was originally news reporting. "Fair use" has some big gray areas that can be traps for people who provide information on the Internet. Don't fall into those traps. It's not difficult to shoot off a quick e-mail asking someone for permission to reproduce her work; chances are, that person will be flattered and will let you make a copy as long as you give her credit on your site.

Standing up for your copyright

You probably don't need to copyright your individual auction listings. However, you may want to consider affixing a copyright notice to your Web pages. It makes your readers think twice about unauthorized copying and puts them on notice that you take copyright seriously. You only need to add the following notice:

```
Copyright 1999 [Your Name]
```

You don't need to use the © copyright symbol. It just makes your notice look more official. You can go a step further and register your work with the U.S. Copyright Office. To register your work, download an application form from the U.S. Copyright Office Web site. A set of forms for different types of work

(available at `lcweb.loc.gov/copyright/forms`) is in Adobe Acrobat PDF
format, so you need Acrobat Reader to view it. (Adobe Acrobat Reader is a
free application that you can download from the Adobe Systems
Incorporated Web site at `www.adobe.com`.) Download Form TX for literary
works. You send the form by snail mail, along with a check for $20 and one or
more printed copies of the work you're protecting, to Register of Copyrights,
Library of Congress, Washington, DC 20559.

If you think someone has violated your copyright, confront him by e-mail or
letter and ask him to remove what he has copied from publication. Alternatively, consult an attorney. Ultimately, you are entitled to protect your copyright against unauthorized use by filing a civil lawsuit in a federal district
court.

Maintaining Privacy

Trust, a concept I mention throughout this book, goes hand in hand with that
other emotion that makes Internet auctions viable: privacy. You depend on an
auction service to not publicize you or sell your e-mail address without your
permission. By the same token, you should maintain your buyers' privacy, too.

Protecting your privacy

eBay goes out of its way to emphasize how it protects its members' privacy.
For one thing, eBay is a member of an organization called Truste (`www.truste
.org`), which has developed a set of privacy standards for online businesses.
eBay won't sell or "rent" information about you to third parties, for example.
This doesn't mean eBay won't ever disclose your identity to third parties,
however. It just means the company is upfront about when it will do so. In
fact, eBay does track users as they move through the site and collects "information about your bidding, buying and selling behavior." eBay's full privacy
policy appears on the Web page (`pages.ebay.com/aw/privacy-policy-
reg.html`) shown in Figure 10-4.

I thought it would be interesting to see how many other auction services go
to the effort of publishing formal privacy policies. I found that few sites actually publish a Web page devoted to their privacy policies. Some don't say
anything about whether they will maintain customers' privacy. Personally, I
feel safer using companies that emphasize privacy and sign on with Truste.
The results of my admittedly unscientific survey are shown in Table 10-1.

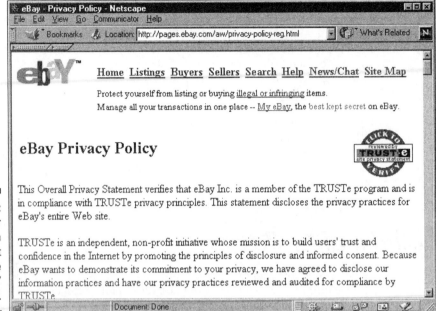

Figure 10-4:
Look for
auction
sites that
value
participants'
privacy.

Table 10-1	Privacy and Security Policies	
Service	**Privacy Statement?**	**Details**
AuctionInc.	No	
Bidder's Edge	One paragraph in FAQ (www.biddersedge.com/FAQ.html)	
eBay	Yes (pages.ebay.com/aw/privacy-policy.html)	Member of Truste
iEscrow	No	Uses secure login and is a bonded business
The Sharper Image	Yes (auction.sharperimage.com/os/info_page.shtml)	
TradeSafe	No	President is former attorney general of Rhode Island
u-Auction-it	No	Emphasizes "caveat emptor" (let the buyer beware)

Service	Privacy Statement?	Details
utrade	Yes (`www.utrade.com/home/privacy.htm`)	Member of Truste
Yahoo! Auctions	yes (`www.yahoo.com/info/privacy`)	Member of Truste

Protecting buyers' privacy

Yes, you should leave feedback for someone, using the appropriate feedback area on an auction site. No, you shouldn't send a mass e-mailing to all the auction customers you can find, telling them someone's personal information.

What about posting bulletin board or discussion group messages about an individual user? You should only do this if you've really been swindled by someone and you have no other recourse. Even then, you're technically invading that person's privacy.

Why should you bother respecting privacy? Call it healthy self-interest: A good reputation and trust will keep you selling online for months or years to come.

Here are some other ways to respect your customers' privacy:

✔ Don't use someone's real name without his or her permission. Stick to the username by which the individual is known online.

✔ Don't put out address or phone numbers without someone's knowledge. Be sure not to sell or give out someone's contact information to a mailing list or newsgroup, either.

Online cookie monsters?

Cookies are part of many Web sites, and you should know what they are and whether to accept them.

An *HTTP cookie* is a bit of information that is transmitted from a server (the computer that stores information on a Web site to which you connect) to your own Web browser. If the cookie is accepted by the Web browser (and most of the latest Web browsers give users the option of declining cookies), it allows the server to "remember" something about the browser. The next time your browser visits the site that issued the cookie, the server retrieves the information on the cookie that it sent earlier. With this information, the server can identify the user.

Should you be worried about a Web site sending a cookie to your computer so it can track you? Probably not. No one's going to come knocking on your door asking for you because of your cookie. Cookies don't record sensitive information like credit card numbers. They can make it more convenient for you to revisit a Web site. The site remembers what you purchased in the past and saves you the trouble of re-registering again. If you're really worried about cookies and want to "block" them, consult your browser's Help files to find out how to do this.

The *Internet Auctions For Dummies* Internet Directory

The 5th Wave

By Rich Tennant

"Cool! My last-second snipe bid for that Swiss chalet you and Mom were admiring earlier made it through."

In This Directory . . .

When it comes to finding sources of support as you start using Internet auctions, the best place to turn is the Internet itself. The *Internet Auctions For Dummies* Internet Directory is a comprehensive yellow pages full of Web sites and other resources that can help you.

- ✔ Compare prices
- ✔ Understand your consumer rights
- ✔ Find auction sales for special types of merchandise
- ✔ Use portals and search engines to locate auction services
- ✔ Locate software to help you format auction listings and Web page content

The *Internet Auctions For Dummies* Internet Directory

● ●

*T*he *Internet Auctions For Dummies* Internet Directory is divided into four sections:

✔ The sites in the first section offer general advice and precautions that will be of interest to anyone wanting to buy or sell at auction.

✔ The second section gives URLs and descriptions of auction sites. I introduce the largest general-merchandise sites and also include a section designed for those of you who are looking for bargains on particular specialty items.

✔ If you can't find the item you're looking for, you can check out the auction site guides and search engines in the third section.

✔ The sites in the last section provide helpful information for business-people who want to get into the auction business or who want to market their products online.

To help you judge at a glance whether a site may be useful for you, this directory includes some handy miniature icons (otherwise known as *micons*). Here's what each micon means:

$ You have to pay an *extra* registration fee to access some services at this site, in addition to the standard fee for posting an item for sale or the commission charged by an auction house when a sale is made. (Virtually all auction houses charge these standard fees, so they aren't noted.)

⟲   This site gives users a way to register buyer or seller feedback, both positive and negative. Many experienced auction sellers regard feedback as an important way to discourage buyers or sellers from committing fraud or backing out of sales.

▯   This site gives you a chance to talk to fellow entrepreneurs, business authorities, or potential customers online.

�’   You can download software or other files at this site.

This site has particularly good hyperlinks that can lead you to other auction outlets or related resources.

This site lets you put up items for sale.

This site allows you to bid on items.

Worthy of a four-star rating, this site is a particularly valuable resource due to its content, links, free software, or all of these.

This site features a search function that lets you look for items at other auction houses, as well as the current one.

People on a tight budget can benefit from discounts and money-saving resources at this site.

General Auction-Related Advice and Resources

Before you venture onto the auction sites I list in this directory, find out how to avoid overpriced merchandise, scam artists, and other Internet hazards. The following sections offer information on comparing prices, using escrow services (to ensure that you get your merchandise before you pay for it), and avoiding consumer fraud. And if you find yourself spending a little too much time and money online, check out the section about online counseling.

Comparison shopping

An informed bidder is likely to get a good deal. One of the best ways to get information is to compare prices of auction items before you even place a bid. Know what constitutes a good deal before you place your first bid. Here are some online resources where you can check prices before you start bidding.

PriceScan

www.pricescan.com

Find the lowest price on any item. PriceScan is an organization dedicated to providing accurate, reliable price information for consumers who are shopping online. Categories of goods covered include books, computers, electronics, movies, music, and video games. The company declares that no vendors pay to be listed, and that coverage includes online and offline businesses. By entering specifications (such as amount of RAM if you're looking for a computer) into a search engine, you can do a price comparison of "functionally equivalent" merchandise.

Consumer protection resources

Better Business Bureau

www.bbb.org

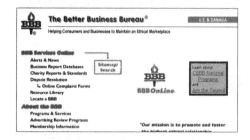

A watchdog agency for online (and offline) business. The site features services, alerts, and news about the newest fraud information; a business report database; charity reports and standards to help you differentiate legit charities from bogus ones; online complaint forms you can use to air your personal grievance with a particular company and a large search engine to help you find information on a particular business. You may become a member of the Better Business Bureau on this site as well. All in all, this is an indispensable tool for both consumers and businesspeople.

Consumer Fraud Alert Network

worldusa.com/fraudalert

A good place to check out legal decisions regarding consumer fraud both online and offline. Scanning the headlines provided on the site's home page can alert you to some organizations you may want to watch out for in the future. The site suggests agencies you can turn to if you feel you have been defrauded, such as the Better Business Bureau (see the previous listing), the Federal Trade Commission, and more. On the downside, the site hadn't been updated in nearly a year when I visited it.

Consumer World

www.consumerworld.org

A great consumer resource for buying advice, product reviews, and other information. Consumer World is a nonprofit site that has gathered many consumer resources that are available on the Internet and has consolidated them for easier access. You can find buying advice and product reviews, comparison shop for bargains, file a consumer complaint with the consumer affairs department of the BBB, read consumer rights booklets, look up wholesale prices, get personal finance tips, and conduct research on the law or a particular company. This site is useful for more general queries about Internet business practices or personal financial advice.

National Fraud Information Center

www.fraud.org

A good place to turn if you suspect you are the victim of Internet fraud. The National Fraud Information Center was originally established to fight telemarketing fraud and now has branched out into other areas of business, including the Internet. The Internet Fraud watch provides you with reports of suspected fraud by online agencies. If you contact the National Fraud Information Center with a suspected fraud, it will investigate for you and, if your claim is legitimate, will help you contact the appropriate government agencies to deal with the problem. Information is available in Spanish or English. This site also features links, news, and specific information about fraud for the elderly (the segment of the population most vulnerable to fraud). This site is good if you have a specific complaint.

NetStoppers: Avoiding Scams

**www.zdnet.com/yil/content/mag/9711/
netstoppers.html**

Find out how to spot Internet scams. This article in ZDNet's NetStopper's column focuses on scam artists and how to avoid them online.

Public Eye

**www.zdnet.com/chkpt/adstlink/www.
zdnet.com/zdtv/moneymachine/
moneyminute/story/
0,3666,2127182,00.html**

This site helps you with money issues regarding the Internet. This site mostly provides information on how to buy on the Internet. It addresses issues such as how to find the best bargain, how to make sure that your financial information is secure, and how to invest online. This site is best for those who want to comparison shop for the best price on an item or who just want advice on how to shop online.

Other Sites to Check Out

www.ftc.gov/bcp/bcp.htm
www.pueblo.gsa.gov
www.whitehouse.gov/WH/
Services/consum.html

Escrow services

i-Escrow Inc.

www.iescrow.com

A popular escrow site that eBay uses. After the auction is completed and the buyer and seller are in agreement, the buyer pays i-Escrow. i-Escrow then informs the seller and instructs her to send the goods to the buyer. Once the buyer has received and approved the merchandise, a check is sent to the seller within five days. The schedule of fees charged by i-Escrow is rather complicated, but what it boils down to is that users have to pay $5 to i-Escrow for items that sell for $100 or less, while items that sell for $100.01 to $5,000 carry a fee of $12.50. By default, the buyer pays the fee, though this can be negotiated by buyer and seller.

TradeSafe

www.tradesafe.com

A more expensive, but still good escrow alternative. TradeSafe's escrow procedure works pretty much the same as i-Escrow's, but fees charged are higher. Items that sell for $400 or less carry a fee of $15 (if you pay TradeSafe in money order or check) or $12 (if you pay by credit card). Items that sell for $401 to $1,300 pay a percentage plus a flat fee. A $5,000 sale costs $95 if you pay TradeSafe by credit card or a whopping $224 if you pay in cash.

Internet addiction counseling

Online auctions can be addictive. Here is a resource to check out if you find you're getting carried away and are in need of counseling:

Center for Online Addiction

www.netaddiction.com/clinic.htm

E-mail counseling, chat room counseling, and telephone counseling for Internet addiction. Internet addiction is a relatively unrecognized condition that can afflict those that use the Internet. The center is run by a clinical psychologist who established the first clinic to help people deal with Internet addiction. This site also has links to books, resources, and events addressing Internet addiction. This is a cheaper alternative to going to a traditional psychology clinic.

Merchandise for Sale

Although a growing number of auctions specialize in everything from postage stamps to travel packages, the dividing line isn't a clear one. If you're trying to find a specific brand or model of a common product, shop around at the auction sites that offer general merchandise. If you are looking for a collectible or specialty item (such as a rare book, a classic car, or a computer printer), you can browse the sites dedicated to specific types of goods, which I list later in this section.

Absentee/telephone bid auction houses

Many traditional auction houses, such as the venerable Christie's, still conduct their bidding by telephone or in person. However, they now allow customers to view the catalog online, but the bidder must submit an absentee bid. These well-established companies are full of experts in many fields, and are certainly good to consult for an appraisal if you need one.

Antique Legacy

antiquelegacy.com

Online auction site specializing in fine antique furniture and housewares. You can use absentee bidding (by phone, e-mail, or regular mail) to try to snatch an item in the catalog, or you can sell items to the auction house that will be professionally appraised and put up for auction. You can view the auction house's catalog online. This site also features many items that are up for direct sale. It has links to other Web sites devoted to specific types of art (like the Contemporary Asian Web site) and fine furnishings.

Butterfield & Butterfield

www.butterfields.com

Online auction house that concentrates on specific items on specific days. This auction house dates back to 1865, so it's been around for a while, though online auction participation is a recent development. Butterfield & Butterfield differs from other auction houses in that it only offers items on specific days, and these auctions occur only every few days. One sale might concentrate on furniture and decorative arts, another on jewelry, another on musical instruments, and so on. It's suggested that you obtain an online catalog of auction items before the sale starts (you can order one online). Online bidders compete on an absentee basis. They fill out an online form and place their bids either beforehand or while the auction is taking place, and then watch the progress online as the bidding occurs "for real" at the location where the auction is actually being held. One nice thing about Butterfield & Butterfield is the free appraisal service — send the auction house a photo of an item either by snail mail or e-mail and it will tell you how much it's worth.

Christie's

www.christies.com

This famous auction house lists merchandise online. A famous auction house that is now online, Christie's specializes in jewelry and fine arts. You can bid on items by submitting an absentee bid to upcoming auctions, though there is no online auction per se. View and research items up for auction on the Web page. This site has a "Lotfinder" feature that helps you search for a specific item, but you must subscribe to the service. You can also subscribe to various auction related, fine arts, or antiques related publications to buy books over this site. Christie's has an appraisal service and the means for you to sell an item, and the information on how to go about accessing those services is posted on this site.

William Doyle Galleries

www.doylegalleries.com

Another auction house online. This site specializes in jewelry and watches, although it also deals in fine furniture and paintings. The Gallery offers two options

for buyers who cannot be at the actual sale at the auction house. You can submit an online bid through Amazon.com/LiveBid (www.amazon.livebid.com) or phone in your bids.

General merchandise that's special

The following sites are catch-alls: They handle auctions of all kinds of things. Go here to find the specific goodies you're looking for, and shop around to get ideas for things you didn't even know you need.

Amazon.com Auctions

www.amazon.com

A relatively new and already well-advertised auction site dealing in everything from musical instruments to jewelry. The newest kid on the block ain't just reading books anymore. Now it offers a huge auction in many categories, from baseballs to books. This auction is worth checking out just because of the number of people who are buying and selling. All of Amazon's eight million users are pre-registered to participate. Currently registered Amazon.com bookstore customers can use their existing registration information to bid on the site's auctions. Amazon offers various types of specialty auctions, such as a charity auction benefiting Kosovar refugees, a Star Wars memorabilia auction, and an auction for art afficionados. This site, like eBay, has an extensive feedback system that fosters a sense of community and also reduces the chances of fraud. It even has an Outrage Policy that guides you through the steps of putting a deadbeat seller or bidder through the wash. All in all, this is an exciting and easy to use resource.

AuctionAddict.com
www.auctionaddict.com

A huge online auction that features many goods and several types of auction options. AuctionAddict.com features person–to-person auctions (and so does not act as a broker and does not guarantee prices or goods) and a classified ad venue with no listing fees. Goods are offered in 400 different categories, including stamps, home furnishings, toys, computers, and more. Besides the standard auction format, AuctionAddict.com offers Fixed-Price items (which are about the equivalent to classified ads) that are posted for sale without auction. Fees are charged exclusively to the seller, though auction goods that don't go for the reserve price aren't billed a commission. A Community Center provides information and feedback on users (so you know what you're getting and who you're dealing with) and offers discussion topics (like what is the best online auction site?) for users who want to chat about auctions. The rest of the Community Center features a general discussion forum, an appraisal area (where other users appraise your items online), a Beanie Baby forum, a collector's forum, and a fraud watch forum (to post information about shady auction houses). Users are billed monthly. This site is very good for the experienced auctioneer and is helpful for those who want in-depth information on a particular topic.

Auction Universe
www.auctionuniverse.com

This site has extremely comprehensive listings. Whether you want to buy or sell a single item or are a passionate collector of just about everything, you'll find what you're looking for here. This site offers links to auctions of everything from antiques to electronics. It also provides a search engine for auctions as well as links to live auctions. This site is very comprehensive and easy to use.

eBay
www.ebay.com

The most famous online auction site. This is the best-known and most successful online auction site, receiving hundreds of thousands of bids each day. You can find anything, new or used, including more unusual items such as tickets to events. eBay features inexpensive, moderate, and big ticket items (such as Harley

Davidsons, Porsches, and diamonds). It provides a history for every buyer and seller, as well as auction insurance. If you're an extrovert, you can chat with other customers and auctioneers; if you're an introvert, you can read the eBay newsletter. This site is the home of Rosie O'Donnell's much publicized charity auctions. You can also bid on eBay merchandise (such as shirts, coffee mugs, and mouse pads with the eBay logo). If you've never visited an auction site before, this is the perfect introductory site.

Keybuy Auction House

www.keybuy.com

One of the few completely free auctions. This auction has no commission and no listing fees, making it one of the only completely free auctions on the Internet. This may change, however, so keep your eyes peeled for new charges. It auctions goods in a wide range of categories, from computer hardware to jewelry, although most listings appear in computer-related categories. The site has a variety of auction formats that you can participate in and has features such as a chat room and a search engine to help you find specific items.

OpenIPO

www.openipo.com

Bid for stock on this site. Whether you want 100 shares or 100,000, you are on equal footing with everyone who puts money on the table. The OpenIPO auction employs a mathematical model that sets the optimal share price for both the company and the investors. The result is a price that reflects what people are really willing to pay for the stock. In OpenIPO auctions, unlike other auctions, bidding is completely secret, and the winning bidders all pay the same price of the lowest winning bid.

The Sharper Image

auction.sharperimage.com/osauction.shtml

The gadget store has an online auction, too. This site auctions Shaper Image goods (ranging from jukeboxes to shoe fresheners) that are brand new, repackaged, refurbished, and/or one-of-a-kind items. The site features AutoBid, which allows you to place a maximum bid on an item so you don't have to be online during the actual auction; Auction Watch, which tracks your bidding history; and MultiBid, which allows you to bid on more than one item at a time rather than bidding on a single item using the individual item bid pages. You can also opt to receive notices from Sharper Image about exclusive deals on products via e-mail.

Sotheby's

www.sothebys.com

Yet another famous, traditional auction house that now has a Web site. This one offers links to live auctions, free catalogs, a calendar of events, and collecting searches. You can search for auctions by date or by country. This is a good site for the international, exotic collector. A form in the back of the Sotheby's auction catalog, which you can view online, authorizes a representative from the Gallery to bid for you; alternatively, you can submit a telephone bid, which does the same thing. This site has an auction glossary that is useful to inexperienced participants. This site also features links to other auction houses. To sell your goods through the Gallery, you must have them appraised by the Gallery.

uAuction

www.uauction.com/index.html

A general auction site with nice extras. uAuction features auctions of antiques, collectibles, sports memorabilia, dolls, books (first edition and new fiction), cars (classic to new parts and tools), computer hardware, general merchandise, music, pet accessories, sports, stamps, and jewelry (vintage and new). You can get the bidding history of an item and view feedback about the quality of merchandise on this site. This site also has tools to start your auction, and allows you to search for items on other online auction sites. It features links for both buyers and sellers, tips on how to successfully bid on an item, and information on how to start your own auction.

Yahoo! Auctions

auctions.yahoo.com

    ★★ ★★

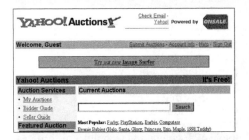

The main rival of eBay for the largest and most comprehensive auction site on the Web. Yahoo! Auctions is the contender for the throne when it comes to Internet auction sites. Its most competitive advantage is that it does not charge sellers a fee to list items for sale. However, it also doesn't attract the range of potential buyers that eBay does, and it lacks a way to register negative feedback on deadbeat bidders, which some say encourages deadbeat bidding. Nevertheless, Yahoo! Auctions is a good alternative to eBay. This huge site provides links to hundreds of online auctions that specialize in virtually everything. It is a great place to start your search for a specific item because it has about a million categories and products to choose from. The site features chat rooms so sellers and buyers can interact online. You can contact other people who share your interest in a specific type of item through the Collector's Clubs. The site has extensive seller and buyer's guides, as well as Automatic Bidding. It's totally free to use, though other auctions it connects you to might not be.

Other Sites to Check Out

www.4sale-or-auction.com
www.biddingtons.com
www.haggle.com
www.auctioninc.com
www.onsale.com
www.auction-sales.com
dir.yahoo.com/Business_and_Economy/
     Companies/Auctions/Online_auctions
www.expressbarter.com

Specialty items and collectibles

Chances are you were drawn to Internet auctions because you were looking for something in particular: that Joe DiMaggio baseball card you've always wanted, or a faster modem to speed up your Web surfing. Check out the following sites to find specific types of goods.

Antiques for young and old

Got your heart set on a hard-to-find antique? Using online auctions to bid on antiques is a fantastic way to save some money and a lot of time. Though most auctions specializing in antiques are run by a specific antique dealer, the prices are usually lower than what you would find in a showroom. Online auctions for antiques almost invariably have a thorough appraisal system as well, so you need not fear getting a worthless product.

Auctions By ABC

www.auctionsbyabc.com

Canadian auction house specializing in antiques. This Canadian auction house features antique bottles and stoneware. It also auctions insulators, crocks, merchant jugs, ginger beers, lightning rod balls, sodas, medicines, milks, poisons, inks, hairs, whiskeys, beers, bitters, flasks, black glass, fruit jars, whimsies; and collections and consignments of antiques and collectibles (including toys, tins, signs, advertising, photographica, glass, china, Disneyana, militaria, primitives, artifacts, oil lamps, and more). All bidding is done in Canadian dollars, so don't be frightened by the seemingly inflated prices. This is an absentee auction (which means that there is no online bidding) and all bidding is done by e-mail, regular mail, or phone. To view the items that are not posted online, you must purchase the catalog ($12, yes, Canadian dollars!). This site provides links to clubs, collectors, and an antique marketplace. All items are appraised by professionals at the auction house. Auctions by ABC also provides an auction insurance option in case of deadbeat bidders or other problems.

John Morelli Auctioneers

www.abcliveauction.com

Weekly online auction for antiques and collectibles. John Morelli Auctioneers features weekly online auctions for antiques and collectibles, computers, coins, glassware, and figurines. A vast quantity of goods are offered, particularly in the collectibles and antiques categories. There is no registration fee for this site, but bid fees range from $1 to $10.

Other Sites to Check Out

www.acaonline.com
www.nidlink.com/~trails
www.antiquesnorth.com
www.ehammer.com

Beanie Babies by the bushel

Beanie Babies have taken the world by storm and have become a focal point for awesome online auctions. Almost all online auctions have some Beanies available, though a few specialize in them. This is a fast, cheap, and easy way to get your hands on your favorite Beanies.

Bidder's Edge

www.biddersedge.com

Online auction has tons of Beanie Babies and auction extras. Bidder's Edge is a Web site that provides "buying tools" for people shopping at online auctions. You can search its database of product and pricing information. Information is primarily about Beanie Babies (the site claims to have 22,000 available for auction), but the site also features computer systems and software, office equipment, and consumer electronics. The site has a feature that allows you to search other online auctions for a specific item. The site also features services such as My Auctions, which tracks the items you are most interested in; Deal Watch, which alerts you by e-mail when items are offered again; and a Bid History page, which allows you to see your comprehensive bidding history or the bidding history of a particular product. You can also personalize the features of the site so a personal page will pop up when you sign in. Warning: This site may be complicated for the auction uninitiated, though the site does feature instructions for new buyers and a tour of the site.

The Collectible Exchange

www.beaniex.com

Welcome to the #1 buy/sell/trade beanie baby website

(Click here to order a replica of **Sally Winey's** first creation.)

Auction concentrating exclusively on beanies. The Collectible Exchange is an all-Beanie Babies, all the time, online auction house. I profiled the family that runs the highly successful company in my book *Starting an Online Business For Dummies.* You can buy, sell, or trade Beanies through this site. The site also features Beanie news and specials, a demo for first timers, and a Beanie price list so you know how much your coveted Beanie is worth. If you want to sell your Beanie to The Collectible Exchange, you should carefully read all the rules, since this site is pretty picky about the condition of the toys (your Beanie should have its tags!).

Books (remember those?)

Online auctions specializing in books are steadily becoming more popular amongst bibliophiles because of the time and money saved. You can bid for rare and historical books and documents that would be difficult and time consuming for the average collector to find. For those interested in more general merchandise, these book auctions also deal in more "popular" books.

Auction Port — Book Listings for Collecting and Selling

www.auctionport.com/book.html

Book site has large selection and search engine. This site features specialized book auctions that run for three to fourteen days, and also has access to live auctions that run up to an hour. Many auctions feature pictures. No auction has a buyer's commission. You only pay your winning bid plus shipping and handling to the seller. This site also helps you locate that book you are looking for: You can compare your list to the Auction Port, and the site will notify you when that book is added to the auctions at Auction Port.

Auctions — Book Collecting — Net Links

collectbooks.miningco.com/ msubauctions.htm

Book auctions for serious bibliophiles. This is a great site for the serious book collector. There are numerous hyperlinks and indexes, as well as a search engine.

E-World Auction

www.EworldAuction.com

Monthly auctions of old and rare books, maps, prints, and other works on paper. You can bid on items and post items for auction on this site. You can also visit the Sale Gallery, where you can buy goods without auction. This site features information on how to create your own Web site and how to find restoration workshops. There are also links to book and map dealers and reference works. E-world charges no commission, registration fees, listing fees, or monthly fees. This site is very easy to use for both the buyer and the seller.

Flea Market Books

www.fleamarketbooks.com/auction.html

Large range of categories and quick service. Flea Market Books is an online book auction that is free to buyers and sellers, though there is a registration fee if you want to join the auction. This is a good alternative to the eBay book site (probably the most popular way to buy books by auction), which is often slow.

Other Sites to Check Out

members.aol.com/MarkB45375/mark.htm
www.bookauction.com

Cars you can drive to the bank

These auction sites deal mostly in used or classic cars, but you can find new cars at considerable discounts on some sites.

Federal Government Car Auctions

eqmoney.com/cars.htm

Seized cars and trucks for dirt cheap. Ever wonder what the government does with all those cars it takes from criminals? It sells them at federal car auctions, silly. Seized cars, trucks, and boats are available at incredible discounts. You can't make a sale online, but you can use this site to get times and places where auctions will be held. What's more, the "Guide to Federal Car Auctions" is free.

NJ Online Auto Auction

www.howellnj.com/auto

Private auctions only at this site. The NJ Online Auto Auction site features one-on-one buyer-to-seller interaction, and all payment terms are agreed on between the two parties; in other words, NJ is not a broker and is not responsible for the conduct of buyers or sellers. There is a $25 registration fee to sell, but there are limited times when the seller registration is free. There is no buyer registration fee. This site's categories include Antique/Classic cars, domestic cars, SUVs, motorcycles, and more.

Clothing to fit you to a T

Don't have a thing to wear? Some online auctions have extensive clothing categories, and a few specialize entirely in clothing. This is a good way to get discounts on quality clothes because you are not supporting a store that needs to mark up items to make a profit. Plus, whatever your idea of style, you're sure to find an outfit that fits.

Clothing Bids

www.clothingbids.com

Online auction specilaizing in wholesale clothing and accessories. All merchandise is sold in bulk only, so this site is best for professional buyers and sellers. New auction lots open daily, and you can bid in several dozen categories.

FirstAuction

www.firstauction.com

Interesting auction options at this clothing site. FirstAuction is a large online auction featuring jewelry, women's apparel, beauty products, furniture, collectibles, housewares, and electronics. This site has interesting features such as the Flash Auction,

a thirty-minute auction instead of the usual week- to month-long online auction. It also offers a forty-eight-hour auction option, which allows you to bid on items for forty-eight hours only. Those of us with a penchant for instant gratification will find these features a godsend. Personal pages and an auction newsletter are also provided. This site has the Auction Guide tool, which is very valuable for the first time user. It walks you through the auction process step-by-step and offers insider's tips.

Other Sites to Check Out

http://www.atlasclothing.com

Coins/stamps/ currency just for fun

Online auctions are a great tool for the avid stamp, coin, or currency collector. These sites have good prices on hard-to-find and rare pieces, as well as numerous links and information that will make the collector smile.

Earl P.L. ApfelBaum, Inc.

www.apfelbauminc.com

One of the most respected stamp firms has an Internet site. Earl P.L. ApfelBaum, Inc. is one of the oldest and largest stamp firms in the world and is now online for auctions. You can view items up for auction online and then phone in your absentee bid to auction house. This site provides links to other online stamp auctions. ApfelBaum's will also buy your entire collection.

Sandafayre

www.sandafayre.com

One of the largest and most comprehensive sites for stamps and philatelic material on the Web. Every week Sandafayre offers an auction with over $1 million of philatelic items online. Sandafayre mostly buys and auctions large collections, not individual pieces. This site also features direct sales and a free catalog.

Stamp Auctions

www.stampauctions.com

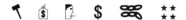

This stamp site has options and extras galore. This site for stamp auctions has many perks, including the Nassau Street directory, which lists links to other stamp related Web sites; a Power Search function that enables sellers to search for lots with a specific catalog number or country; a Seller's Tutorial; a Personal Shopper that gives you e-mail updates on particular items you're interested in; a discussion group for stamp collecting and dealing; a free classified ad service; and a chat group. This site is great for stamp fans who want access to all the news, information, and items for sale and chat about the stamp world on one Web site.

Other Sites to Check Out

www.teletrade.com
www.stampauctioncentral.com
www.philatelists.com

Collectibles you can collect

The best way to get the collectible you want is to go where all the collectors are. These sites have hundreds of items at good prices for buyers, and hundreds of eager customers for sellers.

Auction, Inc.

ai.wwcd.com/auction/wwcd/home.html

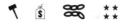

Large, comprehensive auction for all your collection obsessions. Auction, Inc. features autographs, Beanie Babies (the most prominent item on this site), and sports and movie memorabilia. The perks are too numerous to list, but one example is its No Sale, No Fees feature that protects the unsuccessful seller from commission fees. On this site, buyers bid only once, preventing "outbidding." The AutoBid system allows you to keep your maximum bid secret until the last minute and allows you to participate in bidding without being present. What's not kept secret is the seller's reputation among other buyers. What's good for the goose is good for the gander, and sellers may see the bidder's history and feedback rating as well. Auction, Inc. also provides links to person-to-person auctions, one time auctions, and other online auctions.

Box Lot

www.boxlot.com

Over 7,000 active lots of antiques, books, magazines, jewelry, toys and dolls, collectibles, stamps, and coins listed for auction. Box Lot is a large listing agent (not a broker), which is slightly different than a standard online auction house. It acts primarily as a link between the buyer and seller and does not take responsibility for merchandise. Box Lot features links to seller and buyer services.

Up4Sale

www.up4sale.com

Mostly toys and Beanie Babies at this site. Up4Sale is primarily an auction for toys and Beanie Babies, though it also deals in trading cards, music tapes and CDs, and comic books. The site features a news room, links to other sites, and an AOL guide. It also features a member rating so you can vote on member conduct (you even get kicked off if your rating falls too low) and look up bidder and seller histories. The site has free registration and both standard and reserve type auctions.

U-Trade

www.utrade.com

Specializes in collectibles but can fulfill all your merchandise desires. U-Trade is a general merchandise auction site that offers everything but specializes in collectibles. This site gives you the option of setting up your own free Web page from the U-Trade site. Its "Pay for Performance" protects sellers from paying commission fees if their items don't sell. Sellers can also pay to have items placed in a Featured Auction section that displays their item prominently to increase sales. Registration is free, though sellers must pay to post items.

Computers and computer equipment: you need this

When it comes to Internet auctions, computer equipment is hot. Many auction houses do nothing else. They receive equipment from businesses or individuals and then act as a broker to auction the merchandise online. You can often get deals at these places, but be sure to do some price comparisons first. Know exactly what you want and avoid impulse purchases.

Bidnask

www.bidnask.com

For the impatient among you, this site features real-time auctions. This site has a cool real-time "trading floor" where you can negotiate in real time for new products at the best prices. It has a guest tutorial to get you used to the format and is free to buyers. This site also has more traditional online auction formats for those suspicious of the new.

BidOnline.com

www.bidonline.com

Large computer auctions several times a week. This site has a large number of items in a broad range of categories, from motherboards to printers. New, remanufactured, and closeout items are what it's known for. Auctions are held three times a week.

Onsale

www.onsale.com

Brand name computers and accessories for less. Onsale is a huge auction offering computer products, sports and fitness related items, home and office items, vacations, and travel deals. Onsale claims to be the world's largest retail online auction. You can buy from Onsale or from brand name stores such as IBM or Hewlett-Packard. To post items, you must sell items directly to Onsale and the site will post them for auction, acting as the broker. The site also offers the Quick Buy option, which allows you to just go ahead and buy most items up for auction at a set (usually higher than you may pay in a auction) price without having to compete with other bidders. You can also visit the At Cost page and totally circumvent the whole auction process and buy goods at wholesale prices. Onsale features options such as Easy Search, which enables you to find a specific item; Bid Watch, which makes it easy to monitor bidding on various items at once; and Bid Maker, which allows you to participate in the bidding process without actually being present. This site is a little complicated but has helpful features for first-time users.

Outpost Auctions

www.outpostauctions.com

Smaller computer auction site. This site was launched by Internet retailer Cyberian Outpost as this book was being written. All types of computer hardware were being offered, although only about 30 items were currently available. Reserve auctions are held, and automatic bidding is an option. At this writing, all services were free to both buyers and sellers — no fees are charged to list or sell an item.

Surplus Auction by Egghead

www.surplusauction.com

Huge weekly online auction of computer hardware and software run by Egghead, a leading retailer of computers and computer related items. This site features auctions on computer hardware and software, accessories, and peripheral devices, including hard-to-find items. You can also bid on some office products, consumer electronics, sporting goods, and jewelry. The site features an online outlet store (good for cheaper computer items), a newsletter, and links to other online auctions.

3D Auction

www.3dauction.com

Small but fascinating computer auction. 3D Auction features auctions for computers and computer accessories, and has categories ranging from notebooks to upgrades, though the actual product lists are not very comprehensive. This auction is in 3D, which makes it fun if you have the glasses. The site provides Auto Bid, a feature that bids for you when you are not online, and Auction Watch, a feature that allows you to keep tabs on all your past and present bids. Free registration.

D-20 Merchandise for Sale

uBid

www.ubid.com

Good for business buying. uBid is a medium-sized computer auction. You can bid on notebook computers, desktop computers, consumer electronics, and some housewares and sports equipment. To sell to uBid, you contact the site directly with your product information, and it becomes the broker for your item. This site makes good use of current Web technology. You can make a personal page that pops up with all the features and information relevant to you when you sign on. Links to the Business Mall and PC Mall are good for business research.

Other Sites to Check Out

www.auctiongate.com
www.auction-it.net
www.pc-buyer.com
www.hardwarecanada.com

Consumer electronics too good to give away

Although computers are a logical thing to purchase on a computer-based medium such as the Internet, you can also find audio, video, and lots of other electronics equipment at auction, too.

CyberSwap

www.cyberswap.com

Online auction house for computers and consumer electronics, for both personal and office use. You can get good deals on cards, computers, fax copiers, memory, office equipment, and software. This site features some software you can download from the CyberSwap Web site.

Interactive Auction Online

www.iaoauction.com

★★
★★

Buy direct from manufacturers and distributers at this auciton. Interactive Auction Online provides manufacturers, wholesalers, and distributors a unique avenue to increase revenues while liquidating high quality excess inventories. After you buy your consumer electronics on the Web, the site promises to provide vendor support and customer service. This is an easy-to-use and well-organized Web site.

The Mall at WholeSale Products

www.wholesaleproducts.com

★★
★★

Great site for electronics auctions. You can buy Hewlett-Packard calculators (48GX, 48B, and others), palmtops, VCRs, camcorders, and much more. This site offers great indexes for consumer electronics. You can order in English or Spanish. Great service.

Other Sites to Check Out

www.quixell.com (German language site)
www.usauctions.com
www.erauctions.com.au

Fine art for all tastes

Given the popularity and the high prices often associated with purchasing fine art online, it only makes sense that auction houses that specialize in fine art are flocking to the Web. The following are just a few examples.

ADEC Art Price Annual

www.artpriceserver.com

These art world professionals offer great information. This site claims that it has "the most exhaustive databank on cataloged works of art sold at public auctions." ADEC/Art Price Annual has collected and processed these data from an attentive and daily study of movements on the world art market through public sales, with close cooperation of auctioneers and the input of correspondents worldwide. This site is a great reference tool for art professionals, experts, amateurs, and collectors.

ART FORUM — The European Art Market Online

www.cofrase.com/artforum

A French fine art forum and auction featuring private bidding directly between buyer and seller. This auction house only provides contact information and does not act as a broker. This site features links to favorite fine art sites, calendars of upcoming antique shows and art fairs, information on upcoming exhibitions, information on galleries and museums, lists of quality catalogs, and tips for amateurs on the fine points of fine art auctions.

Phoebus Gallery

www.phoebusauction.com

A variety of art auctions here. Phoebus is an auction gallery touting collectibles and antiques. The site features benefit auctions for local charities and specialty auctions (like an erotic art auction and a military auction). On this page, you may preview items coming up for auction, bid on items (through an e-mail absentee bid), and consign items for the Gallery to sell. This site has lots of links to other galleries and auctioneers and provides an option to exchange links with Phoebus.

Other Sites to Check Out

www.gbtate.com
www.lunds.com
www.masterarts.com

Fossils and natural history

Talk about antiques: The site in this section gets into some *really* old stuff — we're talking about meteorites, minerals, and dinosaur bones that might be millions of years old.

NaturalHistoryAuction.com

www.NaturalHistoryAuction.com

Great for the budding archeologist in you. This is a Web page that contains links to auctions listed on eBay for fossils and other natural history-type stuff. A related Web site (www.meteorites.com) deals solely in rocks from outer space.

Glass

If you love antique paperweights and Depression glass or are looking for hard-to-find reference books for glass collectors, check out this site.

Just Glass Auctions

www.justglass.com

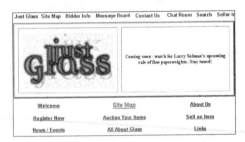

Large auction dealing solely in glass goods. Since this site went online in early 1998, it has received 20,000 bids from people who are looking for beautiful glass items. Chat rooms and message boards are available to help collectors contact one another.

Jewelry that will make you sparkle

If you're looking for special jewelry for a special occasion or are trying to find a particular kind of gem, you'll save lots of time by doing your browsing with a Web browser. Here are some auction sites where you can find a gem of a deal.

Dicker and Dicker

www.dickeranddicker.com

This site provides appraisals of your jewelry and a large selection in its online catalog. Dicker and Dicker is an online jewelry auction house that deals in the sale of privately owned jewelry. Bids are accepted from prospective buyers who compete against one another. All items are shown to jewelers, retailers, and gemologists by Dicker and Dicker before they are put up for auction and are given an estimated value, which is usually the reserve price. All bids are absentee bids at a regular auction at the auction house, but you can get the absentee bid form online, as well as in the catalog.

Interactive Collector

www.icollector.com

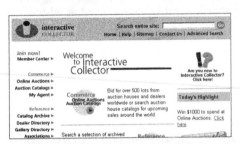

This site has a strong community. Interactive Collector is a large auction house that features jewelry, antiques, and various works of art. You can bid for over 500 lots from auction houses and dealers worldwide or search auction house catalogs for upcoming sales around the world. This site presents live chat with members of the auction community, industry experts, or celebrities. It also features an AutoBid function, which allows you to place a blanket bid on an item so you do not have to be present to raise your bid. This site is good if you want to search several online auctions at once and if you want reference material.

Other Sites to Check Out

www.dupuisauctions.com/GeneralInfo.cfm
www.dgse.com

Maps and prints

Even if you don't plan to buy maps or prints, you'll enjoy the beautiful items in the following site's online catalog.

Paulus Swaen Maps and Prints

www.swaen.com

  $ ⟳

Maps and manuscripts are auctioned here. This company deals in auctions of prints, maps, medieval manuscripts, and antique playing cards. Buyers are charged a premium of 12 percent on purchases of up to $30,000.

Sporting equipment for your active side

From the comfort of your home, you can purchase clothing and equipment to help you have fun and get some exercise when your Web surfing is done.

Basketball Bonanza

www.basketballbonanza.com

Category	Basketball Bonanza		Independent Sellers
	Auction	Store	Auction
Memorabilia			
Photos	(47)	(124)	(0)
Magazines	(6)	(70)	(0)
Programs: Pro	(4)	(172)	(0)
Programs: College	(4)	(46)	(0)
Media Guides	(2)	(50)	(0)

Tons of sporting goods and a large search engine at this site. Basketball Bonanza is an online sports auction featuring hundreds of items, including magazines, media guides, cachets, balls, uniforms, unique items, private signings, and cards. The site has an extensive search engine. Its grading feature establishes the condition of the item for sale, from poor to mint condition. Registration is free. Basketball Bonanza has an AutoBid feature and an AuctionWatch feature (which tracks all your bids, past and present, so you don't have to visit every bid page). The seller's fee is small at this site and there are no commission charges.

Golf Bids

www.golfbids.com

Only golfing goods at this auction. This auction, operated by the Golf Auction Network International, Inc., features a men's, women's, and kid's ProShop that's stocked with golf equipment and apparel. Golf Bids also auctions golfing vacation packages and property in hot golf destinations. Joining the auction is free. The site has an easy-to-use "Starter's Shack" for beginners.

Other Sites to Check Out

www.golfclubexchange.com

Sports memorabilia: Thanks for the memories

Some of the most exciting auctions involve valuable sports-related items. The auctions of home run hero Mark McGwire's baseballs, which were partly held online, are only one example. Here are some sites where you can find some more affordable sports treasures.

Rotman Auction

www.wwcd.com/rotman

Lots 0751-0800 | Lots 0801-0850 | Lots 0851-0900 | Lots 0901-0950

To Request Your Free Catalog Call (508) 791-6710
Fax (508) 797-5398 or E-Mail info@rotmanauction.com

Lots Include: Sport &
Non-Sport Cards, Sports
Memorabilia, Autographs,
Comic Books, Movie Posters,
Pins, Political Memorabilia,
Statues & Figurines and Much
More.

Huge memoriblia auction. This large online
sports auction features autographs and
other sports memorabilia. The site provides a unique grading system that rates
all items for you, so you have an idea of
the relative value of the item you are considering. You may submit absentee bids
through telephone, fax, mail, or e-mail and
can bid prior to the auction day.

Sports Auction

www.sportingauction.com

A safe and reliable auction. A very secure
and private auction on all sorts of sports
memorabilia and other items, this site has
an extensive search engine and also provides an Auction Watch feature. The site
has fixed price items as well as the auction and a "bargain store" where all items
are 30 to 60 percent off. Web entrepreneurs may be interested in the Sports
Auction Affiliate Program, which offers
commissions for leads from your Web site.
This site has been reviewed and approved
by various watchdog agencies.

Stickler's Sports Den

sportsden.hypermart.net

Baseball cards are the speciality here.
Stickler's Sports Den Auction is a huge
baseball card online auction featuring

cards ranging from 1909 to 1998 — all
players and all brands of cards. Bids are
updated twice daily by e-mail only. You
may bid prior to the day of the auction.
Auction insurance can be purchased. The
site features a large chat room and message
board as well as the Baseball Card Ring,
which links you to other card aficionados.

Other Sites to Check Out

www.autografs.com
www.merchantfind.com/fgcards/fgcards.htm
www.curranscards.com
www.baseballplanet.com

Travel that makes getting there fun

Airlines and other travel companies that
have extra seats to fill on regular trips and
more elaborate excursions often try to
auction them off online. The catch is that,
often, you have to be prepared to leave at
a moment's notice. If you're footloose and
looking for a quick getaway, check out
these sites.

First Internet Travel Auction

www.4a.com/auction

Our Sponsor:
4A Travel
1-800-851-1588 or 281-584-0029

1st Internet Travel Auction specializes in marketing inventory in

*Auctions for anything you could possibly
need on your trip.* First Internet Travel
Auction specializes in marketing inventory
in Colorado and Florida for airlines, lodg-
ing facilities, car rentals, and cruise ships.
The inventory is limited, so you must act

fast when it is available. The vendors only auction off inventory for either 24-or-48-hour-long auctions.

Travel Bids

www.TravelBids.com

Save money by getting bids from many travel agents. This site is good for air travel, resorts, and cruises for any dates of travel. For Regular Listings (the most popular type of TravelBids listing), you make a reservation directly with any airline, resort, or cruise company, and then list your trip on this site. Many travel agents from around the United States will then bid on your business, and the winning agent will take over your existing reservation and issue the ticket to you. The idea is that this process will give you the lowest possible fee. You must pay $5 to list a trip, and travel agents wishing to bid must also pay the fee. Only travel agencies that are deemed reputable may post bids, so you can safely pack your suitcase.

Travelfacts Auction

www.travelfacts.com

Bid on cruises, hotel rooms, travel packages, airline tickets, and other travel services and products. New items are added to the current listing of products and services frequently. In the future you will be able to create your own auction for travel products or services. This is a great site with many indexes, FAQs, and vacation offers.

Wine for tasters and collectors

The following sites are good resources not only for bargain hunters but also for those who want to find out more about how to purchase and judge wines.

WineBid.com

www.winebid.com

Online auction dealing in wines. This site holds monthly auctions and includes services such as a free appraisal of your wines, a low seller's commission, and extensive buyer and seller monitoring services. The site features a fine wine newsletter. You can download a wine list for offline viewing. Sellers can get free appraisals of their wines and can use various options to monitor their lots.

Wine Exchange

www.wine-exchange.com

Large private wine auctions. The International Wine Exchange was created to provide wine collectors, merchants, distributors, restaurateurs, and wine lovers with a marketplace where wines can be bought and sold. All bids are continuously posted as they are received and listed in The International Wine Exchange's Open Auction Marketplace. The International Wine Exchange does not act as a broker and is not involved in any transactions. All sales of the wines listed in the database are private transactions that occur between the two parties. The International Wine Exchange only provides a "marketplace" where the continuous open auction takes place and charges a membership fee for this service. This site features The Most Wanted Wine List.

Wine Online

www.winecollector.com

Good auction for those inexperienced in the art of wine. The Wine Online auction site is a joint effort of Phillips Son & Neale Auctions Limited and the Park Avenue Liquor Shop of New York. Each month, the site posts products including special bottlings, new releases, new arrivals, and special packages for auction. You can view a full catalog and a handy guide to "tasting notes" which are useful for inexperienced buyers. As of yet, the auction does not take electronic bids, so you must submit an absentee bid, but the site is very new and assures visitors that live bids will be added in the future.

Wine Spectator

www.winespectator.com

A site featuring wine politics, winery profiles, and a winery locator. This site features late-breaking wine news and a chance to win prizes just for establishing an account. A credit card is not required for registration. The site does not actually have an online auction but may be a valuable tool for both potential auction buyers and sellers since it features daily wine news, weekly features, a forum to meet with others, a library, and information about wineries, dining, travel, and wine auctions.

Nonprofit/charity auctions: It's all to the good

The Golden Triangle

golden-triangle.org

Friendly, easy-to-use charity auction. Golden Triangle Free Nonprofit Auction is a division of and is produced by Ekaya Institute, a nonprofit organization dedicated to the publishing and production of traditional and new media projects and programs that benefit youth, the arts, and the environment. You can donate an item or bid on an item on this friendly site.

Joy and Light Center Online Auction

www.joylight.com/auction.html

This charity auction encourages group participation. This site has developed an innovative program for nonprofit corporations and community organizations to help with your online charity auction and Web page development. Sororities, fraternities, schools, churches, membership organizations, and 501(c)(3)s can participate. This program is one of the most economical means to enter the world of online charity auctions. You don't need your own Web site because the site sets you up with a Web page and online link to your own auction site. You can also get listed in search engines and directories, and get assistance with marketing your auction to your supporters.

Other Sites to Check Out

www.marcon.org/auction.htm
www.celebrityauctions.com

Auction Site Guides and Search Engines

Perhaps you checked out the sites in the preceding section but didn't find the item you want to buy. Or maybe you are getting started in the auction business and you want to make sure that people on the Internet can find your site. Check out the following sections for solutions.

Auction-related portals and search engines

Internet auctions are still a young industry, and there aren't a lot of Web sites that have set themselves up as *portals* to auction sites. A portal is a site that intends to be a starting point or clearinghouse of information about a group of online resources. The sites in this section provide general information such as ratings of auction sites, as well as useful tips for bidders and sellers. Look for more sites to assume the role of auction industry clearinghouse in the future.

The Auction Guide

www.auction-guide.com

Find out how to save 20 to 70 percent on computer hardware. Emphasis is given to auction sites that concentrate on computer equipment. You can find a good page of tips for auction bidders, as well as a directory of online auctions at www.auction-guide.com/directory/index.htm). (This is mistakenly described as a "dictionary" on the site's home page.)

Auction Patrol

www.auctionpatrol.com

This site provides information from other Internet auction users. Auction Patrol helps you make informed decisions while participating in online auctions. This site looks at not only the huge sites, but also the lesser known sites. It brings you information on various sites that it deems notable and alerts the user to interesting goods that are being offered. Auction patrol also brings you tips on various aspects of the auction experience.

BidFind

www.bidfind.com

★ ★
★ ★

Search site devoted exclusively to auction sites on the Internet. BidFind regularly indexes the offerings on dozens of auction sites and stores the listings in its computers;

you enter keywords describing what you are looking for, and the site returns auction listings that match your criteria.

HandiLinks Auctioneers and Liquidators Directory

www.handilinks.com/cat1/a/a415.htm

A large listing of auctions on the Web. This site provides a list of auction houses on the Internet, some of which are accompanied by brief descriptions, many of which have only a name and no description at all. Sites are not rated or evaluated in any way. On the plus side, the very bottom of the list contains some good links to news about auctioneers and liquidators.

General search engines

You're probably already familiar with search engines from the standpoint of a general information consumer: You can find information on just about any topic by using an Internet search service. You can also find items for sale at auction on the search engines. If you augment your auction activities with a business Web site, you need to visit these sites to find out how to get your business listed so that customers can find you more easily. Each site has information that explains how to include your site on its index.

AltaVista

www.altavista.com

One of the larger search engines on the Web helps you find your preferred auction. AltaVista is one of my favorite search engines. It's fast, and it provides users with a wide range of shortcuts to narrow down the information they want. Like other search services, AltaVista presents a directory of Internet sites on a topic-by-topic basis. Its Business and Finance category includes sites for Regulation and Government and Small Businesses.

DejaNews

www.dejanews.com

Search newsgroups for auction info. DejaNews specializes in searching through the thousands of newsgroups that make up the wild, wild world of Usenet. DejaNews can help you locate a group that's related to your area of business. Or you can enter a topic in the Search text box at the top of the DejaNews home page and click Find, and after a short time, a page appears with links to individual newsgroup messages related to your query.

Excite

www.excite.com

Create your own personalized Web pages to receive the news and business information you want. Excite's home page contains lots of current news, weather, and stock information.

HotBot

www.hotbot.com

A fast, fast, fast search engine. HotBot's colorful artwork reflects its creator, Wired Digital, which is now part of the Lycos Network. HotBot is especially good if you are searching for links to your own Web site: Enter your own URL in the search text box, and select Links to This Site from the first drop-down menu under Options. If you're looking for your own free home page or e-mail address, HotBot provides hosting, too.

Infoseek

www.infoseek.com

Search Web sites, news outlets, corporations, and newsgroups. Infoseek has an especially rich selection of international Web directories in different languages. Among other things, Infoseek has a topic heading for small businesses, which may be of particular interest to you.

Lycos

www.lycos.com

Search through the Web, newgroups, and stocks for high quality sites. Lycos is one of the oldest search engines on the Web, which means that it's more than a few years old. Like Infoseek, Lycos has a category listing for small-business resources that you may find useful. It lets you search not only the usual categories like the Web and newsgroups, but also stocks, weather, and even recipes. Its Top 5 Percent rating system attempts to separate higher-quality Web sites from those of the ho-hum variety.

WebCrawler

www.webcrawler.com

Search the extensive classified listings on the Internet. WebCrawler began as a student project in 1994 and has since turned into a mini-industry of its own. One good thing about WebCrawler is that it lets you (or your customers) search through Internet classifieds for particular items.

Yahoo!

www.yahoo.com

★ ★
★ ★

Probably the most popular and best-known site on the Web. Yahoo! is the place to go if you want to find any type of information online. However, Yahoo! is not comprehensive. It doesn't include every single site online; nor does it try to. Rather, its team of reviewers personally checks out sites and decides whether to add them to one of the Yahoo! index pages. The Yahoo! Store is a good place to create a business Web site. Yahoo! is at once a search engine that helps you find sites on the Web, and a well-organized index to Web sites arranged by topic. I probably turn to Yahoo! once or twice during every surfing session, and I always seem to find something interesting.

Web Sites for Auctioneers and Other Businesspeople

This part of the directory is a roundup of various resources for anyone interested in selling goods at auction or starting an auction site. You can find sites where you can publicize the things you want to sell at auction, software you can use to build a Web site or track auctions, and much more.

Classifieds with class

The Web offers countless sources for advertising via classified ads. Included here are guides to the many sites that offer this service, some of which are free and some of which require payment. The beauty of the Web is that you reach a lot more people than you would by advertising in your local newspaper.

America Online Business Directory

downtown.web.aol.com

$

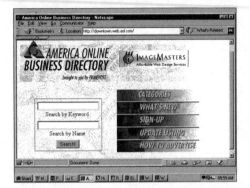

Free classified listings for AOL customers. This is a great resource if you are already a customer of PrimeHost, America Online's Web site hosting service. PrimeHost customers can list their businesses in this searchable classified ad database for free. You only have to fill out a simple online form with your PrimeHost customer number, e-mail address, URL, and site category. Non-customers are charged $125 to place an ad in the directory.

The Grandfather of All Links Free Advertising Directory

ecki.com/links/oclass.shtml

Huge free listing service. This listing of free classified advertising sites takes forever to load, but it is updated and current. Sites are sorted alphabetically and grouped by how long you can run the ad and whether the ad is city- or state-specific. The Grandfather of All Links also includes a directory of non-English sites.

Yahoo! Classifieds

www.yahoo.com/Business_and_Economy/ Classifieds

Browse classifeds by region or category at this popular site. As usual, Yahoo! is a great starting point if you're looking for just about anything — in this case, sites where you can place your classified ads online. Yahoo! enables you to browse by region or by category. You can also find general classified sites that include additional services such as chat rooms, personal ads, and auctions.

Other Sites to Check Out

www.villagesclassified.com
www.classifieds2000.com
classifieds.imall.com/ads.shtml
www.trade-direct.com

eBay help

eBay is practically a world unto itself. It has so many different help, interaction, and search utilities that you sometimes have to search around for them. The following are a few useful aspects of the site whose locations weren't obvious (at least to me). I list them here so you won't have to spend a lot of time looking for them.

About Me

pages.ebay.com/aw/help/ help-t-usr-abot.html

Getting to know you, getting to know all about you. This page provides an introduction to eBay's About Me feature, which lets you create your own Web page so you can supplement your auction listings.

After the Auction: Now What?

pages.ebay.com/aw/help/ help-t-aft-what.html

Answers to the most common auction questions. Visit this page for a particularly good, albeit brief, set of answers to one of the most common questions auction buyers and sellers ask.

Go Global!

pages.ebay.com/aw/global-home.html

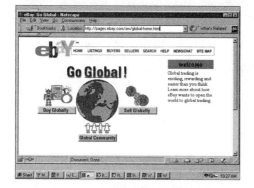

Links to other Web pages. This page features links to separate Web pages for buyers and sellers who have questions about customs, taxes, and shipping overseas.

New User Tutorial

pages.ebay.com/aw/nut-start1.html

Great tutorial for the uninitiated. Go to this page for a step-by-step introduction to eBay, which also serves as an introduction to how Internet auctions work in general.

Legal resources to keep you on the up and up

You don't need to be in legal trouble in order to research the many legal resources in cyberspace. Small-business owners often need to know about copyright and trademark issues, as well as international trade law and state laws.

The Copyright Web site

www.benedict.com

Entertaining answers to copyright questions. This site endeavors to inject a measure of humor into the sometimes-dry subject of copyright. It has a section on Fair Use and Public Domain, and a chat group on copyright issues.

The Internet Legal Resource Guide

www.ilrg.com

A good beginning in your search for answers to legal questions. This is a good general starting point if you're looking for legal information. The ILRG includes an index of lawyers and law firms, in case you need help. It also has extensive databases of legal information, articles, and links.

Nolo Press

www.nolo.com/chunkPCT/PCT.index.html

Lots of information on trademarks. Nolo Press is a well-known publisher in the field of self-help law. This page on patent, copyright, and trademark resources also points you to lots of good information on intellectual property terminology. Scroll down the page and click the Conducting a Trademark Search and Registering a Trademark links to find out about topics that can be especially important to your small business.

THOMAS

thomas.loc.gov

Check on bills pending in Congress. THOMAS (named after Thomas Jefferson) is the official U.S. Congress Web site. Administered by the Library of Congress, THOMAS lets you check on the status of pending legislation. You can search by bill number, title, or keyword.

The United States Copyright Office

lcweb.loc.gov/copyright

★ ★
★ ★

The place to go if you want to apply to register for copyright for your Web site. Registering your copyright gives you an extra level of protection for your business contents, even though copyright law provides for online material to be protected as soon as it is published.

Other Sites to Check Out

www.doc.gov
www.yahoo.com/Government/Law/Federal
www.eff.org
www.findlaw.com/01topics/10cyberspace
www.findlaw.com
www.globalcontact.com

Software that's going, going, gone

For the most part, the auction-related software you can download is designed to help you create full-fledged auction sites. Other programs help auction sellers format their listings. The range of software available should grow as Internet auctions become even more popular.

Auction Broker

auctionbroker.hypermart.net

Software designed to help you set up and run your online auction. Several different products are available, from the Store (which allows you to set up a virtual store) to the Enterprise (which combines both auction and store features). You can customize the software to fit your individual needs by turning on and off any of the Auction Broker options (including Clerk, BidFiler, AutoBidder, Auction Minder, and more).

AuctionEngine

www.auctionengine.com

Create a compelling auction. AuctionEngine provides continuous and simultaneous communication between the auctioneer and the buyers, just like a live auction. This software enables the auctioneer to blend various features for the most effective online auction possible.

Auction Information System

**www.star.net/people/~mga60/
 auction.html**

Reduce the work related to tracking items and producing an auction catalog. This is shareware, which means you can try it out for free and then register the program for $95. The software allows you to know immediately what any bidder has purchased, minimizes record keeping efforts, produces invoices, and more. This software runs on any DOS compatible system with a 386 or higher CPU.

Auction Man

**www.leederassociates.com.au/
 auctnman.html**

Manage all types of multiple-item auction sales. Auction Man has various manifestations: The AuctionMan/PRO is for larger, multiple item auction management; the AuctionMan/LITE caters to smaller auction rooms; and the AuctionMan/JNR is intended for freelance and other auctioneers who are only concerned with one-offering auctions and have no need for stock control. This software has features such as single and multisale operations nodes, a filing system, and invoice prep and printing. This application can be run on basically any system (from D.O.S., to windows, to Novell) and from network and single user applications.

Blackthorne Software

www.blackthornesw.com/Bthome/ default.htm

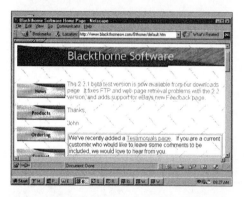

Helps sellers track their listings. This company produces software that helps sellers format and track their listings. Demo versions are available for downloading from the Blackthorne Web site. See Chapter 7 for more information.

Easy Auction

www.EasyAuction.com

Everything (almost) you need to create your own auction site. This site has information and software that enables you to run your

own Internet auctions from your own Web site. The site features Bonsai Software's EasyAuction online auction software. Easy Auction is designed to auction a single lot or grouping of items at a time, so if you want to set up a larger auction, look elsewhere. You link the auction you build to your existing Web site, so if you don't have a Web site, you have to build one before using the software. There is an initial 30-day free trial period during which you can evaluate Easy Auction by running test auctions as well as demonstration pages for viewing the software in action. Auction service is otherwise billed with a $10 flat rate per lot put up for auction at your site or 5 percent of the winning bid.

Open Site Software

www.opensite.com

Online auction software reviewed in Info World; winner of the Internet World Best of Show award in 1998. This site features a variety of merchandise, from software for new online auctioneers with a minimum of time and financial investment, to software designed for small businesses that want to generate additional revenue, to software for larger businesses that want to create sophisticated auctions. The site also features tips on getting started using auction software and demos.

Sold II Software

www.soldii.com

Site featuring auction software. Using SOLD II Auction Software, virtually any kind of auction can be run more quickly and easily. SOLD II offers a family of auction products ranging from single-user auction software right up to 20+ user systems to serve the special needs of some larger auction companies.

Soft Globe

www.softglobe.com/auction/index.htm

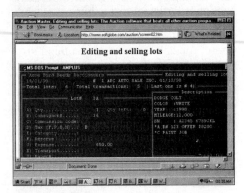

Site that features Auction Master online auction software. You can download a free demo from this site. The software enables you to simultaneously receive goods from consignors, register them, and sell them. The software also helps you monitor expenses, registration, sales, unsold lots, printing invoices, and more. This sofware is good for the serious online auctioneer since it is a little complicated to use.

Part IV
The Part of Tens

The 5th Wave   By Rich Tennant

"Mr. James! Mr. James! I know you're in there—I can hear you breathing over the partition. If you don't stop outbidding me on those Tae-Bo workout videos..."

In this part . . .

*T*his part is for all of you who want a quick summary of the most important auction tips and warnings I can provide, and for those of you who just can't get enough of the number ten.

In this part I offer ten tips for sellers, ten tips for buyers, ten secrets about online auctions that no one except you and I will ever reveal (and I am probably in BIG trouble with the in-crowd), ten things you can do in case of trouble (where is that beanbag baby I won and paid for five months ago?), and the most important ten of them all, the ten mistakes to avoid while in the wonderful world of online auctions. Enjoy!

Chapter 11

Ten Tips for Sellers

Selling at an Internet auction is similar to other forms of electronic commerce, but the field does carry some unique twists. Other chapters in this book discuss how to communicate with customers around the world and create Web pages to supplement your auction listings (see Chapters 7 and 9). In this chapter, I give you some "insider" tips — things you may pick up only after participating in auctions for weeks or months.

Don't Limit Yourself to One Category or Service

Auctions can be habit forming for sellers as well as buyers. When you find a service you like, it's only natural to stick with it. However, the Internet auction field is constantly changing. You can save money and be more successful by not limiting your sales activities to one particular category or auction service. Many of the smaller and newer auction services waive seller's fees to attract business.

Whether you're using a new service or a well-established one, it pays to do some shopping around on the site to see what items (if any) sell particularly well on that site. Concentrate on offering the types of objects that customers are used to finding and are likely to bid on.

Connie Varco has good success selling vintage linens on Yahoo! Auctions. On a larger service like eBay, she's more likely to have success with unusual items that stand out from the crowd. "I don't concentrate on one particular area," she says. "I have made very good profits on the majority of things I've sold — enough to keep me going, take care of necessities, and feed the family."

Set Low Reserves to Encourage High Bids

Time and again, auction sellers tell me that they achieved their highest purchase prices on items they offered at low initial bids and low reserve bids. Here's what Connie Varco describes as her best auction sale:

"The most exciting thing I've sold had to be a depression glass coaster I found at the bottom of an auction box. It was beautiful and had a list price of $32. I set my reserve price low in order to sell it, but I ended up with more than 20 bids, and it sold for almost $200."

Buyers are put off by high minimum bids that are essentially the same as specifying a reserve price, except that the "reserve price" isn't secret. Frequently, you see a valuable item for sale with a minimum bid of, say, $500, and no bids at all. Often, an item like this goes unsold. The seller may then turn around and offer the same object at a slightly lower — but still high — minimum price of perhaps $400. I say: What's the point?

Have confidence in the quality of your merchandise and let the market decide what it's worth. At the very least, keep the minimum bid as low as possible. By all means, if you want to protect your investment, put a reasonable reserve on what you're selling. But just once, experiment with no reserve and see what happens. The words "No Reserve" on a desirable item create extra excitement in bidders' minds. You'll probably be pleasantly surprised by what happens.

Include Good Images in Your Listings

A good digital image is worth a thousand words. What, you ask, constitutes a "good" image? Here are some suggestions (see Chapter 7 for more tips):

- **Small file size.** A good image takes up as little computer space as possible so that it can be transmitted from server to browser and appear on the bidder's computer screen in a matter of seconds. Try to keep the file size less than 20K — smaller, if possible.

- **Small physical dimensions.** Crop an image using a graphics program so it doesn't take up too much physical space on a Web page. Keep the physical size small so viewers can see it easily on a small computer monitor — and so it doesn't distract from your description.

It's often helpful to buyers to include a couple of different views of an object, though having three or four images on the same auction Web page can make the page take longer to load. If you do post multiple images, try to keep them in the 10K to 20K file size range to be kind to your viewers.

Toot Your Own Horn with a Good Description

A good auction description gets to the point right away. In the very first sentence, spell out what makes this piece of merchandise stand out from the crowd. Is it difficult to find, out of print, in exceptionally good condition, or simply a good buy?

Auction bidders are in a hurry because there are so many things to check out online. Be sure to call attention to your item's good points up front. Try organizing your description this way (see Chapter 6 for more tips):

- **Lead with a hook.** Hook shoppers' interest with a couple of descriptive adjectives about the item, along with a sentence that simply describes what the item is.

- **Call on divine provenance.** *Provenance,* in auction-speak, is the history or origin of an item. Tell where you got the object, how old it is, and who has used it.

- **Follow with the flaws.** Avoid misunderstandings by mentioning any flaws or drawbacks — but leave them for the fourth or fifth sentence of your description. (A photo that shows the flaws is an extra-nice touch for prospective bidders.)

- **Finish with a flourish.** Don't end on a down note; provide a closing sentence that sums up why people should be dying to bid on what you have to sell. Tell them if it's brand-new or if it's used but in mint condition, for instance. At the very least, provide a note about shipping costs, payment options, and any restrictions (you won't ship overseas, for example).

The following is a brief example of what I'm talking about:

```
Rich with history, this bottle of 1936 Chateau Backstreet red
table wine is a must for any collector. Comes in an unopened
genuine 32 oz. bottle. Label is a bit frayed and discolored in
lower right-hand corner, and there is a chip in the bottom of
the bottle. Still, this is a rare and valuable find from the
prestigious Backstreet Vineyards of Des Plaines, Illinois.
```

I particularly like descriptions that point out any special shipping options or restrictions, and that go into detail on any special features (good or bad) that the item has.

Avoid unsubtle things like @@@ or !!! Excessive punctuation marks may grab your attention the first or second time you see them in an auction listing title, but after the 20th, 30th, or 100th time, they no longer have any impact. Just let your description speak for itself and give the punctuation keys on your keyboard a rest.

Be Honest

Honesty is without doubt the best policy when it comes to conducting electronic commerce in all its forms, including auction sales. Providing fair and frank descriptions builds credibility, which, in turn, promotes return business.

Honesty also helps you avoid disagreements with buyers who say after they receive the goods that they didn't know of a particular problem or flaw. If you describe an item's problems up front, there's no mystery. If a disagreement arises, you have only to point to your original description as evidence of full disclosure.

Don't Undersell Your Wares

As an auction buyer, I look for bargains. Often, those bargains are goods that aren't top of the line in one way or another. Just because a desirable object isn't in mint condition doesn't mean it won't attract high bids. However, experience tells me that if the seller goes out of his way to point out the flaws *in detail,* bids on the item will be lower than they would otherwise be.

The best descriptions go into detail about an item's good and bad points without seeming apologetic or playing down its real worth. Yes, you should be honest. You should mention problems such as cracks or stains. But avoid the following:

- **Emphasizing the flaws more than the good points.** If you only describe what's wrong with an item, you discourage people from bidding high on it.

- **Don't apologize for the flaws.** If you take the attitude that it's your fault the damage occurred and that the item is somehow second-rate, you overshadow the item's desirability.

A rare antique with a few imperfections is still an object of value. Online shoppers aren't generally looking for perfection; they want convenience and a good deal. Don't reduce your reserve because your item has a crack or chip or some flaking paint. Refer to price guides and get a good idea of the item's worth before you put it on the virtual auction block.

Follow the Rules

By trying to sell some types of objects at auction, you're just asking for trouble. I'm talking about things like police badges, firearms, and "adult" items. You may well get in trouble from law enforcement agencies that don't allow sales of such things, especially to minors. Make sure you insist that bidders be of age, if age restrictions apply.

At the very least, be aware that auction houses like eBay, as well as some law enforcement agencies, place restrictions on the sale of guns online, for example. In early 1999, the government was reportedly investigating unspecified "illegal transactions" on eBay.

 Be sure to read the auction house's rules on questionable sale items so you can be sure you're on the up and up. For example, eBay rules state that any police badge offered at auction on its site must have "reproduction" or "movie prop" clearly listed in the title. The sellers also need to have a scanned letter of authorization from the agency whose badge is reproduced, stating that the reproduction badge does not violate existing trademarks or copyrights.

 Don't violate a copyright by quoting printed material in your auction listings or reproducing printed or digitized images that someone else has published. eBay has instituted a Legal Buddy Program that works to ensure that items listed for auction don't infringe upon the copyright, trademark, or other rights of third parties. One of the best places to research the issue of copyright is the U.S. Copyright Office site at lcweb.loc.gov/copyright. Also visit The Copyright Web site at www.benedict.com.

Provide Payment Options Aplenty

Everyone (well, practically everyone) selling at Internet auctions accepts cashier's checks and money orders. If you can take credit card payments, you can get even more business. Having an account with an escrow service also helps.

The important thing is to give buyers payment options. It's getting easier to obtain a merchant account with a bank so your company (if you have one) can accept credit cards. However, the problem of processing the purchase information is still yours to handle. Setting up a merchant account is getting easier but still involves some work, as does processing the credit card purchases themselves, so such an account makes sense only if you have your own business or conduct lots of transactions.

A software program called Authorizer (www.atomic-software.com) helps your business process payments by automatically sending the data to the bank of your choice. If you want to accept credit cards and let someone else do the processing, check out QuickSite, a program that helps you build a business Web site and provides you with a variety of e-commerce hosting options (primecom.net/quicksite).

Love What You Do

If you plan to sell on Internet auctions for the long haul, keeping a positive attitude is a must because of the time investment required. Selling involves a lot more than just throwing some pictures and a quick description on a Web page.

"I probably receive three to five e-mails a day asking questions, and I might send out at least that many e-mails myself," says seller Connie Varco. "Be professional in every aspect. Always be friendly. It helps and it doesn't cost you a thing. Keeping an open line of communication makes deals go along much smoother. You really have to be committed to what you're doing. If you make yourself open, you will learn many little tips along the way. Other sellers can be a great source of help."

Don't Be Afraid to Be an Auction Entrepreneur

"Don't quit your day job!" You hear it all the time. I still hear it myself, even though I quit my day job several years ago. I'm afraid you're going to hear this old saw one more time from me, but with a twist: Don't quit your day job until you succeed at making online selling your full-time occupation. *Then* quit your day job and make a grab for entrepreneurial success.

I know I'm going out on a limb here. That's why my recommendation is to make auctions your nighttime and weekend activity until you make enough money to reach your financial goals. Then take the plunge and make it a full-time occupation. Plenty of people have done so, and you can, too. The Internet is still in its formative years, and the field is still open for entrepreneurs. So give it a try.

You have to search a bit in order to find examples of success stories that center on individual users. You can search through the archives of past press releases at www.ebay.com/aboutebay/releases/index.html. Also check out the eBay Community Member Profiles at www.ebay.com/aboutebay/community/profiles.html for examples of traders who found success through online auctions. One reporter describes his own computer auction success in an article at europe.cnn.com/TECH/computing/9805/19/online_auction/index.html.

Chapter 12

Ten Tips for Buyers

The saying *caveat emptor* (Let the buyer beware) appears on the Help pages of many Internet auction sites. But to my mind, the saying isn't quite right. Let the buyer be *aware* is more appropriate.

I'm talking about being aware not only of pitfalls but also of services and tricks that can make your shopping experience go more smoothly and successfully. You don't need to feel as if you're stumbling around in the dark when you embark on your first virtual auction adventure. In this chapter, I provide ten tips for making purchases successfully and profitably without falling victim to online scams or other pitfalls that can leave you bidding for trouble.

Shop 'Til You Drop

Don't get stuck using a single auction service to find everything you want. As I write this, I discover new auction services going online practically every few days. Many of these services specialize in a particular area rather than offering everything under the sun, so you may be able to find better deals or, at the very least, more informed descriptions of auction merchandise, at smaller, more narrowly focused Web sites.

If you see an item you want, take a few minutes before you bid to make sure that a duplicate item isn't available somewhere else at a lower price. Shop around using auction-specific services such as BidFind (www.bidfind.com) to get the best deal on what you're looking for.

Don't Believe Everything You Read

Good auction sellers describe their wares in glowing terms and play down any faults their offerings may have. Don't take these claims at face value, no matter how honest or knowledgeable the individual seems to be.

By all means, don't be taken in by overused descriptors like Rare! Unusual! One-Of-A-Kind! and the ubiquitous L@@K! The object in question may indeed be rare and valuable, but you should determine that for yourself rather than relying on a stranger's word for it.

Be sure to raise any questions you have with the seller before placing a bid. If the auction description doesn't include an image of the object for sale, be sure to ask for one. If you need a second opinion, consult with one of the auction discussion groups mentioned in Chapter 3, or ask a retailer in your area who buys or sells the type of merchandise you're considering.

Take Your Time

The Internet is the ultimate shopping network for impulse buyers, and auctions take impulse shopping to a new level by promising dramatic savings or rare objects you can't find anywhere else.

Remember that time and the Internet are on your side as a shopper. You have the advantage of time because most auctions last at least a day. First of all, make sure you really want something before you start placing bids and getting caught up in the action. Take the time to print out an auction listing and do research either online or at your local library to determine whether an item is really worth buying. Call some retail outlets and see if you can get a better deal down the street before you start placing bids around the world.

The Internet itself is an advantage because as auctions become more popular, you're more likely to find what you want. If you aren't able to win at auction the first time, don't worry: What you're seeking is sure to turn up again sooner or later.

Some bidders place a small bid early on in the auction just in case the seller decides to end the auction early, or to gauge the level of interest in the merchandise. They increase bids as the end nears when they have a better idea of how hot the competition is. This and other bidding strategies are discussed in Chapter 4.

Do Your Homework

Impulse purchases lead to financial disasters. A little research can go a long way toward ensuring that you buy what you want at a price you can afford. Print an auction listing, take it to the library, and look up the product in a consumer catalog or a guide to antiques or collectibles. Check prices for similar items at a retail store. Get an appraisal. Whatever you do, know what the item is worth and what constitutes a good buy before you click the Submit Bid button. (See Chapter 4 for more tips and resources for researching prices.)

Besides researching the item you're interested in, you should research the person selling it. Be sure to check out the seller of the item you're bidding on, and give preference to folks who are frequent online auctioneers and receive positive feedback. Use the feedback system and other techniques described in Chapters 3 and 4. After the auction is over, keep in touch by e-mail or phone so the buyer knows you have mailed your payment, or that you have received the merchandise.

Network with Other Auction Hounds

I shopped on eBay for many months before I discovered the various bulletin boards for current and new users. I wish I hadn't waited so long to wise up! These boards are chock-full of great tips and the latest insider analyses of trends and problems.

If nothing else, lurk in the background and check out what others are saying. If you do have a question or a problem, post a message. Joining the online auction community takes some extra effort, but the rewards can be substantial. You may make some new friends, and you can certainly get some useful tips and find people to turn to for help when you need it. (See Chapter 3 for more information.)

Beware of Shill Bidders

I frequented online auctions for quite a while before I heard the term "shill bidder." A *shill bidder* is someone who makes arrangements with a seller to bid on merchandise in order to drive up the price. The bidder may even be the seller herself, using a different username, password, and e-mail address.

How do you recognize a shill bidder? Such a person may never have completed a transaction (on eBay, she has the feedback number zero (0) after her username), or the bidder's username or e-mail address is similar to the seller's. Sometimes a shill bidder keeps outbidding every high bidder, although in truth, it can be really difficult to tell whether the person is cheating or simply really wants the item. If you suspect that shill bidding is taking place, think twice about continuing to bid. Consider dropping out and waiting for the next item you're interested in.

Identifying shill bidders is difficult, although LabXPro, a site that auctions scientific and lab equipment, claims to use a "complex algorithm" to detect shill bidders (read about it at www.labx.com/v2/labauction/livebidhelp.cfm).

Besides being unfair, shill bidding is grounds for expulsion from many (if not all) auction services. Be aware that it can happen and, if something "fishy" occurs during, or especially near the end of an auction, raise the issue with the service you're using at the time.

Pay Extra for Escrow Protection

An *escrow service* is a business that helps buyers and sellers complete transactions carried out over the Internet. The service receives the buyer's payment for an item and holds her money until she notifies them that she received the item in satisfactory condition; the service then releases payment to the seller. This way, the buyer and seller don't have to rely on trust, and each receives what she needs to complete the deal.

Yes, arranging for escrow protection takes more work, and yes, it costs a little extra. However, the peace of mind you get from using an escrow service is well worth a few extra dollars. To find out more about escrow services and how they work, see Chapter 5.

Why Wait? Post a Want Ad

Why wait until the treasure you're looking for appears online? If you're looking for something rare or obscure, post a notice to tell potential auctioneers what you want.

For example, you can be proactive by posting an ad on eBay's Wanted Board. Go to the Buyer Services page (pages.ebay.com/aw/ps.html) and click the Wanted Page link.

Newsgroups and bulletin boards are a natural resource for want ads. Check out the descriptions of collectors' gathering spots in Chapter 3, visit some of these groups, and post a message detailing your needs.

Don't Let Auctions Get the Better of You

The suspense and excitement of Internet auctions can be addictive. On one level, they can take time away from your family and friends. On another, they can threaten your financial and psychological well-being. It's important to realize that you can easily get carried away, and to recognize the signs that you have a problem. Take the Center for Online Addiction's quiz on Internet auctions at `www.netaddiction.com/resources/auction_houses.htm` (see Figure 12-1) to find out whether you have a hobby or a serious problem.

Internet auctions should be a fun and positive addition to your life, not an obsessive addiction that takes it over. If you can't stop bidding, selling, or obsessing over auctions, take a break and seek help if you need it. For example, you can get help from Center for Online Addiction's Virtual Clinic (`www.netaddiction.com/clinic.htm`).

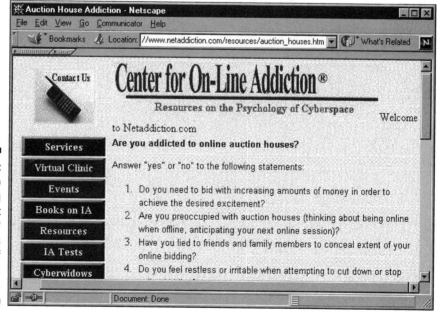

Figure 12-1: Can't stop thinking about auctions? Take this quiz to see if you have a problem.

Don't Let Shipping Be a Shocker

Often, what seems like a bargain when the auction closes turns out to be something else when you get your credit card bill and realize how much the auction service added for shipping. If you purchase something substantial such as a computer monitor, you can easily add $20 to $50 in shipping charges to your purchase price.

The solution: Before you start bidding, read the fine print on the auction site that tells you about how much actually receiving the merchandise will cost. Most sites that auction electronics equipment, computer components, and other consumer goods to high bidders provide this information. If you're using a person-to-person service, you can do a rough estimate of the shipping costs using an online shipping calculator if the seller doesn't mention shipping charges in the item's description. See Chapter 8 for more information.

You may want to consider not bidding on any auction listing that doesn't specifically provide information about shipping and handling. Otherwise, make sure you get an exact shipping cost from the seller by sending the individual an e-mail inquiry before you bid.

Chapter 13

Ten Little-Known Facts about Internet Auctions

· ·

*L*ike most things, Internet auctions aren't always what they appear to be. As with other business deals and communications, shady things happen, and loopholes to standard practices abound. In this chapter, I share ten secrets about online auctions that can help you avoid unpleasant situations and get the best deals — even if you sometimes have to be a little sneaky to do so. All's fair in love and Internet auctions!

Shipping Costs Can Sink Your Bargain

Shipping costs are often the hidden "gotcha" that turns a deal into a disappointment. Some sellers, whether they are individuals or auction services, charge exorbitant amounts for shipping. Suppose you place the winning bid on a rare Buddy Holly record from someone overseas for a mere $5 but discover to your surprise that having it sent to you costs $15 more dollars. Ouch!

Don't be shocked by shipping add-ons. Read the background information on the auction site that explains how merchandise is sent to you. If you need more specific information, don't hesitate to ask.

Some sellers routinely add a set fee, such as $20, for any shipments to other countries: "$20 extra for shipping to Canada," for example. You can calculate the exact overseas shipping charges by using the U.S. Postal Service's online shipping rate calculators (ircalc.usps.gov).

You Can Find Out What Your Buyer or Seller Has to Say about Others

A great way to check out a buyer or seller is to research the feedback he leaves for others — not the feedback he receives, but the comments he *leaves*. This can be very revealing. Many people who receive a lot of positive feedback don't take the time to leave any comments themselves.

Here's how you can call up the feedback from eBay's Web site:

1. **Connect to the Internet and go to the eBay Web site** (www.ebay.com).

2. **Go to the Web page that contains the User ID of the seller you want to investigate.**

   If the person is a seller, go to the page that presents the object he's selling. If the person is a buyer bidding on your item and he's the high bidder, go to your item's Web page, where his User ID is displayed as the current high bidder.

3. **Click the feedback number (the number beside the username) of the individual you want to investigate. For example, to look into the feedback left by greg@site.com(6), click the number 6.**

   A URL appears in the Location (Netscape Navigator) or Address (Internet Explorer) area of your browser window as eBay retrieves the Feedback Profile for that individual. This is the feedback he's received from other users.

4. **Click the URL just after the word *feedback* and type the word** left.

   For example, if you check the feedback left by someone with the username *meteorite*, the URL looks like this:

   ```
   http://cgi.ebay.com/aw-cgi/eBayISAPI.dll?MfcISAPICommand=
   ViewFeedbackLeft&userid=meteorite
   ```

5. **Press Return.**

   In a flash, eBay does another search and presents another Web page with the feedback comments left by the same user about other eBay sellers or buyers.

Sometimes, the feedback comments you uncover aren't terribly revealing. You may well discover that the person you're investigating leaves the same exact comments for everyone with whom he does business. But occasionally you discover something useful in helping you decide whether to do business with an individual.

Changing Your Mind Is a Seller's Prerogative

Once you put your merchandise on the virtual auction block and open the bidding, you're pretty much committed to making the sale, right? Well, not exactly. It's not generally good practice to back out of a sale you initiated, but it isn't impossible.

Sometimes things just don't work out: You have second thoughts about selling something, your 6-year-old daughter drops the item and breaks it, or perhaps a long-lost relative offers you $10,000 for it. (The same sort of thing applies to buyers. See the next section to find out how to back out if you're a bidder.)

eBay's rules state that you are required to carry the auction through to its conclusion and sell the item to the high bidder. However, if you become the high bidder, you have no problem. Simply make a winning bid and immediately close the auction. You win, keep the item, and get to stay on eBay for not violating the rules! The only penalty is that you have to pay eBay the sales commission for the final bid price.

On Amazon.com Auctions, sellers can cancel a sale if no bids have yet been received, or if no bidders meet your reserve in a reserve price auction. If you have a reserve price specified and a winning bidder, you can still cancel but the company cautions that this should be done rarely and is likely to invite negative feedback. In any of these cases, sellers are still obligated to pay Amazon.com the listing fees.

You should back out of a sale only if you have no other alternative. Backing out is likely to earn you negative feedback, which can influence sales you want to hold in the future.

Bidders Can Back Out, Too

Backing out of a sale when you're the high bidder doesn't necessarily put you in the "deadbeat bidder" category. You may have very good reasons for having second thoughts or getting cold feet after you come out at the top of the bidding heap.

Sellers are human beings. They usually respond in a reasonable manner if you quickly tell them you're very sorry, but you can't afford the item. If you must do this, offering to pay for the listing fee and sales commission that the auction service charged is an especially good idea.

There's a possibility, however remote, that if you are courteous and honest about your situation and offer to reimburse the seller for the sales fees, he may let you go without submitting negative feedback about you. It's more likely that your feedback record will be blotched by some thumbs-down comments, but if you can't afford to pay, say so as soon as possible so that the seller knows what's happening and can either relist the merchandise or approach the next-highest bidder. You guarantee yourself negative feedback if you simply disappear without any comment.

The Second-Highest Bidder Can Be a Winner

Usually, coming in second is considered a losing proposition. However, under certain circumstances (such as those described in the previous section) the second-highest bidder can get the prize. If the high bidder backs out for some reason, the seller on eBay can approach the second-highest bidder and ask him to follow through on the bid.

On Amazon.com Auctions, a seller can cancel a high bid if the bidder has received a substantial amount of negative feedback and if the seller has doubts about the validity of that person's bid. The company's Help pages don't say anything about subsequently contacting the second highest bidder, but I don't see why you couldn't do this if you wanted to. However, bidders' names are hidden until the reserve price is met (if one is specified). Click the Bid History link on the item's auction listing page to see the bidders' nicknames. Then click a nickname to get contact information for that individual.

This doesn't happen often, however. Most transactions are either completed successfully or, if the transaction doesn't go through, the item is relisted. If you're the second-highest bidder and are contacted by the seller, don't feel obligated to follow through. You may no longer want the item or (more likely) have found a substitute. Often, though, second bananas are happy to get a second chance to buy something on which they lost out earlier.

Your Virtual Acquaintances Have Feelings, Too

You may not realize it, but your account with an auction service can be terminated if you post "inappropriate or non-auction-related feedback" (Amazon.com Auctions says this in its Community Rules) about another user. Because you seldom, if ever, meet your online acquaintances in person, you can lose sight of the fact that they're human beings just like you. Think before you harshly criticize (in Internet-speak, *flame*) someone; it can get you in trouble as well as hurt someone else, too.

People communicate online in ways they never would if they were talking to someone face to face. People sometimes flame someone else by sending an outrageously angry e-mail message. Folks in a chat room may get much more intimate than they would otherwise.

If something goes wrong with one of your person-to-person auctions, don't explode in a rage. Most of the people you deal with are not auction professionals, and they can make mistakes just as you can. Act with courtesy and patience — above all, take a deep breath and wait an hour or so before firing off that angry e-mail message you were contemplating.

Bidding Low Can Make You a Winner

A Dutch auction is very different than a conventional Yankee-style auction in which the highest bidder wins. In a Dutch auction, everyone pays the same price, which is the same as the *lowest* bid. The lowest bidder and the next highest-bidders win multiple items being offered at the same time. (See Chapter 1 for more details about Dutch auctions and other type of auctions.)

The trick is to avoid being the low bidder, who is said to be *on the bubble*. There's no problem being the low qualifying bidder when the auction ends. The problem occurs when you're the low qualifying bidder while the auction is nearing its end, because you run the risk of someone outbidding you and kicking you off the list of winners at the last minute. Instead, bid at the last minute and place a bid that makes you the second-lowest bidder. Just make sure you're in the winner's circle without being in the low bid position.

eBay's explanation of how Dutch auctions work is at `pages.ebay.com/aw/help/help-faq-format.html`. The eBay Underground FAQ page also contains a good explanation of this strategy (`www.frii.com/~afs/ebay`).

Sniping May Not Be Nice, But It Works

Sniping, the practice of placing a bid just a few minutes or seconds before an auction ends so that other bidders can't place a counter-offer, is popular for a reason: On some sites like eBay, it *can* help you win auctions. Sniping isn't illegal, but it is sneaky.

I blush to admit it, but I've done this myself and won. I've also *been* sniped and lost (it hurts!). Here's how sniping works:

1. **Refrain from getting into the auction until the last few minutes.**

   Keep reloading your Web page to check the progress of the auction. (In Microsoft Internet Explorer, choose View➪Refresh or press F5. In Netscape Navigator, choose View➪Reload or press Ctrl+R.)

2. **Place a bid just before the auction ends.**

   Bid the absolute maximum amount you're willing to pay. Why? You have no idea whether the high bidder's currently posted bid is really the maximum he'll pay. He may have already placed a proxy bid that's far higher than the amount you see on screen.

   The exact time that you place your snipe bid depends on your comfort level. Some snipers wait until the last five minutes, and some even wait until the last few *seconds.*

3. **Frantically reload the auction listing Web page to see whether anyone counter-bids you at the last minute.**

   Hopefully, when you reload the page and see that the auction is over, your name will be listed as the high bidder.

Some sites, like Amazon.com Auctions, have instituted defenses against sniping: If bids arrive in the last five minutes of an auction, for example, the auction is automatically extended to give other bidders a chance to respond.

Sniping is a strategy that can blow up in your face if anything happens at the critical moment: Your computer crashes, your Internet connection fails to work, the auction service fails to respond, or your modem starts to crawl slowly. If you really want something badly, try some semi-sniping: Place a bid 20 or 30 minutes before the sale ends, rather than in the last minute or two.

Whether you get a bargain as a result of sniping is another matter: You have to outbid the current high bidder, and you have to meet the seller's reserve price if one is specified, just as you do if you bid an hour or a day in advance. See Chapter 4 for more bidding strategies.

Pseudonyms Aren't Just for Authors

Although I don't recommend this, in the interest of making you aware of all there is to know about Internet auctions, I have to include the fact that you can register more than once at an auction site. I'm talking about adopting a new "identity" in the form of a new username and password so you can escape negative feedback or other trouble you ran into under your previous username and password.

Until Microsoft, Intel, or another computer giant finds a way to track individual users through computer chip or software serial numbers, you're still able to surf pretty much anonymously, at least if you use one of the thousands of Internet Service Providers around the world to get online. A remote Web site can tell what computer you used to connect to the Net, but it can't tell who you are or where you live. However, if you use a proprietary online service like America Online to connect to the Internet and participate in online auctions, your chances of being "tracked down" if you do something wrong skyrocket.

There are plenty of warning signs here that you should pay attention to. For one thing, if you register with two different usernames but use the same e-mail address, street address, credit card information, or other personal data, someone at the auction house or an inquisitive bidder may raise questions, and you could be thrown off the service altogether. You'll certainly incur the wrath of anyone you want to do business with.

Auctions Aren't the Only Game Online

Auctions are definitely the hot form of electronic commerce as I write this, but if you're simply looking to sell something online, consider placing a classified ad on a Web site.

The procedure for posting online classifieds is simpler and more straightforward than putting merchandise up for auction. Basically, you compose a short ad, set a price, and provide a phone number or e-mail address. The rest is up to the potential buyers who see your ad and respond. Some sites charge a flat fee for placing ads, but many let you post notices for free.

Some of the classified Web sites specialize in specific types of popular collectibles are Cellular Recycler for buying and selling cellular phones (www.cellular-recycler.com) and Trader Publishing Company for cars, trucks, RVs, and other vehicles (www.traderonline.com). You can find a lengthy list of classified sites at internetclearing.com/classified.asp.

Chapter 14

Ten Responses in Times of Trouble

● ●

*M*ost Internet auction interactions are smooth as silk. That's why so many people become regular auction buyers and sellers.

But auction transactions do occasionally go sour for one reason or another. And when that happens, guidelines for how to respond may be hard to find. In the "real" world, you have a variety of traditional recourses (the police, lawyers, small claims court, and so on). However, few of these avenues are applicable to fraud in cyberspace.

Chances are that you will never have a problem, but if you do, all is not lost. As this Part of Tens section demonstrates, you have a number of places to turn if you run into trouble, whether you're buying or selling.

Use Feedback Wisely

Feedback is what makes person-to-person auction services such as eBay work. Feedback encourages buyers and sellers to behave with courtesy, and acts as the "enforcer" to threaten those who break the rules.

Because any feedback you give can have great impact, I encourage you to think twice before leaving negative feedback. Yes, you should leave negative feedback if it's appropriate. I'm just saying that you should make sure you do the following:

- ✔ Wait until you are certain that the buyer or seller is not going to respond or follow through and that all your efforts to elicit either the payment or shipment you want have failed.
- ✔ When you do leave negative feedback, be specific and straightforward without being abusive or unprofessional.

Remember that the feedback you leave reflects your own level of professionalism, and that clever auction users can review your comments. (See Chapter 13 for instructions on retrieving the feedback a person has left for others, as opposed to the feedback an individual has received.)

Complain to the Auction Service

If your high bidder never sends a check, your first instinct may be to call out the big guns. But, before you complain to state or national agencies, contact the auction service involved. All auction sites have (or *should* have) customer service or technical support personnel you can approach when you have questions or urgent problems. Newer services especially are on the lookout for problems and may be even more receptive to hearing your story than more established services.

On Amazon.com Auctions, go to the Community Guide page and click the Reporting Fraud link. A Reporting Fraud page appears with tips on resolving disputes, as does a single link to a page where you can contact Amazon.com. This page simply tells you to send an e-mail message to investigations@amazon.com with detailed information about the problem you encountered.

On the Yahoo! Auctions home page (auctions.yahoo.com), click the Bidder's Guide link. When the Bidder's Guide page appears, click the Community Guide link and then click the Your Community link. Click the Ask Our Customer Care Team link at the bottom of the Your Community page. A Web page appears containing a form you can fill out with a description of the problem. Click the Send button at the bottom of the form to send your complaint to Yahoo! Auctions.

eBay provides a number of places where you can turn for help: Clicking the Help link at the top of any page on the eBay Web site takes you to the Starting Point page. If you have a question that needs immediate attention, scroll down and click the Got a Question? link to go to the Support page, which has links to the following helpful resources:

- **The eBay Support Q & A Board.** A question or complaint posted on this message board gets a response from eBay staff. You can read about similar problems other users have reported and check out notices about service outages or other technical glitches.

- **eBay Live Support for New Users.** There's no such thing as a dumb question, and if you have a basic concern such as how to make a link to an image or how Dutch auctions work, you can post it on this message board to get a response from eBay personnel.

- **The eBay User to User Q & A Board.** In theory, this message board is a place where users with questions can get advice and help from other users. In practice, it's a social venue like the eBay Cafe message boards (see Chapter 3). You *can* get help here from other eBay users here, however.

- **SafeHarbor Investigations.** This part of the SafeHarbor customer service area is the place to turn if you have been defrauded by a buyer or seller and want eBay to look into the problem.

✓ **The Emergency Contact message board.** This is a forum where you can post messages if you don't have phone or e-mail contact information for a user and need to reach her in a hurry. To get to this board, go to the eBay News & Chat page (`pages.ebay.com/aw/newschat.html`) and click the Emergency Contact link.

Other auction services offer a smaller range of support options. Yahoo! Auctions maintains a Support page at `help.yahoo.com/help/auctions`. Auction Universe (`www.auctionuniverse.com`) also has a Customer Support page with a FAQ and an e-mail link to the customer support staff — that's about all. Click the Customer Support link at the top of any Auction Universe page to get there.

Voice Your Complaint Far and Wide

Whether a site has a lot or only a few support options, if a seller is truly uncooperative, you still may not get your money back or receive your missing merchandise.

In this case, you have no choice but to go beyond the auction service and contact a wider range of agencies that can hear your complaint and do something about it. Here are just a few suggestions:

✓ If you did not receive a shipment sent by U.S. mail, contact the U.S. Postal Inspector's Office (`www.usps.gov/ncsc/locators/find-is.html`) to find a local inspector in your area and file a Mail Fraud Complaint. The Postal Service then notifies the seller that such a complaint is being investigated, which is likely to intimidate him into giving you a refund or shipping the goods you purchased.

✓ You can also file a complaint with the National Fraud Information Center (`www.fraud.org`) or the Federal Trade Commission (`www.ftc.gov`).

Book dealer Tessa Hebert provides the preceding suggestions and many more on two informative Web pages she maintains for eBay users who need somewhere to turn in case of trouble. Sellers can find a page full of tips at `www.mindspring.com/~bookdealers/nopay.html`. Buyers can find lots of useful suggestions at `www.mindspring.com/~bookdealers/ripoff.html`.

Start Using Escrow Services

If you're once burned and twice shy or if you're just a cautious sort of person, I urge you to strongly consider using an escrow service. The level of security you get can be worth the extra steps and service fee the buyer pays.

In addition, using an escrow service that accepts credit card payments essentially lets buyers pay by credit card rather than limiting them to the usual cashier's check/money order options specified by most sellers. See Chapter 5 for more information on how escrow services work and how much they cost.

Set Firm Guidelines

Do everything you can to avoid misunderstandings in the first place. Many problems arise because sellers don't provide enough information to prospective buyers. It's always a good idea to be clear and complete in your specifications to buyers.

Provide as much specific information as you can in your auction description. The more specific you are in setting down rules, the less likely it is that you will become engaged in a dispute. I'm not bothered when sellers specify that they take only money orders, that they ship exclusively with a particular company, or even when they won't haggle over price if the reserve price is not met. Such rules reduce my level of uncertainty and give me less to worry about.

If you sell through person-to-person auctions, don't be afraid to lay down the law and run the sale the way you want. It's good for both you and your winning bidder(s).

Get It Off Your Chest

Misery loves company. Sometimes sharing your problem with someone in a similar situation helps. Whether you're a buyer who was outbid or a seller who encountered a deadbeat bidder, talk to other users about it. Together you may come up with a solution that you wouldn't find on your own. At the very least, you'll feel understood.

At this writing, eBay is the only auction service that provides its users with message boards where they can hold virtual conversations. By the time you read this, other auction services may likely have their own user discussion forums, and some enterprising auction users will create a Usenet newsgroup in the .alt category (see Chapter 3).

When Things Get Drastic, Go Plastic

Using a credit card gives you an extra level of protection when it comes to auction sales. If you purchase items with plastic and they turn out to be damaged, you may be able to get a refund from your credit card issuer.

If you made a purchase with a credit card and the seller never shipped your goods, you can threaten to have the seller's merchant account status revoked by filing a complaint with the Federal Trade Commission (FTC). The FTC has a rule that goods must be shipped within 30 days of purchase; see Chapter 5 for more information.

Berate Your Service in Auction Ratings

 Tattling is not bad if it prevents bad things from happening to others. If you receive poor (or nonexistent) customer service from an auction service, you can complain to a site on the Web with a considerable amount of influence over that service's success: Talk to one of the Web sites that provides lists and ratings of the different auction companies on the Internet.

Many of the following sites provide descriptions and ratings of auction sites:

- ✔ BidFind (`www.bidfind.com/af/af-list.html`) provides detailed descriptions about auction services, especially computer auction houses. (By complaining to BidFind, you may be able to influence those descriptions.)

- ✔ PlanetClick (`www.planetclick.com`) lets individual users rate auction services as well as other Web sites on a scale of 1 to 10. This site is especially good for descriptions of tiny, home-grown auction Web pages.

- ✔ The Mining Company (`www.miningcompany.com`) also rates auction sites chosen by someone who visits and evaluates the site beforehand.

- ✔ Auction Patrol (`www.auctionpatrol.com`) has a set of community forums called The Station where users can comment on their own auction experiences. It also provides a Wall of Fame that rates particularly good auction sites, as well as other features.

Also check this book's Internet Directory for descriptions of auction sites.

Choose Your Weapon: E-mail

Okay, "weapon" is a bit strong here, I suppose. The point is that e-mail is your primary tool when it comes to convincing uncooperative individuals to follow through on their commitments, sharing complaints, conveying information about sales items, and getting help from your fellow auction users.

Be sure to save any e-mail messages you receive from an auction service that relate to transactions that go bad. As an extra safety measure, print out the messages so you have a tangible "paper trail" to call on in case your computer data is lost. Also save any e-mail messages you received from the person who isn't following through on your deal.

Get a Refund and Start Over

Sometimes the easiest thing for a seller to do when a buyer disappears is to fold her cards, so to speak, and start over. Getting a refund of your selling fee from your auction service won't bring back the time and energy you lost, but it does save you from losing money.

You can then either re-list your auction merchandise or try to approach the second-highest bidder on your auction. The individual who lost out before may well be overjoyed to hear that she still has a chance to get what she wanted, even if the purchase price is a bit higher than her original bid.

Bonus Tip: Connect with an ISP

Here's a brief 11th suggestion to round out this Part of Tens chapter: Complain to the Internet Service Provider that gives your uncooperative buyer or seller access to the Internet.

Most ISPs have strict guidelines about how customers can use the Net, and these usually include rules about conducting fraudulent or criminal activity online. If you complain to the ISP, the company may cancel the individual's account or at least issue a warning that may encourage her to "shape up" and follow through on your deal.

Chapter 15

Ten Things that Can Spoil the Auction Experience

● ●

*Y*ou, dear reader, just want to do it right. You want to buy and sell successfully. You want to avoid the Internet auction horror stories the media loves to hype.

I want you to avoid trouble, too. That's why I've gathered ten examples of common problems you can avoid. This chapter isn't intended to scare you away from Internet auctions. Rather, my hope is that by being aware of potential problems, you can take a few precautions. So without further ado, here are some descriptions of worst-case scenarios, along with tips for keeping your auction experiences happy and safe.

Your Deal Falls Through

This discouraging experience affects both buyers and sellers and is probably the most common difficulty that regular Internet auction users run into.

I'm not going to pretend that I have the perfect solution here. The success of Internet auctions, like other areas of online commerce, depends on the honesty and cooperation of human beings who are subject to human nature. You may run into high bidders who disappear without telling you that they're having second thoughts about what they just purchased. Sellers may take your money and then not ship what you purchased and ignore your e-mail messages.

You can avoid such dilemmas by dealing only with individuals who have high positive feedback ratings (see Chapter 3). Escrow services (see Chapter 5) also provide protection.

You Become Addicted to Auctions

When I first got started with Internet auctions, they totally dominated my thoughts for several weeks. I found myself interrupting activities to run upstairs and connect to auction sites to check on certain items I was eagerly following. Thanks in part to the protests of my wife and children, I got a grip and took an extended break from auctions.

Shawn Morningstar knows what I'm talking about. She had nothing but positive experiences collecting antique telephones through Internet auctions, but after a while, she began to realize that participating in auctions was becoming addictive.

"I guess it was the thrill of the auction and learning strategies to try to outbid rivals," Shawn says. "That, combined with always having e-mails about the progress of my bids to look forward to, made it hard not to keep checking in with the site.

"Another fairly addictive aspect is the feedback forum," she says. "It's fun to see nice things written about you by people you have dealt with. Also, knowing that there were something like 70,000 new items listed each day made it really intriguing to keep up with the listings. I soon began to realize that this was becoming a major habit and that my collection is just fine as it is. Luckily, I hadn't spent too much money by that time."

Shawn found lots of nice treasures, but she, too, had to take a break from the action. You can take auctions so seriously that the thrill disappears and they become an obsession rather than an activity that enriches your life.

My advice is simple: Either relax and have fun, or turn off your computer and take an extended break until your compulsion dies down. Don't be afraid to take a breath of fresh air in the event that you (or your family) sense that things are getting out of hand. If your auction participation has already escalated into a problem, check out this book's Internet Directory for Internet addiction counseling resources.

You're Careless with Feedback

Feedback is a serious part of online auction participation. Comments left by buyers and sellers about their dealings with one another are closely scrutinized and evaluated by both the subjects of the comments and people who are thinking of doing business with them.

Remember that when you leave feedback, you publish words that can be read by anyone who connects to the auction site. Be courteous and specific in your comments and avoid profanity and childish comments that can cause you embarrassment. Write a draft of your comments to be reviewed by a friend, or to be reread when you have a little more perspective. Send feedback only when you're sure it's appropriate, well-written, and accurate.

You List Before You're Ready

Be absolutely certain that you want to sell the merchandise you're about to place on the virtual auction block. If the object belongs to someone else, make sure that individual knows your intentions and agrees with the reserve price you intend to set.

You can end an auction immediately after having second thoughts, but when you do so, you risk getting a bad reputation and negative feedback. What's your hurry? Wait a day or two before placing your stuff online until you're sure you're ready to sell.

You Bid Too Eagerly

It's easy to get carried away with placing bids when you see something you really want. If you're involved in a bidding war with someone else, competitive feelings can take over.

Remember, you're bidding with your own hard-earned money. Don't bid with too much emotion. If the minimum bid gets too high for your wallet, remember that no matter how rare the item seems, thousands of new things go up for auction everyday, and you're likely to find a comparable item sooner or later — possibly at a price that doesn't bruise your budget.

The Bidder's Check Bounces

One of the biggest disasters a seller can face is finding out that a bidder's check bounced. This pitfall is surprisingly easy to avoid, however. You can require cashier's checks or money orders as payment. Even better, if you use an escrow service, you can have your buyer pay the escrow service by credit card so that in return, you receive a check from the escrow service.

The Package Gets Lost

This common problem is easy for buyers and sellers to avoid. Many shipping services, including Federal Express, United Parcel Service, and the venerable U.S. Postal Service, provide tracking of shipments. (See Chapter 5 for a list of shippers that offer Internet-based package tracking.)

If you're a seller, always ship using a tracking number, and e-mail the tracking number to your buyer after you ship. That way, both of you can keep an eye on the whereabouts of your merchandise, and you can save yourself some anxious e-mails from buyers as well.

If you're a winning bidder, look out for your interests and suggest that your seller ship the package to you a certain way: with insurance, or by two-day service rather than a slower option, for example. As long as you offer to pay for the extra charges, sellers shouldn't have a problem with such requests.

You Forget About Shipping Costs

Computer equipment, electronic gadgets, household appliances, and other goodies that seem like bargains at the end of the auction turn out to be less of a deal when you find out how much the service is going to charge to ship the merchandise to you.

If you're planning on purchasing an especially heavy item, be sure to calculate the shipping cost yourself and build that into the purchase price before you even bid. That way you'll know when you have a real steal and when you should stop bidding.

There's nothing wrong with inquiring about shipping charges before you even place a bid on a piece of merchandise. Be sure to save such e-mail exchanges, as well as the important ones that you send and receive after the auction, in case the seller attempts to make a few extra bucks by attempting to inflate shipping charges.

You Don't Do Your Homework

It's like a bad dream: You eagerly open the box you just received and end up groaning when you see what you actually purchased at auction. Or, after you start using what you bought, you see something online that is newer, better, faster, and possibly cheaper. You immediately start contemplating ways to resell your purchase.

How do you avoid buying a future white elephant? Make sure that what you purchase is really what you want. Do some comparison shopping and research your desired treasure before you place a bid. Chapter 4 tells you what you need to know to become a savvy shopper.

Your Kids Get In on the Auction Action

The Yahoo! Auctions Terms of Service agreement requires users to be at least 18 years of age before they can place bids or offer items for sale. So do the Community Rules on Amazon.com Auctions. eBay's User Agreement notes the risk of dealing with "underage persons" but doesn't say anything about an age limit.

I don't know any foolproof ways to verify the age of auction participants. Young people go online without their parents' knowledge. One notorious case involves a 13-year-old New Jersey boy who placed fraudulent bids of more than $3 million on eBay. According to an Associated Press article, the boy's parents had no idea this was taking place and immediately removed his Internet privileges when they were notified of his expensive extracurricular activities.

Although you can't keep tabs on what other people's children are getting into online, you can and should keep an eye on the computer activity of the young people in your own house. If you want to limit their access to certain Web sites, look into products like SurfWatch (www.surfwatch.com), which allow you to block specified Web sites that contain explicit sex, violence, and other objectionable material. You can customize the program to block content that you specify. A user who attempts to access sites that contain the content, or that have been specifically blocked, can't view them.

Appendix

About the CD

. . . .

*C*hances are good that one of the reasons you're attracted to online auctions is the prospect of finding bargains. You're probably on a tight budget and don't have lots of money — or time — to purchase software.

The CD-ROM that accompanies *Internet Auctions For Dummies* provides you with software you don't have to wait minutes (or sometimes even hours) to download. You can install and use the programs right away. I gathered programs that are geared toward the needs of someone who wants to go online and start buying or selling at auction with a minimum of fuss. Here's some of what you can find:

- ✔ MindSpring Internet Access, a popular Internet service provider
- ✔ Paint Shop Pro, a great shareware graphics program for Windows
- ✔ HotDog Professional 5.5 Webmaster Suite, a popular and full-featured Web page creation program for Windows
- ✔ AuctionAssistant to help sellers publish multiple auction listings on eBay
- ✔ AuctionTicker to help buyers and sellers alike keep track of auctions via a scrolling "ticker" that appears in their Web browser window
- ✔ EZ-Ad-Pro, a simple Web page form that automatically creates formatted auction descriptions that look professional and hopefully encourage more bids
- ✔ Auctioneer and EveryAuction, programs that enable ambitious entrepreneurs to create their own full-featured auction Web sites

System Requirements

Make sure that your computer meets the minimum system requirements listed below. If your computer doesn't match up to most of these requirements, you may have problems using the contents of the CD.

- A PC with a 486 or faster processor, or a Mac OS computer with a 68030 or faster processor.

- Microsoft Windows 3.1 or later. (If you use Windows NT 4.0, you need to have Service Pack 3 or later installed.) On a Macintosh computer, you need System 7.55 or later.

- At least 8MB of total RAM installed on your computer. This is a bare minimum. For best performance, I recommend that Windows 95-equipped PCs and Mac OS computers with PowerPC processors have at least 16MB of RAM installed. In my experience, Windows 98 works best with 32MB or more of RAM.

- At least 75MB of hard drive space available to install all the software from this CD. (You need less space if you don't install every program.)

- A CD-ROM drive — double-speed (2x) or faster.

- A sound card for PCs.

- A monitor capable of displaying at least 256 colors or grayscale.

- A modem with a speed of at least 14,400 bps.

If you need more information, check out *PCs For Dummies,* 6th Edition, by Dan Gookin; *Macs For Dummies,* 6th Edition, by David Pogue; *Windows 95 For Dummies,* 2nd Edition, by Andy Rathbone; *Windows 98 For Dummies* by Andy Rathbone; or *Windows 3.11 For Dummies,* 3rd Edition, by Andy Rathbone (all published by IDG Books Worldwide, Inc.).

Using the CD with Microsoft Windows

To install the items from the CD to your hard drive, follow these steps:

1. **Insert the CD into your computer's CD-ROM drive.**

2. **Windows 95/98/NT users: Choose Start➪Run.**
   Windows 3.1 users: In Program Manager, choose File➪Run.

3. **In the dialog box that appears, type** D:\SETUP.EXE.

   Replace *D* with the proper drive letter if your CD-ROM drive uses a different letter. (If you don't know the letter, see how your CD-ROM drive is listed under My Computer in Windows 95/98/NT or File Manager in Windows 3.1.)

4. **Click OK.**

   A License Agreement window appears.

5. **Read through the license agreement, nod your head, and then click the Accept button if you want to use the CD — after you click Accept, you'll never be bothered by the License Agreement window again.**

   The CD interface Welcome screen appears. The interface is a little program that shows you what's on the CD and coordinates installing the programs and running the demos. The interface basically enables you to click a button or two to make things happen.

6. **Click anywhere on the Welcome screen to enter the interface.**

   Now you are getting to the action. This next screen lists categories for the software on the CD.

7. **To view the items within a category, just click the category's name.**

   A list of programs in the category appears.

8. **For more information about a program, click the program's name.**

   Be sure to read the information that appears. Sometimes a program has its own system requirements or requires you to do a few tricks on your computer before you can install or run the program, and this screen tells you what you may need to do, if necessary.

9. **If you don't want to install the program, click the Go Back button to return to the previous screen.**

   You can always return to the previous screen by clicking the Go Back button. This feature allows you to browse the different categories and products and decide what you want to install.

10. **To install a program, click the appropriate Install button.**

    The CD interface drops to the background while the CD installs the program you chose.

11. **To install other items, repeat Steps 7–10.**

12. **When you've finished installing programs, click the Quit button to close the interface.**

    You can eject the CD now. Carefully place it in the plastic jacket at the back of the book for safekeeping.

In order to run some of the programs on the CD-ROM, you may need to keep the CD inside your CD-ROM drive. This is a Good Thing. Otherwise, the installed program would have required you to install a very large chunk of the program to your hard drive, which may have kept you from installing other software.

Using the CD with Mac OS

To install the items from the CD to your hard drive, follow these steps.

1. **Insert the CD into your computer's CD-ROM drive.**

   In a moment, an icon representing the CD you just inserted appears on your Mac desktop. Chances are, the icon looks like a CD-ROM.

2. **Double-click the CD icon to show the CD's contents.**

3. **Double-click the License Agreement icon.**

   This file contains the end-user license that you agree to by using the CD.

4. **Double-click the Read Me First icon.**

   This text file contains information about the CD's programs and any last-minute instructions you need to know about installing the programs on the CD that aren't covered in this appendix.

5. **To install most programs, just open the program's folder and double-click the Installer icon.**

6. **To install some programs, just drag the program's folder from the CD window to your hard drive icon.**

   After you install the programs that you want, eject the CD and carefully place it in the plastic jacket in the back of the book for safekeeping.

Using the Directory Links

For your convenience, links to all the URLs in the *Internet Auctions For Dummies* Internet Directory are included on the CD. You can open the links in your Web browser with a simple mouse click.

To use these links pages, follow these steps:

1. **With the CD-ROM in your drive, connect to the Internet and launch your Web browser.**

2. **In your Web browser, choose File⇨Open or whatever option lets you select a file.**

   An Open dialog box appears.

3. **Select the Links.htm file.**

   If you're using Windows, type **D:\LINKS.HTM**. (If your CD-ROM drive is not D:\, be sure to use the correct letter for your drive.)

   If you're using the Mac OS, use the Open dialog box to display the contents of the CD-ROM. Select the Links.htm file and press Return or Enter.

4. Click a link for any site that you want to visit.

Doing so opens a second browser window that takes you to the Web site you selected. The links page remains open in the original browser window that you can toggle back to it to select another link. Each time you click a new link, the Web site selected pops up in that second browser window — so don't worry that you're going to end up with several browser windows open at one time.

What You'll Find

Here's a summary of the software on this CD. If you use Windows, the CD interface helps you install software easily. (If you have no idea what I'm talking about when I say "CD interface," flip back a page or two to find the "Using the CD with Microsoft Windows" section.)

If you use a Mac OS computer, you can enjoy the ease of the Mac interface to quickly install the programs.

Accounting software

These easy-to-use business programs will help auction sellers keep track of income and expenses for tax purposes.

Simple Business Invoicing & Inventory and Simple Business Accounting by OWL Software

For Windows 95/98. Simple Business Accounting is designed to let people with no prior accounting experience keep track of income and expenses, and it uses the single-entry accounting system favored by the IRS. Simple Business Invoicing & Inventory is a complete sales management system that helps you with inventory tracking, invoicing and billing, and mailing list management. For more information, visit www.owlsoftware.com.

Auction software

The *Internet Auctions For Dummies* CD-ROM contains a good selection of programs to help both buyers and sellers step up to the auction block. The following programs will help you place bids, create auction descriptions, or track sales in which you are particularly interested.

AuctionAssistant by Blackthorne Software

For Windows 95/98/NT. AuctionAssistant is designed for busy eBay sellers who want to put multiple items on the auction block at the same time. The program is designed to help you track bids on as many as a dozen or more items on eBay. AuctionAssistant can automatically upload image files to accompany your listings and perform many other functions as well.

Auctioneer by Netmerchants Inc.

For servers running Windows NT 3.51 or higher. This program lets you create auction sites that provide for registration, bidding, and e-mail communications, as well as chat and live bidding. Auctioneer supports ODBC (Open Database Connectivity) so you can graduate to a powerful database program as your auction site becomes more popular. The program allows you to administer your site from your Web browser.

AuctionTicker by Blackthorne Software

For Windows 95/98/NT. AuctionTicker is designed for busy Web surfers who want to keep up on auctions while surfing other sites at the same time. The program keeps you informed through a scrolling ticker that appears in your browser window. It automatically checks on a selection of auctions throughout the day, and works the same whether you want to track bids on things you're selling or things you're bidding on. The evaluation copy only lets you track one auction at a time.

EveryAuction by EverySoft

For systems running Perl 5.0. EveryAuction is an application that uses the popular cross platform programming language Perl to create your own auction site. Developers need to have Perl 5.0 in order to use EveryAuction, but Perl is freely available on the Internet (you can find out all about Perl and get instructions on how to download it from the Perl Institute Web site at www.perl.org/perl.html). With EveryAuction, you can create a site that allows users to register and choose validated passwords, place bids, list items, end auctions, and more.

EZ-Ad-Pro by Electronic Technologies

For Mac and Windows users. EZ-Ad-Pro is an application that provides users with a simple Web page form into which they can enter the information for their auction sales listings. The program formats the listing by automatically adding a background color, creating a heading, and arranging an image (if you have one) along with your text.

Virtual Auction Ad Pro by Virtual Notions, Inc.

For Windows 95/98/NT. Virtual Auction Ad Pro enables you to create formatted auction ads that grab attention with colors, special fonts, backgrounds, and other Web page elements. You can choose from six preformatted auction listing designs. You enter your description, price information, and other data in a user-friendly form, and the program assembles your listing without requiring you to enter any HTML commands. In contrast to AuctionAssistant, which only works with eBay, Virtual Auction Ad Pro creates listings that can appear on Amazon.com Auctions, Yahoo! Auctions, and many other Internet auction sites.

Graphics software

Images are essential to attracting bidders. After you capture your digital image, whether you scan or photograph the object or let the photo lab do the work, be sure to crop the image and adjust the contrast or brightness so it appears clearly in a Web browser. The following graphics programs enable you to retouch computer images like a pro in no time at all.

GraphicConverter by Thorsten Lemke

For Mac OS. GraphicConverter is a useful graphics tool for editing images and converting them to GIF or JPEG format. It also provides drawing tools so you can create simple graphics from scratch or edit existing files.

Paint Shop Pro by Jasc Inc.

For Windows 3.1 and Windows 95/98/NT. Paint Shop Pro is a powerful shareware graphics editing and viewing tool. The program lets you create original computer graphics or edit existing graphics files. Check out www.jasc.com for more information.

Internet software

The programs in this category are designed to connect you to the Internet, send and receive e-mail, and browse the Web so you can start shopping or selling at online auction sites.

Eudora Light by QUALCOMM Inc.

For Windows 3.1, Windows 95/98/NT, and the Mac OS. E-mail is an essential part of online auctioning; you need to have an e-mail address before you can register with an auction site. Eudora Light is a freeware version of one of the most popular e-mail programs around for several years, Eudora Pro. Find out more about Eudora Pro and Eudora Light at www.eudora.com.

Internet Explorer 5.0 by Microsoft

For Windows 3.1, Windows 95/98/NT, and Mac OS. This is a full-featured Web browser from Microsoft. You can use the version on the CD for all your Web surfing needs. For more information and the latest version, check at www.microsoft.com/ie/default.htm.

MindSpring Internet Access by Mindspring Enterprises, Inc.

For Windows 3.1, Windows 95/98/NT, and Mac OS. MindSpring Internet Access is a free commercial product that gets you signed up with the MindSpring Internet service provider. If you don't already have Internet access, MindSpring is an excellent ISP that offers Internet access for a low monthly fee. MindSpring also has different Web hosting options depending on the kind of account you have. If you're already on the Internet but would like to learn more about MindSpring and the diferent service options it offers, you can go to its Web site at www.mindspring.com.

When you install MindSpring on a Mac, the installation program asks you for a key code. Enter **DUMY8579** in the dialog box. Make sure to use all capital letters, just as it's shown here.

If you already have an Internet service provider, installing MindSpring may replace your current settings. You may no longer be able to access the Internet through your original provider.

Netscape Communicator 4.5 by Netscape Communications

For Windows 3.1, Windows 95/98/NT, and Mac OS. Netscape Communicator is a sophisticated suite of Web browsing and Internet tools. Communicator includes e-mail, newsgroup, and address book software you're sure to find useful in your daily online business activities. For more information and the latest version, visit www.netscape.com.

Web page editors

Web page content is an important supplement to many auction listings. You can create a Web page about yourself, your business if you have one, or about the favorite things you collect, buy, or sell. This book's CD-ROM provides you with options for Web page tools. All of them let you create Web pages without having to learn HyperText Markup Language (HTML). But some contain the bells and whistles only professionals will love.

Dreamweaver 2.0 by Macromedia, Inc.

For Windows 95/98/NT and Mac OS. Dreamweaver is a powerful Web site authoring tool that lets you create text using style sheets (which help you apply the same features from page to page) and Dynamic HTML (which adds interactivity through Web page scripts).

FrontPage Express by Microsoft Corporation

For Windows 3.1, Windows 95/98/NT, and Mac OS. FrontPage Express is a simple yet full-featured Web page editor that comes bundled with Microsoft Internet Explorer. It's based on Microsoft's commercial Web site development software, Microsoft FrontPage.

HotDog Express by Sausage Software

For Windows 95/98/NT. HotDog Express is an HTML editor for Windows users that automatically adds HTML tags to text and images. You click buttons and choose menu options; the software adds the HTML for you. If you like the trial version on the CD, you can either purchase the program or check out the other versions of HotDog at Sausage Software's Web site: `www.sausage.com`.

HotDog Professional 5 Webmaster Suite by Sausage Software

For Windows 95/98/NT. HotDog Professional 5 is a dramatically upgraded version of HotDog, which for several years has been one of the most popular Web page editing tools around. The Professional version includes Web site management features in addition to the more basic utilities you need to create HTML Web pages. To find out more about HotDog, visit `www.sausage.com`.

If You Have Problems (Of the CD Kind)

I tried my best to compile programs that work on most computers with the minimum system requirements. Alas, your computer may differ, and some programs may not work properly for some reason.

The two likeliest problems are that you don't have enough memory (RAM) for the programs you want to use, or you have other programs running that are affecting the installation or running of a program. If you get error messages like `Not enough memory` or `Setup cannot continue`, try one or more of these methods and then try using the software again:

- **Turn off any anti-virus software that you have on your computer.** Installers sometimes mimic virus activity and may make your computer incorrectly believe that it is being infected by a virus.

- **Close all running programs.** The more programs you're running, the less memory is available to other programs. Installers also typically update files and programs; if you keep other programs running, installation may not work properly.

✔ **In Windows, close the CD interface and run demos or installations directly from Windows Explorer.** The interface itself can tie up system memory or even conflict with certain kinds of interactive demos. Use Windows Explorer to browse the files on the CD and launch installers or demos.

✔ **Have your local computer store add more RAM to your computer.** This is, admittedly, a drastic and somewhat expensive step. However, if you have a Windows 95/98 PC or a Mac OS computer with a PowerPC chip, adding more memory can really help the speed of your computer and enable more programs to run at the same time.

If you still have trouble installing the items from the CD, please call the IDG Books Worldwide Customer Service phone number: (800)762-2974 (outside the United States: (317) 596-5430).

Index

• *F* •